PAPERS IN LINGUISTICS
IN HONOR OF LÉON DOSTERT

JANUA LINGUARUM

STUDIA MEMORIAE

NICOLAI VAN WIJK DEDICATA

edenda curat

C. H. VAN SCHOONEVELD

INDIANA UNIVERSITY

SERIES MAIOR

XXV

1967

MOUTON

THE HAGUE · PARIS

PAPERS IN LINGUISTICS
IN HONOR OF
LÉON DOSTERT

edited by

WILLIAM M. AUSTIN

ILLINOIS INSTITUTE OF TECHNOLOGY

1967

MOUTON

THE HAGUE · PARIS

© Copyright 1967 in The Netherlands.
Mouton & Co. N.V., Publishers, The Hague.

No part of this book may be translated or reproduced in any form by print, photoprint, microfilm, or any other means, without written permission from the publishers.

Printed in the Netherlands by Mouton & Co., Printers, The Hague.

DEDICATION

It is somewhat difficult at this time to assess the true relationship between Léon Dostert and linguistics, a field he entered by the back door, a *linguiste malgré lui*. He entered it, as in everything he did, with style and flair, however, and the effect of his presence has been considerable. There is hardly a major linguist today in this country or Europe who does not know him personally, hardly a segment of linguistic endeavor that has not been touched by his thought, guidance or initiated programs.

It is likewise difficult to name Léon Dostert's principal achievement, but in the opinion of the editor it was the introduction of natural language to the computer, a halting step in the form of the "classical" Georgetown-IBM machine translation experiment of January 1954, a step he took with Paul L. Garvin, who evaluates that experiment in this volume. Most of linguistic, and much of computational, activity since has been sparked by that event. Not only machine translation, but information retrieval, transformational and other types of generative grammar, natural language and the computer are largely derived therefrom. Perhaps the most important scientific task for the remainder of this century, and probably the next, will be the enabling of computers to handle natural language. The name of Léon Dostert is engraved on this arduous path.

One could mention other things: the linguistically guided and highly effective "Georgetown method" of language learning and teaching, simultaneous translation at Nüremberg and the United Nations, the binaural device for language learning, the teaching of foreign languages to the blind, but these too are widely known.

It is to Léon Dostert, belatedly for his sixtieth birthday, that this volume is warmly and respectfully dedicated. Without him, who knows?

William M. Austin
Illinois Institute of Technology

TABLE OF CONTENTS

DEDICATION, BY WILLIAM M. AUSTIN	5
LÉON DOSTERT, BY R. ROSS MACDONALD	9
WILLIAM M. AUSTIN	
Logicalism and Formalism in Linguistics	15
JOHN DEFRANCIS	
Syntactic Permutability in Chinese	23
W. NELSON FRANCIS	
A Modified System of Phonemic Transcription for One Idiolect of English	37
PAUL L. GARVIN	
The Georgetown-IBM Experiment of 1954: An Evaluation in Retrospect	46
BOZENA HENISZ	
Experimental Machine Translation	57
ARCHIBALD A. HILL	
The Typology of Writing Systems.	92
CARLETON T. HODGE	
Hausa Personal Pronouns	100
HENRY M. HOENIGSWALD	
Champion or Star?	106
WINFRED P. LEHMAN	
The Gothic Genitive Plural -$\bar{e}$: Focus of Exercises in Theory	108
KEMP MALONE	
On the Etymology of *Scarf*	112
ALBERT H. MARCKWARDT	
Lexical Redistribution in Modern English *say* and *tell*	118
RAVEN I. MCDAVID, JR.	
Language, Linguistics and the Three Cultures	123
MILOS PACAK	
Computational Morphology	134

HERBERT PENZL
>   The Phonemic Interpretation of Early Germanic Names 145
GEORGE L. TRAGER
>   Semology, Metalinguistics and Translation 149
EDITH CROWELL TRAGER
>   Linguistics and the Design of Psycholinguistic Experiments 155
RUTH H. WEIR
>   Some Thoughts on Spelling 169

LÉON DOSTERT

R. ROSS MACDONALD

Léon Dostert was born May 14, 1904, at Longwy, France, the son of Léon Emile Dostert and of Eugénie Marie (Hollet) Dostert.

In 1914, a few months after he had passed his tenth birthday, war broke out between Germany and France, and the town of Longwy, situated as it is near the fortress of Verdun, was overrun by the German armies. It became necessary for everyone attending school in Longwy to study German.

When Léon Dostert had finished elementary school, he had to begin working. He was set, at first, to unloading supplies for the occupying forces. He had acquired the German language so well during his enforced studies, however, that he was assigned to act as interpreter between the German soldiery and his co-workers.

In the course of time the German forces were driven out of Longwy and American forces arrived. Léon Dostert began immediately to study English, and, after some months, spoke sufficiently well to serve the American troops as an interpreter in their dealings with the French.

Eventually the Americans also left Longwy, but a number of them had formed such a high opinion of the abilities of young Léon Dostert that they decided to aid him, if possible, to come to America to further his education.

For a time Léon Dostert's health, which had been almost ruined by the privations of the war years, prevented travel. But it was finally arranged that he come to Pasadena, California, in 1921. He was enrolled in the South Pasadena High School. At first a program involving a number of courses in English was arranged for him, but this soon proved unnecessary. Indeed, he was excused from taking courses in English grammar and composition because his formal English was markedly superior to that of his American classmates.

In 1924, having finished high school, he enrolled at Occidental College and studied there for two years. He then transferred to Georgetown University, where he began working as an Instructor in French, and where, in 1928, he received the degree of Bachelor of Science from the School of Foreign Service. By 1930, he had been granted the degree of Bachelor of Philosophy by Georgetown, and in the following year he was granted the degree of Master of Arts. During this period he continued to teach at Georgetown University and began to move up the academic scale.

He spent the summer of 1929 at La Sorbonne.

In 1932, he began classes with The Johns Hopkins University, and, by 1936, had finished his course work for the degree of Doctor of Philosophy. By 1939 he was Professor of French at Georgetown and Chairman of the Department.

In September 1939, France again became involved in a war with Germany, and Léon Dostert, still a French citizen, was called to the colors of the French infantry. He served his tour of duty as an Attaché at the French Embassy in Washington. The fall of France, in July 1940, released him from military duties, but he continued to serve as Attaché at the French Embassy until August of 1941, when he became an American citizen.

Returning to academic life, he accepted the position of Professor of French Civilization at Scripps College, remaining there for one year.

In 1942, he enlisted in the American army, was appointed, with the rank of Major, to be a Staff Officer. He served both as Liaison Officer to the French Commander-in-Chief, until 1944, and as interpreter to General Eisenhower, until the end of hostilities.

In 1945, Colonel Dostert was put in charge of organizing the simultaneous interpretation system, the concept of which he was largely instrumental in developing, at the Nuremberg War Crime Trials.

As a result of his military career, Colonel Dostert received from the United States the Legion of Merit with Oak Leaf Cluster, the Bronze Star with Oak Leaf Cluster, and the European Theater Ribbon with four Combat Area Stars; he received from France the rank of Knight of the Legion of Honor, as well as the Croix de Guerre with two Palms; he was made a Commander Ouissam Alaouite by Morocco and a Commander Nisham Iffikar by Tunisia. In addition to these military honors, he was appointed Officier d'Académie by the French Government.

In 1946, Colonel Dostert was invited to organize the simultaneous interpretation system at the United Nations. The following year he became an Administrative Counselor to the International Telecommunications Union, and, in 1948 he served as Secretary General of the International High Frequency Broadcasting Conference in Mexico City under the auspices of the United Nations.

In 1949, the Reverend Edmund A. Walsh, S. J., Regent of the School of Foreign Service at Georgetown University, and Professor Dostert collaborated in the founding of the Institute of Languages and Linguistics of the School of Foreign Service of Georgetown University. This Institute was designed as a school where those who were training for the Foreign Service of the United States might develop a solid background in specific languages, as well as an understanding of the characteristics of language in general. One of the features of the new Institute was the extensive use of tape recorders as a learning aid. (Recordings had been used in language teaching at a number of centers previous to this, especially at Cornell University in the mid-thirties, but it was only with the development of the tape recorder that extensive language laboratories became technically practical.) Professor Dostert was to serve as Director of the Institute of Languages and Linguistics from 1949 until 1959.

During this period he held the post of Professor of French Civilization at Georgetown University and of Chairman of the Department of Foreign Languages in the School of Foreign Service of Georgetown University.

It would be difficult to over-emphasize the variety and quality of the activities which developed at the Institute of Languages and Linguistics over the next few years. Many of the more estimable names in contemporary linguistics and language study became associated with the Institute either directly or in the capacity of consultants.

Almost immediately, Professor Dostert organized the Annual Round Table Conference on Languages and Linguistics, which has now become a regular contribution of the Institute to the fields of Linguistics and Language Teaching. At the same time, the Monograph Series on Languages and Linguistics was begun; the proceedings of the Round Table Meetings were reported in the Monograph Series, and a number of other contributions to scholarship were published there as well.

In 1952, Professor Dostert organized, in collaboration with the Mutual Security Agency, a program for teaching English in Yugoslavia. This program was designed to give technically competent Yugoslavs a background in English so that they could profit as quickly and as much as possible from their studies in the United States without having to undergo a preliminary period of learning English in the United States.

It was for this project that Professor Dostert developed his binaural apparatus for teaching languages. With the aid of this machine, a student can have available for listening two synchronized texts, one in the language he is studying, at one ear, and the other in a language he knows, at the other ear. The student turns down the volume on the language he knows and listens only to the language he is learning; he endeavors to understand it as he hears it. At any time he is able to raise the volume of the language he understands so that he can immediately discover the content of the more difficult passages in the language he is learning, and without recourse to instructor or dictionary.

In 1953, Professor Dostert was instrumental in organizing a similar English language project in Turkey. This Turkish project, which is still under Professor Dostert's direction, has since developed many facets, and has come to include the training of English Language Teachers in Turkey, and the preparation of textbooks, as well as a literacy program for the Turkish Army.

In 1953, also, Professor Dostert became interested in the problem of machine translation, and was put in charge of the research and organization of an experiment to determine whether translation could actually be effected by machine. This venture, in which Georgetown University collaborated with the International Business Machine Corporation, bore fruit in the first actual mechanical transfer from one language to another in January, 1954.

In 1955, a growing interest in machine translation led to the establishment of the Machine Translation Research Project of Georgetown University with Professor Dostert as its director. This project was originally under the sponsorship of the

National Science Foundation and of the Central Intelligence Agency. It is currently sponsored by the United States Atomic Energy Commission, and by the Research Directorate of EURATOM.

In 1957, Franklin and Marshall College conferred on Professor Dostert the degree of Doctor of Letters (honoris causa).

In 1958, Georgetown University conferred on Professor Dostert the degree of Doctor of Laws (honoris causa).

In 1959, Professor Dostert was invited to serve as Chairman of the Northeast Conference on the Teaching of Foreign Languages. In 1959 also, he relinquished the Directorship of the Institute of Languages and Linguistics in order to devote his time more fully to Machine Translation. The Machine Translation Research Project had expanded rapidly and developed associations with other machine translation groups, both in the United States and abroad. The details of this development are set forth in the General Report (1952-63), Georgetown University Machine Translation Research Project Paper No. 30, June 1963. In the preface to this paper, Professor Dostert gives an account of the basic thinking behind the developments in the Machine Translation Research Project at Georgetown.

In 1960, Occidental College conferred on Professor Dostert the degree of Doctor of Letters (honoris causa).

In 1960, Professor Dostert served as President of the National Federation of Modern Language Teachers' Associations.

Also in 1960, during a series of discussions as to how the blind could be trained in various types of work, Professor Dostert suggested that they might be trained in various language skills. As a result, a research and development project, under the sponsorship of the Department of Health, Education and Welfare, was established to train blind students as transcribers of spoken Russian. Later, the project was extended to include similar training in German, and to try methods by which the blind might be trained as teachers of these languages. This training and research are still being carried on.

During the academic year 1963-64 Professor Dostert was on leave from Georgetown University; he has accepted an invitation to lecture in French at Occidental College, where he began his university career. At present he is chairman of the Modern Language department of that Institution.

Professor Dostert is a member of a number of scholarly associations, including Phi Beta Kappa and the Phi Beta Kappa Associates; he also belongs to the Modern Language Association, to the Linguistic Society of America, to the American Association of Teachers of French, and to the National Federation of Modern Language Teachers' Associations.

Professor Dostert has served as the Editor of the Georgetown University French Review (1932-39), as Chairman of the Committee on Publications of the Institute of Languages and Linguistics of Georgetown University since the founding of the Institute, and as Editor of the Monograph Series on Languages and Linguistics of

Georgetown University since 1951; in addition to supervising the editing of all of the Monographs, he personally edited the Monograph on Machine Translation (Number 10).

A list of Professor Dostert's publications follows.

PUBLICATIONS BY LÉON DOSTERT

"Machine Translation and Automatic Language Data Processing" *Vistas In Information Handling*, Volume 1, "The Augmentation of Man's Intellect by Machine" (1963).

"Approaches to the Reducation of Ambiguity in Machine Translation", *Journal of the Society of Motion Pictures and Television Engineers* (April, 1959).

Français, Premier Cours (Milwaukee, Bruce Publishing Co., 1958).

Français, Cours Moyen (Milwaukee, Bruce Publishing Co., 1961).

Spoken French, Basic Course, Units 1-6, *MB* 600. (Nine reprints since 1955). Prepared for the United States Armed Forces Institute (1955), 125 pp., 24 ill.

"Foreign Language Reading Skill", *Journal of Chemical Education*, Vol. 32 (March 1955).

"The Georgetown-IBM Experiment", included in collection of essays, *Machine Translation of Languages*, edited by William N. Locke and A. Donald Booth (Technology Press of Massachusetts Institute of Technology and John Wiley and Sons, Inc., 1955).

"Certain Pedagogical Concepts for the Use of Audio Aids in Language Teaching", *The French Review*, Vol. 27, no. 6 (May 1954).

"French in the Service of the Church", *La France et la Chrétienté*, Golden Jubilee Symposium, Assumption College (Worcester, Mass., 1954).

"The Georgetown Institute Language Program", *Publications of the Modern Language Association of America*, Vol. 63, no. 2 (April 1953).

"The Language Laboratory", *Report on the Second Annual Round Table Meeting on Linguistics and Language Teaching*, edited by John De Francis, No. 1, of *Monograph Series on Linguistics and Language Studies* (Georgetown University Press, September 1951), pp. 73-29.

"Languages in Preparedness: Link or Obstacle?", Armor of *The Calvalry Journal*, Vol. 60, no. 3 (May 1951).

"The Wilsonian Ideal and World Reconstruction", *World Affairs Interpreter*, Vol. 13, no. 2 (July 1942).

France and the War, No. 24 in the series, *American in a World at War* (New York, Oxford University Press, 1942).

"Paul Bourget et les Etats-Unis", *Georgetown University French Review*, Vol. 4, No. 3 (May 1936).

"François Mauriac", *Georgetown University French Review*, Vol. 4, No. 1 (December 1935).

"The Catholic Movement in Contemporary French Thought and Literature", *Georgetown University French Review*, Vol. 4, No. 1 (December 1935).

Georgetown University

LOGICALISM AND FORMALISM IN LINGUISTICS

WILLIAM M. AUSTIN

> Let U = the University, G = Greek, and
> P = Professor, then GP = Greek Professor
> Lewis Carroll

The above spoof by a famous logician expresses what many linguists feel about mathematical linguistics, that it is a fashionable and pretentious way of saying what linguistic forms already say better and that it will not lead to any new discovery procedures or, in mathematical terms, that the formulas are *sterile*. While at the moment this has not been entirely disproved, it should be remembered that mathematics has been of great importance to most sciences. Physics is an extreme example of this, of course, but biology and anthropology have also been affected. The very nature, and indeed, status of linguistics as a science is involved here. Twenty-five years ago one heard statements like "linguistics is a classsificatory science" and linguists, secure in a brave new world of taxonomy, went about classifying and labeling items, like Linnean botanists and hurling epithets of mild contempt like "philogist" at those who did not do this or did it badly. Now, as is well known, the tables have been dramatically, and some feel justifiably, turned and "taxonomist" has become a term of opprobrium.

A *détente* of sorts now exists between the analytic descriptivists or "traditional American structuralists" and the predictive descriptivists, who are for the most part transformationalists. An analytic description enables one to assign non-contradictory labels to all items in a system while a predictive description enables one to specify all-and-only the expressions of a system, e.g. "generate" or create sentences in a language.[1] Holders of the latter view claim that an analytic description, essentially an IC analysis, phrase structure (PS) or something similar, is alright for a limited corpus such as Gothic but fails to answer (or lacks "explanatory power" for) all three of these fundamental questions:[2]

(1) What are the fundamental facts of a language possessed by a speaker?

---

[1] This distinction, as well as the later exposition of a directed graph, is from an excellent but somehow unpublished paper by Charles Fillmore and Andreas Koutsoudas entitled "The Directed Graph in Language Description".

[2] From Jerrol J. Katz, "Mentalism in linguistics", *Language* 40, (1964) p. 130. The title is somewhat fatuous as mentalism is not used in its usual, or theological, connotation.

(2) How are these facts put into operation for communication?
(3) How are these facts learned?

Structuralism may answer the first, it is claimed, but not the last two. Whether transformational grammar answers the last two questions or, if it does, if it provides the best of possible answers, is debatable. But one thing is crystal clear. Predictive or generative grammar is here to stay. Taxonomy, an early phase of scientific development and a necessary one, if that science is to remain empirical, will continue. But in the computational scientific climate of today it will not be the sole interest or for a while, at least, the main focus of linguistic endeavor. The guideposts along this path of change are clear: Harris (1952),[3] Georgetown-IBM (1954),[4] Pike (1954)[5] and Harris and Chomsky (1957).[6] The newer logical approach contained an implicit (by now explicit) attack on the older definitional one. This can be stated briefly in logical terms: are statements of the order $X \rightarrow Y$ in environment $W-Z$ sufficiently powerful to explain linguistic phenomena? The attack first centered on IC analysis which was downgraded to the PS rules of this order, a preliminary and less explanatory part of a grammar essentially transformational. The second attack, on the cornerstone of structural linguistics, has come fairly recently.[7] We will take this up first. This will be followed by a discussion of several other basic conceptions of transformational grammar.

(1) *The Elimination of the Phoneme.* It is at once apparent that phonemic theory is logically of the form $X \rightarrow Y$ in env $W - Z$ (English $/p/ \rightarrow [P^{\prime}]$ in $\#\underline{}\acute{V}$). If the fundamental unit of language is of this form the question arises, why not all the rest? Two solutions have been found for the threat.

One: A direct transition from "morphophonemes" (vaguely defined, or not at all; usually an ad hoc combination of "archiphoneme", phoneme, and morphophoneme;[8] nor is the possibility of a morphophoneme without an a priori phoneme raised) to a *finite* string of phonetic data. *Finite* is here italicized for "it is obvious that" the tree past + go → went → u̯ent', 'u̯ent' *or* 'u̯ent̪, etc., etc., are a non-finite set of possibilities. What we call a "phone" is actually a phonetic type, a peak of Gaussian curve and has

---

[3] "Discourse analysis", *Language* 28, pp. 1-30; "Discourse analysis: a sample text", idem, pp. 474-494.
[4] The "Classical" original machine translation experiment with Léon Dostert and Paul L. Garvin the principal investigators.
[5] *Language in Relation to Unified Theory of the Structure of Human Behavior*, ch. 7 (Glendale, California, 1954).
[6] Zellig S. Harris, "Co-occurrence and transformation in linguistic structure", *Language* 37, pp. 283-284; Noam A. Chomsky, *Syntactic Structures* (The Hague, 1957).
[7] See Robert P. Stockwell's chapter "The transformational model of generative or predictive grammar" in Paul L. Garvin, ed., *Natural Language and the Computer*. He writes, p. 43, "An interesting aspect of their shape i.e. phonetic rules is that they evidently do not require an independent 'phonemic' level intermediate between the morphophonemic and phonetic levels." For a fuller discussion see Emmon Bach, *An Introduction to Transformational Grammars* (1964), pp. 123-134.
[8] Cf. Robert B. Lees, *The Phonology of Modern Standard Turkish*.

no reality at all. Phonemicists sin here also, but the sin is trivial. Without the phoneme this would not be.

Two: Distinctive features are used to produce the sounds of the system. It is generally agreed that there are nine distinctive oppositionsin English, namely vocalic/non-vocalic, consonantal/non-consonantal, compact/diffuse, grave/acute, flat/plain, nasal/oral, tense/lax, continuant/interrupted and strident/mellow. How are these oppositions to account for the potently manifest points of articulation for the voiceless stops p, t̪, t, k̪, k, ʔ, ? Or, conversely, how are these (and the rest on a comparable scale) going to produce the nine oppositions? If one listed ŋ on the X axis for Italian, for example, it would be marked + for the Italian features of consonantal/non-consonantal, compact/diffuse, nasal/oral and would thus have the same status as, say, k and g. But ŋ is the completely predictable (hence non-existent) shape of n before k and g. It should be clear to everyone that distinctive features are a tautology arising from an already determined phonemic system. They are created from what they are supposed to produce.

To take a more positive point of view, what about something as unshakable as Grimm's law? The *classes* of sounds represented by Indo-European /p t k/ → Germanic /f θ x/. These are not phones nor are they morphophonemes. Latin /múltum/ was morphophonemically //multom// but the result is Italian *molto*. The second *v* in Latin *vivere* would have to be the morphophoneme *v/k* in view of *vīxī* (and *nix, nivis*) and this would differ from the *v* in *novem* (cf. *nōnus*) or the /k/ in *exemplum*. The derived Italian forms *vivere, nove, essempio* make it clear that the sound changes involved are other than morphophonemic. It would seem that the cornerstone of language, the phoneme, remains unshaken, and in the logical form X → Y in env W — Z. The attack on it does, however, throw some light on the intellectual integrity of the attackers, or on their soundness of methodology, or on their emotional bias, or on all three.

(2) *The Real Structure is Disguised.* Advocates of transformational grammars claim that a signal grammar does not reveal the underlying structure which is responsible, for example, for the differences in the following:[9]

talking machine	machine which talks
eating apple	apple for eating
washing machine	machine for washing things
boiling point	point of boiling
laughing gas	gas which causes laughter

Now one can do this with just about anything in the language, as:

| French toast | toast that has been fried in egg |

---

[9] From Robert B. Lees, "The Grammar of English Nominalizations", *IJAL*, Part II, vol. 26 (1960) quoted by Stockwell *op. cit.*

	French perfume	perfume from France
	French doughnut	fried hollow torus of dough
	French leave	leave without permission
or	kitchenette	a small kitchen
	bachelorette	a female bachelor
	layette	a (lay-away?) of small clothes
	leatherette	resembling leather

But Lees' examples could be a trick of glossing. One could say "a machine for talking", "an apple for eating", "a gas for laughing" although "point of boiling" would remain. And the signals Adj + N are the same *on one level*; on another they are $Adj_{999} + N_{1000}$, $Adj_{1000} + N_{1001}$, etc. The signals are different and distinguishing. The collocation of "French" and "leave" accounts for "French leave". It is what it is, not from any transformation (which would be impossible), but from its form and the total environment of that form in the culture.

"Walker", we are told, can be one who walks or a machine for walking because we can say "I walk" and "I walk the baby". But "stroller" can also be two things and I am not aware of "I stroll the baby". Obviously both forms were created because the system permits the sequence V + {er}. A small thing, perhaps, but so were the slight irregularities in the orbit of Mercury.

(3) *Only Well-formed Sentences and* (4) *Elegance of Statement*. These two facets of logicalism are lumped together because they require the same reply. It is astounding to read in Emmon Bach, "What we describe in our grammar is a partially idealized system. To show how this system is used in actual discourse is a further problem." This is followed six pages later by "linguistics in an empirical science".[10] M. W. Bloomfield and Leonard Newmark[11] insist that "sophisticated linguistic attitudes" should be prior to "factual material". Transformationalists, uneasy at having their cake and eating it too, are quick to assert that they are not prescriptionists. They are not, but they are restrictionists. A vast amount, perhaps a majority, of spoken language must be rejected because it is not composed of grammatical or well-formed sentences. The test of grammaticality? We inductively adjudicate that "Who was that fly you were talking to?" is less grammatical than "Who was that girl you were talking to?" On this basis "It even smells whiter" and "Us Tareyton smokers would rather fight than switch" must be highly grammatical. We are thus led back to the *Grammaire générale et raisonnée* of Port Royal of 1660. Restrictive or prescriptive, the result is the same; data will be admitted if they do not disturb the elegance or universality of statement. We are led there through the same path that they were, through the fashionable rhetoric of the time.[12]

---

[10] Op. cit. p. 91 and p. 97.
[11] *A Linguistic Introduction to the History of English*, vii f., This point was noted by James Sledd in his review, *Language*, 40 (1964), pp. 465-483.
[12] This has been beautifully stated by Richard M. Weaver in "Concealed Rhetoric in scientific

The generative approach just criticized can be characterized as logicalist. Titles in the field make this fairly explicit: Chomsky, "The Logical Basis of Linguistic Theory", *The Logical Structure of Linguistic Theory*, Dixon, "A Logical Statement of Grammatical Theory" and so on. This can be contrasted with formalism, a system based on form alone, that is, a data oriented, signal grammar. Several attempts have been made in this direction but none have been as well systematized as the logicalist approach. The best known is that of Pike's tagmemic formulas. Harman has shown that by removing some of Chomsky's arbitrary restrictions, a generative grammar using PS rules alone can be obtained.[13] Hockett has a similar but less rigorous statement.[14] An unfortunately less well-known schema is that of the directed graph, most recently advocated by William B. Newcomb.[15] The basic apparatus is simple: it consists of nodes (slots) which may be empty (take any exit) and directed lines.

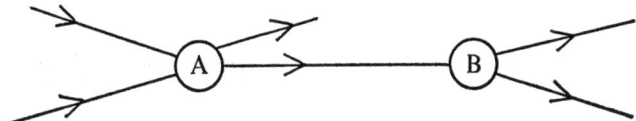 would generate all the expressions contained in A and B. In a graph of the form

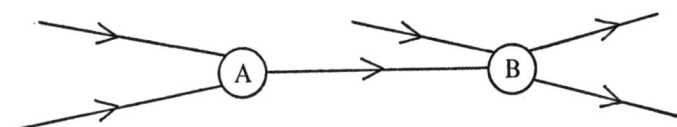

B is said to depend on A, that is, the only way to B is through A. We have the reverse in

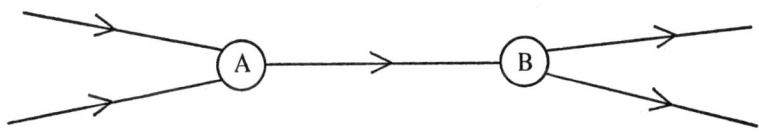

where the only exit from A is through B, A determines B. When we have a combination of the two

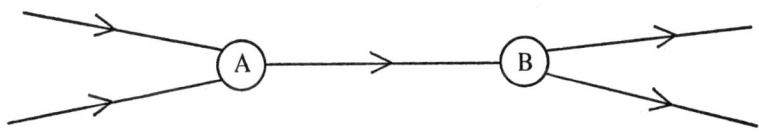

---

sociology", quoted by Paul L. Garvin in his review of "Structure of Language and its Mathematical Aspects", *Language*, 39 (1963), pp. 669-673 "My thesis is that in making this decision they were acting not as scientists, but as rhetoricians, because they were trying to capitalize on a prestige and share in an approbation, in disregard of the nature of the subject they were supposed to be dealing with."

[13] Gilbert H. Harman, "Generative grammars without transformation rules: A defense of phrase structure", *Language*, 39 (1963), pp. 597-616.

[14] Charles F. Hockett, "Grammar for the Hearer", *Proceedings of Symposia in Applied Mathematics*, vol. 12 (1961), pp. 220-236.

[15] In an unpublished paper given at the Kentucky Language Conference 1963. The application of a DG to linguistics was first suggested by Fillmore and Koutsoudas, op. cit, fn. 1.

A and B are said to be interdependent. Finally we may have a node with an iterative loop (repeat until all members of the node are exhausted)

A nominal phrase would be generated as follows:

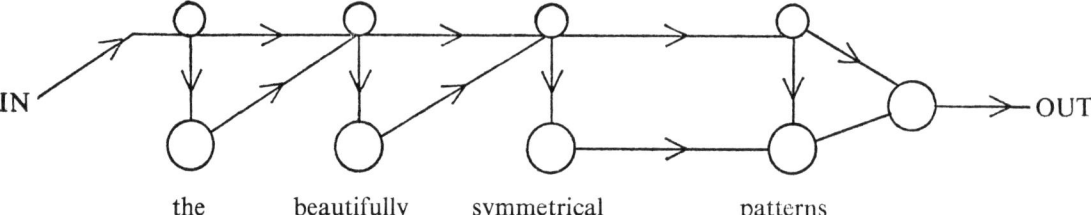

the   beautifully   symmetrical   patterns

Sentence structure on the highest level is of the following form in English:

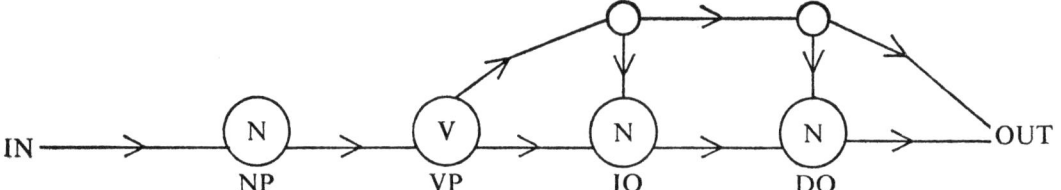

There are only two major syntactic blocks in English, a Nominal and a Verbal. Direct and indirect objects are identical in internal structuring with the subject. Their occurrence or non-occurrence determines such things as Vt, Vi, Vio. In "We felt bad" and "He felt badly" the only distinction between Vsens and Vmot is made by the filler of the final node.

This system is, of course, simply a more convenient way of treating tagmemic formulas. It is also in logicalist terms a finite state grammar of the form $Si \to aSj$ where a is the connecting line between the two nodes. A finite state grammar has been too airily rejected, usually with the introductory phrase "Chomsky has shown..." Chomsky has not shown. His original dismissal was based on the complications of nestings and the fact that sentences can be infinitely long. The most complicated nesting I can think of is something of the order of "A really very beautifully symmetrical pattern" and sentences of infinite (in the ordinary, let alone the mathematical sense) length do not occur. The longest I have heard of, and this is cited as a freak, is an eleven page one of 4,284 words of Nicholas Murray Butler in a 1943 presidential report.[16] An immensely long "sentence" like one beginning with "The items in the Library of Congress are the following: ..." would involve nothing more complicated

---

[16] Mentioned in Charles C. Fried, *The Structure of English*, p. 11.

than an iterative loop. Of course this system, or a similar one, would generate such grammatical sentences as "The bicycle rode the boy" as well as "The boy rode the bicycle". This is unavoidable unless the system is provided with a parallel one, the culture, as it is with users of language. I recently heard someone say, to loud applause, "Plymouth rock should have landed on the Puritans". This, and how much more, would the transformationists deny us.

Conclusion. A formalist, geometrical device such as the above seems to me to have the following advantages:

(1) It would generate all-and-only the expressions of the system, sentences and non-sentences.

(2) It would be data oriented.

(3) It would be completely in accord with the principles of structural linguistics.

(4) It is in accord with the ambience of modern science, particularly with prestigeous physics, where explanatory statements are increasingly geometrical, e.g., gravitation can be completely explained in terms of curvature.

(5) It accounts for language learning and linguistic innovation in a more satisfactory manner than does logicalism. A small child says "There is a dog in the back yard", "There is a lion in the back yard". The child is neither lying or exhibiting an unusual imagination. He is playing with the language machine, that is, filling slots. Once the system has been imprinted in the brain all learning consists of just this. A small boy standing on a curb once surprised me with "Mister, will you cross me?" It seems unlikely that he had previously used some such phasis as "cause me to cross". He was simply filling a node already occupied by "help", "lift", etc. The recent creation "front lash" makes no sense from any transformational point of view. Still more difficult from that point of view would be "purple-lash" (conservative Catholic reaction to recent ecumenical changes).

(6) Language errors, "sentence fragments" and so forth are more readily explained. "it's not that she's ... no, really ... what can he do ..." Short (brief) circuits have been interrupted and others substituted. Short sections of "ungrammatical" sentences are always in proper order no matter what the toxic state ("Play Melancholy Baby").

(7) The advantages for machine translation are obvious. Except for translation choice the English output would be the same for any input language, that is, repeated compatative syntactic analyses would not have to be made. The input language would only have to provide information about subject, object and agreement.

(8) The system can be readily computerized. It practically constitutes a program as it is.

(9) It provides a highly suggestive model of the neural structure of the brain. A DG is a stylized schema of neurons and dendrites.

The argument is not between taxonomy and mathematical (or logical) theory. In any isolation of the two lies disaster for both. Both taxonomic and theoretical (increasingly mathematical, as in all science) aspects of linguistic research will continue with some linguists concentrating in one and others in the other. There will be mutual beneficial feedback. Highly theoretical lectures of de Saussure in 1910 greatly influenced what data gatherers were gathering in America thirty years later. The inexorable data of an empirical science act as a wholesome check on a continual refinement of abstraction. Linguistics should be better off than many sciences in this respect: the data do not constitute a continuum.

Illinois Institute of Technology

SYNTACTIC PERMUTABILITY IN CHINESE*

JOHN DeFRANCIS

Chinese has often been characterized as a language in which word-order plays an exceptionally important role. A contrast is frequently made between highly inflected languages with relatively free word order and Chinese as a language in which a fixed word order compensates for the lack of inflection. The contrast is mentioned particularly often by writers of Slavic background.

Thus a Czech sinologist speaks of Chinese as 'a language with fixed word order'.[1] An explicit contrast with Russian is made in the following comments by a Russian scholar:

In Russian the syntactic function of a word ordinarily does not depend on the position which it occupies in the sentence, since the elements of a sentence possess definite formal-grammatical tokens. Hence *in Russian a free order of words in the sentence is permitted.*

In Chinese the elements of a sentence ordinarily lack definite formal-grammatical tokens, and the syntactic function of a word depends on the position which it occupies in the sentence. Hence *in Chinese there exists a definite order of words in the sentence.*[2] (Italics in original)

In the same vein the eminent Chinese linguist Li Jinxi points out that 'I love him' can be expressed in Russian either as *Ya lyubyu yevo* or as *Yevo lyubyu ya*, whereas the Chinese equivalent cannot be subjected to such changes in word order without changing the meaning.[3]

The factor or 'meaning' underlies all these references to the fixed word order of Chinese, but meaning, as is well known, is a peculiarly difficult thing to handle. Initially we might well forego consideration of meaning altogether in discussing word order in Chinese.

A convenient starting point might be to ask how many acceptable sentences can be formed from a sentence of n syntactic elements by a simple rearrangement of these

---

* This paper is a product of the National Science Foundation Project on Linguistic Transformations at the University of Pennsylvania. In its preparation I have benefitted from discussions with Zellig Harris and Henry Hiż.
[1] Jarmila Kalousková, "Des Catégories des Mots dans la Langue Chinoise", *Archiv Orientální*, XXV (1957), p. 291.
[2] V. I. Gorelov, *Prakticheskaya grammatika kitaiskogo yazyka* (Moscow, 1957), p. 7. Similar views are to be found in M. K. Rumyantsev, *Predlozhenie-podlizhashcheye v sovremennom kitsaiskom yazike* (Moscow, 1957), pp. 45-46.
[3] Li Jinxi, *Hanyu Yufa Jiaocai* (Peking, 1957), p. 4.

elements (without repetition of the elements).[4] AB is a sentence made up of the two elements A and B. Is the permutation BA also a sentence? Take a set of three syntactic elements A, B, and C. We inquire as to whether the following are sentences in the language:

ABC ACB BCA CBA

For *n* elements there are n! permutations.

TABLE I-A

Permutations of Sentence 1: Tā yòng kuàizi chī Zhōngguo-fàn
'He eats Chinese food with chopsticks'

A: tā   C: kuàizi   E: Zhōngguo-fàn
B. yòng D: chī   ( ): permitted sentences

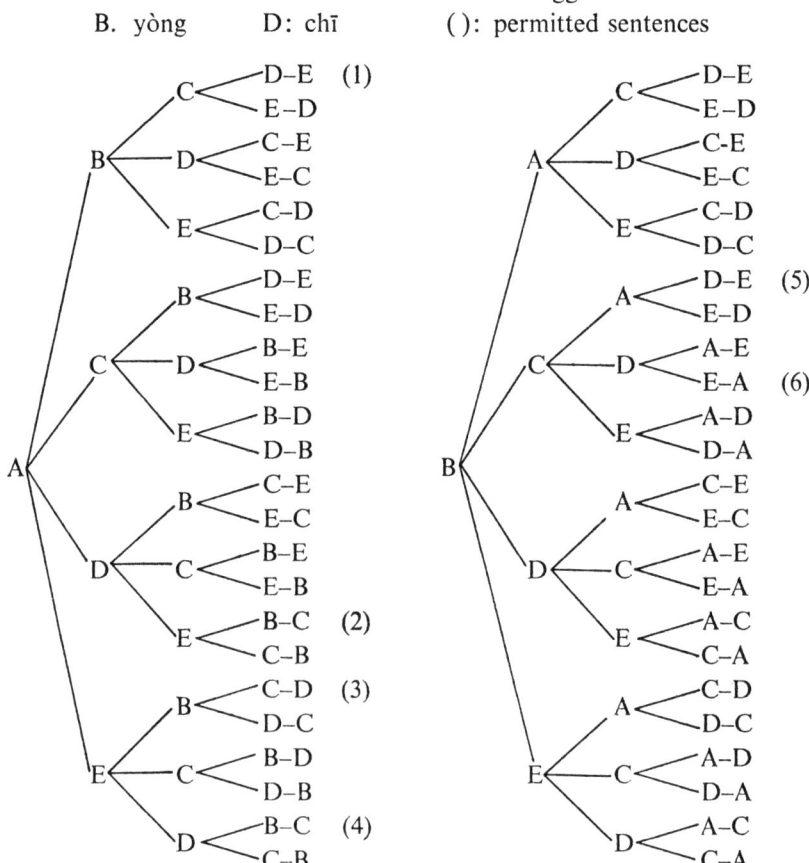

[4] For present purposes it is not necessary to define strictly such terms as 'syntactic element', 'sentence', and 'acceptable'. It will suffice if the first of these is glossed as 'word' or 'compound word', with the decision being made rather arbitrarily as to what a word is since this is a subject of considerable controversy in Chinese. A sentence is an utterance preceded and followed by a full pause. 'Acceptable' is defined as something a native speaker will acknowledge he might say in a specifiable situation.

SYNTACTIC PERMUTABILITY IN CHINESE

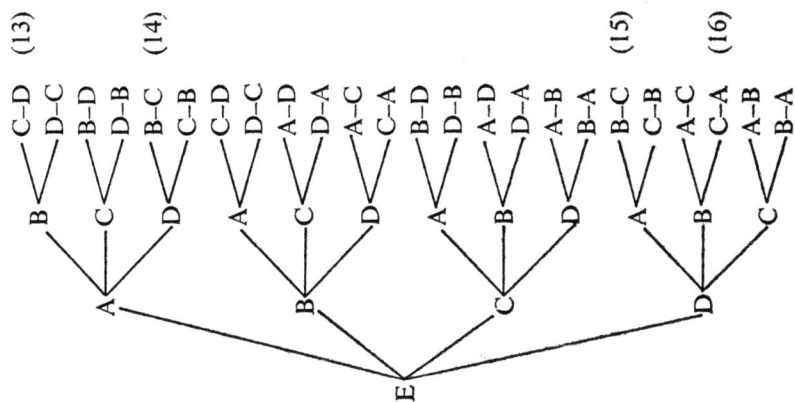

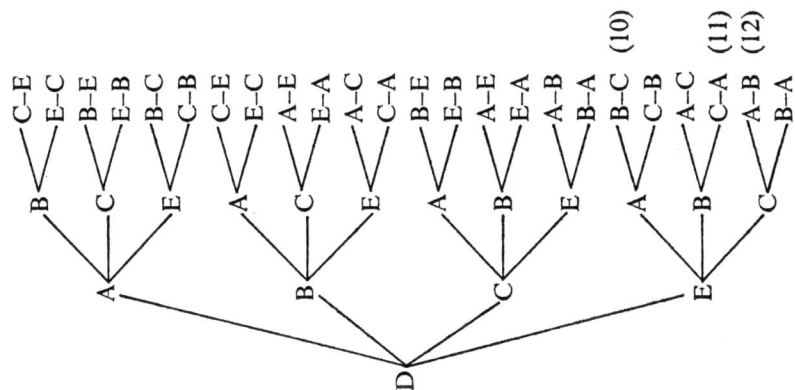

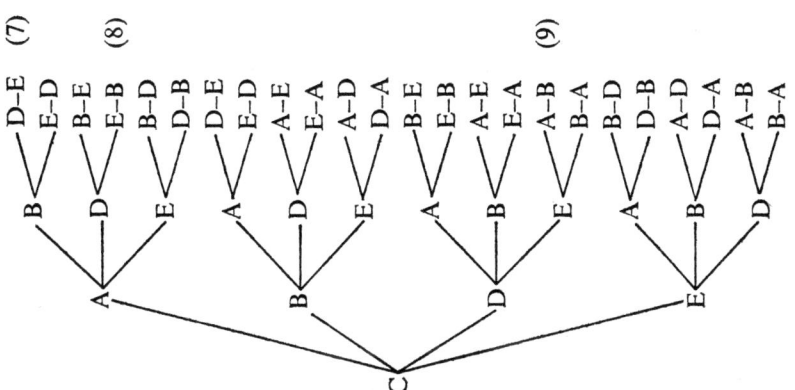

The Chinese sentence

(1) *Tā yòng kuàizi chī Zhōngguo-fàn* 'He eats Chinese food with chopsticks'

can be analyzed as having five syntactic elements. These have 5! or 120 permutations. We need a systematic procedure for generating these permutations so as not to overlook any in our search for sentences. One possible procedure would be to start by assigning a letter code to each of the five elements:

  A   tā   he
  B   yòng   uses, with
  C   kuàizi   chopsticks
  D   chī   eats
  E   Zhōngguo-fàn   Chinese food.

We present above the 120 permutations of these elements, indicating by numbers in parentheses those permutations, sixteen in number, which are acceptable as sentences. (See Table IA.) These sixteen sentences are presented in Table IB.[5]

TABLE I-B Sentences

(1) Tā yòng kuàizi chī Zhōngguo-fàn
(2) Tā chī Zhōngguo-fàn yòng kuàizi
(3) Tā Zhōngguo-fàn yòng kuàizi chī
(4) Tā Zhōngguo-fàn chī yòng kuàizi
(5) Yòng kuàizi ta chī Zhōngguo-fàn
(6) Yòng kuàizichī Zhōngguo-fàn ta
(7) Kuàizi tā yòng chī Zhōngguo-fàn
(8) Kuàizi tā chī Zhōngguo-fàn yòng
(9) Kuàizi chī Zhōngguo-fàn tā yòng
(10) Chī Zhōngguo-fàn tā yòng kuàizi
(11) Chī Zhōngguo-fàn yòng kuàizi ta
(12) Chī Zhōngguo-fàn kuàizi tā yòng
(13) Zhōngguo-fàn tā yòng kuàizi chī
(14) Zhōngguo-tàn tā chī yòng kuàizi
(15) Zhōngguo-fàn chī tā yòng kuàizi
(16) Zhōngguo-fàn chī yòng kuàizi ta

In the case of the sentence

(2) *Tà huì bu huì yòng kuàizi?* 'Can he use chopsticks?',

in our search for sentences, instead of going through the whole of the laborious procedure mentioned above, we can take some short cuts. Thus it is immediately apparent that no permutation beginning with *bu* 'not' will be acceptable as a sentence. By such procedures we obtain a number of trees, presented in Table II, which include those permutations, fourteen in number, which are acceptable as sentences.

Supposing now we combine the two original sentences to produce the new sentence

---

[5] Not all these sentences will be equally acceptable to all native speakers of the language, but they are attested to as sentences by at least one such speaker, Mrs. Teng Chia-yee, a native of Peking whose assistance is hereby acknowledged. One of the difficulties in accepting some of the sentences is that in the form given they lack much information (stress, juncture, intonation) which exists when they are spoken correctly. The non-acceptance of a number of sentences would not materially affect the main points of this discussion.

SYNTACTIC PERMUTABILITY IN CHINESE

TABLE II

Permutations of Sentence 2: Tā huì bu huì yòng kuàizi?
  'Can he use chopsticks'?

```
                ┌─ huì ──────┬─ bu huì yòng kuàizi?              (1)
                │            └─ yòng kuàizi bu huì?              (2)
     tā ───────┤
                ├─ kuàizi huì ┬─ bu huì yòng?                    (3)
                │             └─ yòng bu huì?                    (4)
                └─ yòng kuàizi huì bu huì?                       (5)

                ┌─ bu huì ──┬─ tā yòng kuàizi?                   (6)
     huì ──────┤            └─ yòng kuàizi ta?                   (7)
                └─ yòng kuàizi bu hui tā?                        (8)

     yòng kuàizi ┬─ huì bu huì tā?                               (9)
                 └─ tā huì bu huì?                               (10)

                 ┌─ tā ─┬─ huì ─┬─ bu huì yòng?                  (11)
                 │      │       └─ yòng bu huì?                  (12)
     kuàizi ────┤      └─ yòng huì bu huì?                       (13)
                 └─ huì bu huì yòng tā?                          (14)
```

TABLE III

Permutations of Sentence 3: Tā huì bu huì yòng kuàizi chī Zhōngguo-fàn?
  'Can he eat Chinese food with chopsticks'?

```
        ┌─ huì ──┬─ bu huì ──────┬─ yòng kuàizi chī Zhōngguo-fàn?    (1)
        │        │               └─ chī Zhōngguo-fàn yòng kuàizi?    (2)
        │        ├─ yòng kuàizi ─┬─ chī Zhōngguo-fàn bu huì?         (3)
        │        │               └─ bu huì chī Zhōngguo-fàn?         (4)
        │        └─ chī Zhōngguo-fàn ┬─ yòng kuàizi bu huì?          (5)
        │                            └─ bu huì yòng kuàizi?          (6)
        │
        ├─ kuàizi huì ─┬─ bu huì yòng chī Zhòngguo-fàn?              (7)
        │              └─ yòng chī Zhōngguo-fàn bu huì?              (8)
        │
        ├─ chī Zhōngguo-fàn ─┬─ huì ─┬─ bu huì yòng kuàizi?          (9)
   tā ─┤                    │       └─ yòng kuàizi bu huì?           (10)
        │                    └─ yòng kuàizi huì bu huì?              (11)
        │
        ├─ Zhōngguo-fàn chī ─┬─ huì ─┬─ bu huì yòng kuàizi?          (12)
        │                    │       └─ yòng kuàizi bu huì?          (13)
        │                    └─ yòng kuàizi huì bu huì?              (14)
        │
        └─ yòng kuàizi ──┬─ chī Zhōngguo-fàn huì bu huì?             (15)
                         ├─ huì ─┬─ chī Zhōngguo-fàn bu huì?         (16)
                         │       └─ bu huì chī Zhōngguo-fàn?         (17)
                         └─ Zhōngguo-fàn huì ─┬─ chī bu huì?         (18)
                                              └─ bu huì chī?         (19)
```

Table III (continued)

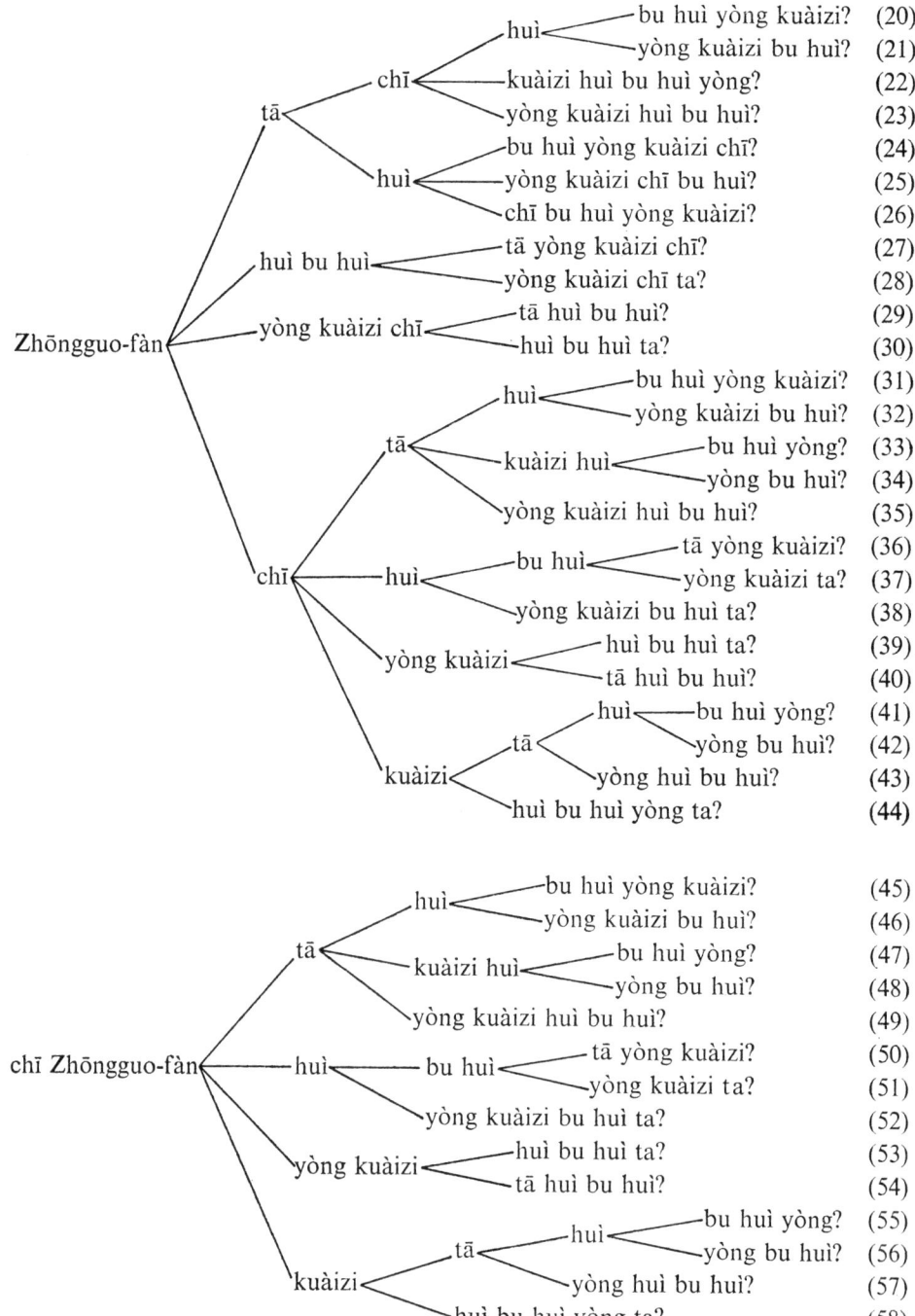

Table III (continued)

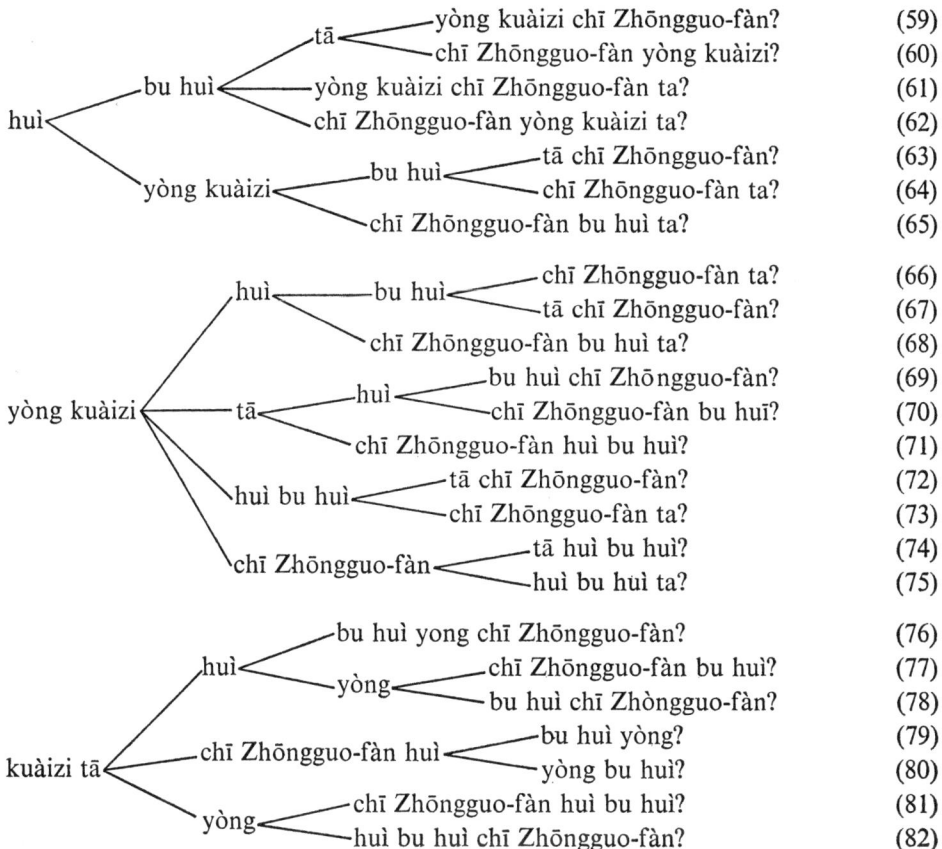

(3) *Tā huì bu huì yòng kuàizi chī Zhōngguo-fàn?* 'Can he eat Chinese food with chopsticks?'

Of the 20,160 permutations, 82 turn out to be sentences. These are presented in Table III.

The rather surprising picture of syntactic permutability suggested by these few examples leads us to inquire whether the permutations indeed involve changes in meaning. This inquiry is central to the more critical examination which is clearly called for into the view of Chinese as a language with fixed word order. Such an examination, which would be an exceedingly complex task, is beyond the scope of this article, the aim of which is merely to draw attention to the magnitude of the problem and to suggest some possible lines of inquiry.

Although it will not be easy to answer, one of the most important questions which must be raised is how the permutations are related to each other in meaning. Let us look for a moment at the 82 sentence-permutations of Sentence 3. A minimal statement that can be made is that the 82 sentences are not arbitrary sentences with phonemically similar words, but are syntactically closely related to each other in that they contain the same elements in the actor-action relation. In all 82 sentences the action of eating is performed, the person who does the eating is *tā* 'he', what he eats is *Zhōngguo-fàn* 'Chinese food', and what he uses to eat is *kuàizi* 'chopsticks'. To say that this large number of sentences describe the same objective situation is already saying a great deal even if it should turn out that there are different subjective shades.

Looking now into the question of aspectual differences among these sentences, we find that there are at least a few which are completely identical even in this respect. Consider the following permutations of Sentence 3 in Table III, noting especially the position of *bu huì* 'cannot':

Tā huì bu huì yòng kuàizi chī Zhōngguo-fàn? (No. 1 in Table III)
(4) *Tā huì yòng kuàizi bu huì chī Zhōngguo-fàn?* (No. 4 in Table III)
(5) *Tā huì yòng kuàizi chī Zhōngguo-fàn bu huì?* (No. 3 in Table III)

It appears that there are three possible positions for *bu huì*: (1) immediately after *huì* 'can' (2) after the first verb-phrase *yòng kuàizi* 'with chopsticks' (3) at the end of the second verb-phrase *chī Zhōngguo-fàn* 'eat Chinese food', which means in this case at the end of the sentence. In all cases *bu huì* is spoken in close juncture with what precedes, and the morphophonemic features of all three sentences are not affected by the shift in position. Nor is there any difference in shade of meaning among the three sentences.

In some cases the question as to whether or not the sentence-permutations involve different shades of meaning cannot be answered in quite so clear-cut a fashion. Consider Sentence (1)
Tā yòng kuàizi chī Zhōngguo-fàn 'He eats Chinese food with chopsticks' and its permutation No. 2 from Table I:

(6) *Tā chī Zhōngguo-fàn yòng-kuàizi* 'In eating Chinese food he uses chopsticks'.

I think the English glosses reflect the Chinese with fair accuracy. Is there some aspectual difference between (1) and (6)? The answer is probably the same for both Chinese and English, and it is probably affirmative, but I would be hard put to define the difference. Is it some secondary feature of emphasis, of style?
Consider also the following permutations of (3)

Tā huì bu huì yòng kuàizi chī Zhōngguo-fàn? (No. 1 in Table III)
(7) *Tā chī Zhōngguo-fàn huì bu huì yòng kuàizi?* (No. 9 in Table III)

Sentence (3) means 'Can he eat Chinese food with chopsticks?' Sentence (7) can be rendered in two ways:[6]

---

[6] I wish to thank William S. Y. Wang for drawing my attention to this difference.

(7a) 'In eating Chinese food can he use chopsticks?' and
(7b) 'In eating Chinese food is he likely to use chopsticks?'

The difference between (3) and (7a) is the same as whatever difference is defined for (1) and (6). But the difference between (7a) and (7b) is more substantial. Hence when (3) is permuted to (7) we get an ambiguous sentence: one meaning (7a) is the same or very close to that of the original sentence, another (7b) involves an aspectual change which can be indicated by English 'can', 'know how to' versus 'is likely to'.

The aspectual difference noted above seems to be the extreme limit of the differences among the 82 sentences under discussion. That the difference is not greater comes as something of a surprise when considered from the viewpoint of Li Jinxi's previously quoted comparison of Russian and Chinese. On closer examination of Li's comparison of the Subject-Verb-Object (SVO) construction in Russian and Chinese, it appears that when Li states that *Ya lyubyu yevo* can be expressed also as *Yevo lyubyu ya*, whereas Chinese[7]

(8) *Wǒ ài tā* 'I love him'

cannot be inverted to

(9) *Tā ài wǒ*, which actually means 'He loves me',

he is stacking the cards against Chinese. The implication is that SVO in Chinese is never expressed as OVS. It is true that (8) cannot be inverted paraphrastically, but we find on examining our 82 sentences that (3)

Tā huì bu huì yòng kuàizi chī Zhōngguo-fàn?

has a permutation (No. 28 in Table III) which interchanges S and O:

(10) *Zhōngguo-fàn huì bu huì yòng kuàizi chī ta?*

Although there may be some slight differences in subjective shades between (3) and (10) it appears that basically they are paraphrases of each other. Furthermore there is no ambiguity here or possible conflict with a fairytale situation such as might result in English if we handle the inversion of S O to O S mechanically and translate (10) as 'Can the Chinese food eat him with chopsticks?'

[7] The changeover from Li's version of these sentences, which are in Chinese characters, to a transcription version introduces the by no means unimportant but here secondary problem of phonemic detail. Pronouns in subject position sometimes, in object position generally (unless stressed) lose their original tones. Whether or not tones are indicated would not affect the discussion, and for purposes of simplifying things for the non-sinological reader who might be thrown off by changes in the transcription, I have chosen to write in the tones uniformally here. In Tables I-III, however, I indicated the shift from *tā* in initial position to *ta* in final position. Besides tones, other secondary features of juncture, stress, and intonation are not always preserved in the permutations. A thoroughgoing study of syntactical permutability in Chinese would have to take changes in secondary features into consideration.

The inversion of subject and object without change in meaning is also to be found in the case of sentence (2)

Tā huì bu huì yòng kuàizi?

which has as its permutation No. 14 in Table II:

(11) *Kuàizi huì bu huì yòng ta?*

Again there is no ambiguity or possibility of this sentence meaning 'Can the chopsticks use him?'

On the other hand (8)

Wǒ ài tā 'I love him'

cannot be expressed as (5)

Tā ài wǒ

and the reason why it cannot is clear. *Wǒ* and *tā* belong to the same form-class (singular personal pronouns) and cannot be interchanged without changes in meaning. The interchanged elements in the permutations of sentence (2) (i.e. *tā* and *kuàizi*) and of sentence (3) (i.e. *tā* and *Zhōngguo-fàn*), though belonging to the general class of substantives, fall into separate sub-classes and can be interchanged without ambiguity or change in meaning.

This does not mean, however, that it requires only a difference in form-class for two elements to be able to change position without change in meaning. Although sentences (2) and (3) have paraphrastic permutations in which S and O are inverted, sentence (1) has no such inverse despite the fact that *tā* and *kuàizi* are in different sub-classes. I don't know why (1) lacks this inverse. Perhaps the question should be put more positively: What is it about sentences such as (2) and (3) which permits the inverse permutation?

The question why the permutation which reverses Subject and Object is permitted in some cases and not in others is part of the more general and extremely important question having to do with restrictions on permutability. In the first place, obvious though this is, it is worth reminding ourselves that of the 20,160 mathematically possible permutations of sentence (3) only 82 are acceptable as sentences. Chinese *does* have serious restrictions on permutability, and investigation should pay attention both to what is not as well as to what is permitted.

Along these lines it would be helpful to look into sentence-permutations from the viewpoint of the specific situations in which they might be used. For example, given a specific contextual situation such as a direct reply to a question, in how many ways can one give answers which are paraphrases of each other, using the same syntactic elements? I suspect that in languages generally, Russian as well as Chinese, not much variety is permitted in such cases.

Study of restrictions on permutability leads also to an examination of similarity or partial similarity among permutations. For example, given sentence (3) with its eight elements (seven if we disregard repetition of *huì*), what partial or complete similarity do its transformations share with other seven- or eight-element sentences? With other sentences of fewer or greater number of elements? Or, to put the question in another form, what sentences can regularly be derived from others?

We saw earlier that the permutation of S V O to O V S was possible in the case of sentences (2) and (3) but not in the case of sentence (1). On the other hand the permutation of S V O to O S V is possible for all these sentences:

(12) *Zhōngguo-fàn tā yòng kuàizi chī* (No. 13 from Table I)
(13) *Kuàizi tā huì bu huì yòng?* (No. 11 from Table II)
(14) *Zhōngguo-fàn tā huì bu huì yòng kuàizi chī?* (No. 24 from Table III)

The permutation of S V O to O S V is much more common than the Subject-Object inverse permutation, but it still is not universal. If S and O are both personal pronouns, for example, the indicated permutation is not permitted.

The study of restrictions on permutability involves another area which needs to be studied, namely the reversibility of verb phrases. In this connection we may note that Y. R. Chao[8] distinguishes between the 'coordinate syntactic construction' and 'verbal expressions in series'. In the former 'the order is usually reversible', whereas the latter has 'a fixed order'. As an example of the coordinate syntactic construction Professor Chao cites a pair of sentences which can be transcribed and translated as follows:

(15) *Tā tiāntiār huì kè xiě xìn* 'He receives callers and writes letters every day'.
(16) *Tā tiāntiār xiě xìn huì kè* 'He writes letters and receives callers every day'.

His examples of verbal expressions in series include:

(17) *Ná dāo gěi ta* 'Take a knife and give to him, —give him a knife'.
(18) *Gěi tā ná dāo* 'Give him take knife, —Take a knife for him'.
(19) *Lí tā tài yuǎn* '[It's] too far from him'.

When Professor Chao speaks of coordinate expressions such as sentences (15) and (16) above as being reversible he apparently means that no change, or at least no significant change, in meaning results. In his examples (17) and (18) we have cases in which the verbal expressions cannot be reversed without changing the meaning. But note that they *can* be reversed if we accept a change in meaning. The reason for pointing this out is to contrast '(17) and (18) on the one hand with (19), where the two verbal expressions *lí tā* (separated) from him' and *tài yuǎn* 'too far' cannot be reversed under any conditions.

It thus appears that verb phrases can be characterized somewhat as follows:

A. Reversible
   1. Without change in meaning (coordinate expressions), e.g. Nos. 15, 16;

[8] *Mandarin Primer* (Cambridge, 1948), pp. 38-39.

2. With change in meaning (verbal expressions in series), e.g. Nos. 17, 18;
B. Non-reversible (verbal expressions in series), e.g. No. 19.

Now consider again sentence (1):

Tā yòng kuàizi chī Zhōngguo-fàn 'He eats Chinese food with chopsticks'.

and sentence (6)

Tā chī Zhōngguo-fàn yòng kuàizi 'In eating Chinese food he uses chopsticks'. (No. 2 from Table I)

The question was raised earlier as to whether these two sentences were the same or different in meaning. Here the same question can be put in the form of asking whether they belong to A1 or A2 above. The same question applies to sentence No. 3

Tā huì bu huì yòng kuàizi chī Zhōngguo-fàn?

and to

(20) *Tā huì bu huì chī Zhōngguo-fàn yong kuàizi?* (No. 2 from Table III).

Sentence (3) can be rendered as 'Can he eat Chinese food with chopsticks?', and Sentence (20) as 'Can he use chopsticks in eating Chinese food?'

It will be helpful in examining these sentences and their possible relationship with those cited by Professor Chao if we modify some of them slightly so that they can be fitted into the following formal pattern:

	S	V_1	O_1	V_2	O_2
(a) = (15)	Tā	xiě	xìn	huì	kè
(b) = (17)	Tā	ná	dāo	gěi	ta
(c) = (1) = (3)	Tā	yòng	kuàizi	chī	Zhōngguo-fàn

In all three cases the verbal expressions can be reversed, resulting in the following sentences:

	S	V_2	O_2	V_1	O_1
(d) = (16)	Tā	huì	kè	xiě	xìn
(e) = (18)	Tā	gěi	ta	ná	dāo
(f) = (6) = (20)	Tā	chī	Zhōngguo-fàn	yòng	kuàizi

The translations of these sentences are as follows:

(a) 'He writes letters (and) receives guests'.
(b) 'He takes knife gives him, —He gives him a knife'.
(c) 'He uses chopsticks eats Chinese food, —He eats Chinese food with chopsticks'.
(d) 'He receives guests (and) writes letters'.
(e) 'He gives him take knife, —He takes a knife for him'.
(f) 'He eats Chinese food uses chopsticks, —In eating Chinese food he uses chopsticks'.

The Chinese sentences suggest the following transformations:

$$S \quad V_1 \quad O_1 \quad V_2 \quad O_2 \quad \leftrightarrow \quad S \quad V_2 \quad O_2 \quad V_1 \quad O_1$$

(a) = (15) ↔ (d) = (16)
(b) = (17) ↔ (e) = (18)
(c) = (1) = (3) ↔ (f) = (6)

Sentences (a) = (15) and (d) = (16) belong to category A1, that is to coordinate expressions which can be reversed without change in meaning. Sentences (b) = (17) and (e) = (18) belong to category A_2, that is to verbal expressions in series which can be reversed with change in meaning but otherwise have a fixed word order. To what category do (c) = (1) = (3) and (f) = (6) belong? The meaning of the sentences does not provide a ready answer, as there is some question as to whether (c) and (f) are the same or different in meaning. It would be helpful if some formal means could be found for distinguishing and categorizing these and other sentences.

If we take the pattern $S \ V_1 \ O_1 \ V_2 \ O_2$ and manipulate it in various ways, such as rearranging its elements or inserting constants, we find, not surprisingly, that not all sentences belonging to this same general pattern behave in the same way. As noted earlier, some sentences do not permit the inversion of $V_1 \ O_1 \ V_2 \ O_2$ to $V_2 \ O_2 \ V_1 \ O_1$. This is the B category of sentences.

There is another category of sentences which permit the insertion of *yímiàn* 'on the one hand' in the following way: *yímiàn* $V_1 \ O_2$ *yímiàn* $V_2 \ O_2$. All such sentences belong to category A_1, those displaying the coordinate syntactic construction. Our sentences (c) and (f) share with those of the A_2 category the characteristic of not fitting into the pattern with *yímiàn*. On the other hand (c) and (f) have some points in common with the A_1 sentences which are not shared by those in the A_2 category. Thus sentences (a), (c), (d), (f) all accept the structure *méi* $V_1 \ O_1$ *yě méi* $V_2 \ O_2$ 'didn't $V_1 \ O_1$ and also didn't $V_2 \ O_2$'. In addition, (c) and (f) have at least one distinctive feature not shared by the other sentences, namely that they permit all three of the following question forms involving *huì bu huì* 'can or cannot'?

(g) huì bu huì $V_1 \ O_1 \ V_2 \ O_2$?
(h) huì $V_1 \ O_1$ bu huì $V_2 \ O_2$?
(i) huì $V_1 \ O_1 \ V_2 \ O_2$ bu huì?

The remaining sentences permit (g) and (i) but not (h).

The fact that sentences (c) and (f), which contain the verb *yòng* 'use', share some features with other sentences but also have some unique characteristics, supports the intuitive feeling that there is something special about this verb. It has frequently been placed in the category of 'coverb', a category of imprecise definition and doubtful validity, but it clearly differs from other 'coverbs' in having a good deal more freedom and independence. Perhaps this explains the large number of permutations of sentence (3).

It would be desirable to test many other sentences of pattern $V_1 \ O_1 \ V_2 \ O_2$ to see what insightful sub-groups can be distinguished. If we extend the inquiry beyond simple permutations and take up permutation combined with zeroing we can expect to get still further insights. A case in point involves zeroing leading to ambiguity, as in the expression *X chī le*. If in this sentence *X* is the logical subject of *chī* 'eat' and the object has been zeroed, the expression means *X ate*. But if *X* is the logical object of the verb and the subject has been zeroed, the expression means *X was eaten*. Here are two sentences illustrating this:

(21) *Wǒ chī le* 'I've eaten'.
(22) *Fàn chī le* 'The food's been eaten'.

These are derived from

(23) *Wǒ chī fàn le* 'I've eaten (food)'

by zeroing *fàn* 'food' in (21) and by permutating *fàn* and zeroing *wǒ* 'I' in (22).

The objective in this sort of analysis is of course to discover patterns and rules, transformational and otherwise, which will throw light on the workings of the language. From this point of view the mere listing of permutations, such as the impressive number noted for sentence (3), is only a first step in the analysis. We must eventually go on to the more difficult task of trying to reduce these sentences to some semblance of order. In this connection it is worth asking whether there is any point in trying to divide these sentences into groups which differ in meaning from each other but in which the members of each group have the same, or approximately the same, meaning. Or shall we say that a difference in word order is ipso facto evidence of difference of meaning? In either case we must state how differences in word order affect the meaning.

Perhaps a careful examination of the 82 sentences will lead to the conclusion that each of them has a unique meaning and has a fixed word order to express this meaning. In that case Chinese may indeed turn out to have 'a fixed word order' —like English and other languages. A conclusion arrived at as a result of such an examination would carry a good deal more weight than the weakly-based contentions cited at the beginning of this article.

In any case it is abundantly clear that we cannot simply dismiss Chinese as having 'a fixed word order'. Whether it is relatively more fixed than other languages is debatable. Far more useful than such generalized statements and comparisons would be a searching examination, along some such lines as those noted briefly in this paper, on how word order functions in Chinese. This is a task which merits a good deal more attention than it has received to date.

University of Pennsylvania
Seton Hall University

A MODIFIED SYSTEM OF PHONEMIC TRANSCRIPTION FOR ONE IDIOLECT OF ENGLISH

W. NELSON FRANCIS

For some years now I have been teaching students phonemic transcription of English according to the system presented by George L. Trager and Henry Lee Smith, Jr.[1] I incorporated this system into my own book, where I called it "the most up-to-date and compendious treatment of English phonemics" and stated that it seemed "well on the way to general acceptance as the standard treatment".[2] My prediction was not much amiss; the system is widely used in this country for instruction in English phonology, and has been adopted in many texts for teaching English to non-native speakers. There has been much discussion of the system, most of it centering on its claim to be an "overall analysis" which "by extrapolation" is "the analysis for the total pattern for all the dialects" of English.[3] It is thus put forward as a generalized scheme of transcription which accommodates all dialects. Most of the criticisms of the system have taken the form of demonstrations of idiolects or dialects which do not fit into its overall pattern.[4] But the acceptance of the system and of its underlying analysis has been widespread and general.

In the light of this widespread acceptance, it seems a bit presumptuous to propose a method of phonemic transcription differing in some essentials as well as in some details. But since the alternative system presented here has a solid foundation going back to Bloomfield's *Language* and other classic documents, and since others have proposed some of its features informally and independently (notably F. W. Householder and A. A. Hill), it cannot appear as a very radical innovation. Nor is it put forward in a generalized sense as an alternative overall pattern. Instead, it is modestly offered as a phonemic analysis of one idiolect (my own), which attempts to replace the more troublesome features of the Trager-Smith system in a way that may make it easier to learn and to use phonemic transcription, especially for those who are not primarily linguists and whose use of phonemic transcription is practical rather than theoretical. I have tried it out on colleagues and on a class of students in a course in modern English phonology. Their reception of it leads me to venture to present it to a larger and possibly more critical audience.

[1] *Outline of English structure* (Norman, Okla., 1951).
[2] W. Nelson Francis, *The structure of American English* (New York, 1958), fn. 1, p. 128.
[3] Trager and Smith, *Outline*, 22, 9.
[4] See, for example, the discussion in *First Texas conference on problems of linguistic analysis in English* (Austin, 1962), especially pp. 77-130.

In attempting to teach the Trager-Smith system to a good many students, I have found that certain points almost inevitably cause trouble. Since many of those who boggle at these points are both intelligent and perceptive, I have been led to the conclusion that there must be weaknesses in the system itself, rather than in my teaching or my students' learning. The principal trouble spots are these:

1. The inclusion of /ɨ/ ("barred i") in the vowel system as a contrastive vowel phoneme.

2. The treatment of syllabic resonant consonants — /m n ŋ l r/ — as biphonemic, composed of vowel + consonant, imposing the necessity of choosing between /ɨ/ and /ə/ as the vowel, and obscuring the phonetic (and possibly sometimes phonemic) distinction between syllabic consonants and VC sequences.

3. The assignment of various phonetic features, especially vowel length and central off-glides, to the phoneme /h/. This was avoided by Gleason, who set up /H/ as a separate phoneme — a solution involving just about as many difficulties as it solves.[5]

4. The treatment of certain syllabic nuclei, especially high-front-tense and high-back-tense-round, as diphthongs with /y/ or /w/ as semivocalic off-glides, in spite of the fact that for many speakers these are pure vowels.

5. The concept of suprasegmental phonemes, whose phonetic realization is also part of the phonetic realization of segmental phonemes occurring simultaneously. In terms of the usual concept of allophone and phoneme, students find it hard to accept such things as /+/ ("plus juncture") and weak stress as phonemes.

6. The difficulty of distinguishing secondary from tertiary stress, or tertiary from weak, and especially of attributing one or the other to syllables in ordinary discourse which does not include discussion of lighthouse-keepers or elevator-operators.

What follows, then, is a theory of my own speech and a system of transcribing it which grew out of the attempt to find a more satisfactory way of handling these persistently recurring transcription problems.

To begin with, let us recognize that the phonological system of a language shares with the other systems — the lexico-grammatical (or morpho-syntactic) one, the semological one, and the graphological one — a certain kind of structure. Each of these systems has two parts: (1) an *inventory*, consisting of a finite set of discrete contrastive units; and (2) a *tactics*, consisting of a finite set of rules or patterns governing the arrangement of these units in larger structures.

The units of the phonological inventory are the phonemes. In any idiolect there is a *finite set* of these; they can be counted and one cannot improvise new ones on the spur of the moment. They are *discrete*; that is, they do not overlap, blend, or merge into one another, but are separate and distinct, following one another in orderly sequence. They are *contrastive*: within the phonological structure that underlies (or may be abstracted from) any actual utterance, every phoneme is different from all the others, and structurally just as different from one as from another. Phonetically, of course,

---

[5] H. A. Gleason, Jr., *An introduction to descriptive linguistics*² (New York, 1961), pp. 33f., 38.

their realizations may differ in greater or less degree; [p] is more like [b] than it is like [z]. But phonemically there are no degrees of contrast.

Phonemes, then, are entities of considerable abstractness. They cannot be spoken or heard; they are not sounds. But they are manifested (or realized) as sounds (phones) when somebody speaks. Furthermore, the same phoneme may be manifested by different sounds, which are its allophones. The customary requirement is that these different allophones be *phonetically similar*; that is that they center around an articulatory and acoustic norm, and that all the allophones of a given phoneme be phonetically nearer to that norm than to the norm of any other phoneme. We also require that the distribution of these allophones be either predictable in terms of the phonemic environment (i.e. in complementary distribution) or irrelevant to the interpretation of the whole utterance (i.e. in free variation).

The concept of allophones as the phonetic realization of phonemes requires that every phoneme in the structured string underlying an utterance must have a specific phonetic segment as its realization. For this reason, I prefer to limit the term *phoneme* to what are commonly called *segmental phonemes* — those whose phonetic realizations occupy a specific fraction of the speech continuum. The so-called suprasegmental phonemes, whose phonetic realization is conceived of as some change in or special selection of the segmental allophones, I prefer to consider as *tactical features* — manifestations of the arrangement-rules rather than discrete contrastive units of the inventory. More about them later.

The segmental phonemes may be classified in two principal ways: according to the articulatory (or acoustic) nature of their allophones (a phonetic classification) or according to the positions they occupy in phonological constructions (a distributional classification). The first kind of classification gives us three principal types: obstruents, resonants, and glides. The obstruents are those whose articulation involves some form of close stricture, either complete, as with the stops, or partial, as with the fricatives. The resonants are those whose articulation involves a relatively free passage. They subdivide into the central oral resonants, or *vocoids*, the partially restricted oral resonants, or *liquids*, and the *nasals*, which have total oral stricture but an alternative open channel through the nose. The glides are those whose articulation involves movement from one position to another of greater or less stricture, and includes flaps and trills as well as vocalic glides like /y/ and /w/.

The second, or distributional, classification gives us two principal groups, *syllabics* and *non-syllabics*. These depend on recognition of the syllable, with its three parts — onset, peak, and coda (to use Hockett's terminology) — as a phonologic unit or minimal construction. Those phonemes which occur as peaks of syllables are syllabics; those which appear in onsets and codas are non-syllabics. In English it is convenient to call those phonemes which are always syllabic *vowels* and the rest *consonants*. An intermediate class, never themselves syllabic but always immediately contiguous to and closely allied to the syllabic, are *semivowels*. The class of vowels turns out to be identical with the articulatory class of vocoids. The class of consonants divides into three groups: the semivowels, just mentioned; the consonantal resonants, which are sometimes syllabic and sometimes not; and the remainder, the pure consonants.

These two classifications are both useful, but they must be kept distinct. The articulatory classification is most useful when we are considering the realization of phonemes as sounds, with their various articulatory and acoustic features. The distributional classification is most useful when we are considering phonological constructions and their status as allomorphs in the grammatical system of the language. Languages differ in the relationship between the two types of classification. In English generally, and in the idiolect here being described in particular, the vocoids are all vowels and vice versa; the obstruents are always non-syllabic consonants;[6] the semivowels are glides, and the consonantal resonants are either syllabic or non-syllabic depending on their environment.

The full repertory of the phonemes of my idiolect is as follows:

8 vowels: /i e æ ə a u o ɔ/
2 semivowels: /y w/
5 consonantal resonants: /m n ŋ r l/
6 stops: /p t k b d g/
9 fricatives: /f θ s š v ð z ž h/

At this point I should, perhaps, insert a parenthetical note about my rather peculiar idiolect. I was born in Philadelphia and lived there (except for four years at college in Massachusetts) for the first 27 years of my life. My speech is thus basically East Midland, sub-variety Philadelphian. But both my parents came from New England — one from coastal Maine and the other from northeastern Massachusetts — and I acquired some features of my vowel system from them. I cannot be put down as truly characteristic of any well-marked regional variety. But I have encountered a good many other East Midland speakers whose speech is basically the same as mine, so this analysis seems suitable for that variety of American English.

The eight vowels are divided into three sets: three front, three back, and two central:

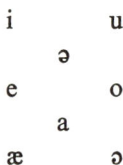

The square is similar to the Trager-Smith one except for the absence of high-central /ɨ/, whose territory is divided between /i/ and /ə/ (though the highest allophones in the central region, which I hear constantly in my adopted home in Rhode Island, are not present at all). All eight of these vowels appear as simple syllabics: as in *pit*, *pet*, *pat*, *put*, and *putt*, in *balm* and *bomb*, and in *only* as contrasted with *lonely*. I differ from

---

[6] Actually fricatives, especially /s/, are occasionally syllabic, as in /pst/ or /s+ku:l/ (*it's cool*). The distribution rules given below can be slightly modified to take care of these.

most East Midland speakers in having low-back-round /ɔ/ rather than low central /a/ in the "short-*o*" words like *pot*. This means that the /a/ vowel is relatively rare in my speech, except before /r/, but the contrast is clear: *lager* is a kind of beer and a *logger* is a man that cuts down trees (/lágr ≠ lɔ́gr/). Likewise from my New England parents comes the use of simple /o/ as a syllabic; it is not widely distributed, but it occurs in *whole* contrasted with *hole* and *home* contrasted with *Rome*. On the other hand, the high central vocoid which I sometimes use in *children* and *pretty* is simply a free or stylistic variant of /i/, which I always use in *chilblains* and *pity*.

Of these eight, six — the three front and the three back — may show the tactical feature of *length*. This is not a very good name for it, since it has three different phonetic components, only one of which is actual duration. But it is a useful and traditional term, which may be symbolized by the usual /:/. The three components of length — or, more precisely, the phonetic features of the allophones that appear when length is present — are

1. *Duration*: the allophone lasts longer in time;
2. *Raising*: the allophone is either higher phonetically throughout or ends in a higher glide, front for front vowels and back for back vowels;
3. *Tension*: the allophone is articulated with a good deal more muscular tension.

All three of these features are present when length is. Raising appears as a higher allophone for the lowest phoneme of each set (i.e. /æ:/ and /ɔ:/) and as a higher off-glide for the two higher phonemes of each set (/i: e: u: o:/).

The six long vowels, in contrast with their short partners, are illustrated by *meet* ≠ *mitt*; *bait* ≠ *bet*; *can* (n) ≠ *can* (aux); *fool* ≠ *full*; *hole* ≠ *whole*; and *caught* ≠ *cot*. It will be observed that these are all treated as diphthongs by the Trager-Smith system: /iy ey æh uw ow ɔh/.

Normally only the long vowels and the two central vowels, in which length is not contrastive, appear in final position, as in *see, say, yeah, coo, crow, law, sofa, aha*. But in a few words such as *idea* short /i/ appears finally, in which case it always has a centralized off-glide. Since this glide is predictable allophonically, it does not need to be considered a phonemic entity or to appear in the transcription. The same glide appears in *theater* (which rhymes neither with *neater* nor *fitter*) and in one pronunciation of *real* which contrasts with both *reel* and *rill*. These are best considered as dissyllabic, with the sequence /iə/.

There are five, or alternatively six, diphthongs, instead of the multiplicity called for by the Trager-Smith system. These consist of simple vowel + front or back semivowel. In all cases the vowel is from a different row than the semivowel: front and central vowels appear with /w/, back and central vowels with /y/. The five are /ay aw oy iw əw/. The last of these, /əw/, is in free (or stylistic) variation with /o:/, a situation which I attribute to the mixture of Philadelphia and New England to which I alluded above: Philadelphia has /əw/ and New England /o:/ (except for those relic areas which still say /bot/ and /rod/ for *boat* and *road*). The version of /ay/ before voiceless consonants has a considerably higher allophone of the vowel; it could be called /əy/ with perhaps somewhat clearer adherence to the phonetic facts.

The three fronting and three backing diphthongs are nicely balanced, but not perfectly symmetrical, as the diagram shows:

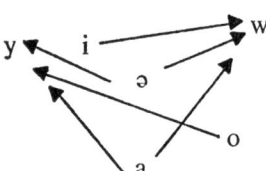

It would be prettier if I had an /ew/ to match /oy/, but except when imitating one variety of British RP, I don't use it. There may, however, be a /uy/ to match /iw/ in a few words like *ruin*, though I believe this usually has two syllables, /rú:win/.

The consonant system is the standard Trager-Smith one, with two exceptions. The first of these is that the affricates of *church* and *judge* are handled as clusters rather than unit phonemes. Try as I may, I cannot conjure up the contrasts on which Hill establishes their existence as units contrasting with stop + fricative clusters; *Dutchy* and *duchy* are alike for me and are transcribed /də́tši:/.[7] The argument from phonotactics balances out; unitary treatment is better for initial affricates, avoiding a unique pair of stop + fricative initial clusters, while cluster treatment is better for final position, where the parallel pair of /ts/ and /dz/, as well as other stop + fricative clusters, regularly appear.

The second difference in the consonant system is that, as already suggested, the consonantal resonants — the three nasals and two liquids — can be syllabic. It is not necessary, however, to posit an extra phoneme or feature of syllabicity, since the syllabicity of these consonants is predictable from the environment. To see how it is we need to consider the tactical feature of *open transition*. This is called a phoneme — "plus juncture" — in Trager-Smith phonemics. But its phonetic realization is not a unique segment of the phonetic continuum; it is a retardation of tempo combined with the selection of characteristic final and initial allophones of consecutive phonemes. It has no explicit phonetic content of its own. For this reason I think it belongs to the tactics; not a phoneme itself, it governs the selection and arrangement of the allophones of other phonemes. The distinction between *a name* and *an aim*, for example, is primarily in the choice of a glottalized onset for the /e:/ vowel in the second case — an allophone of that vowel (as of all vowels) which is characteristically initial. When it occurs, the transition from the preceding phoneme, the /n/, is open. In transcription it is simplest to leave a space, though sometimes to avoid ambiguity we may have to

---

[7] A. A. Hill, *Introduction to linguistic structures* (New York, 1958), p. 36f. In an unpublished 'Proposed phonemically based notation for American English as a second language, generalized form,' Hill states that this distinction involves "a very few contrasts ... which make no semantic difference" (p. 4).

use the /+/ symbol. Similarly in the set /ə tó:l/, /ət ɔ́:l/, and /ətɔ́:l/, the aspirated /t/ of /ə tɔ́:l/ indicates a preceding open transition; the unaspirated /t/ and glottal vowel onset in /ət ɔ́:l/ indicate intervening open transition, and the partially voiced flap of /ətɔ́:l/ indicates no open transition on either side. The choice of allophones indicates the presence or absence of open transition.

Returning to the consonantal resonants, we find that they are syllabic whenever they occur between two consonants (excluding the semivowels), between consonants and open transition or vice versa, and between two open transitions. Diagrammatically:

$$\left.\begin{array}{c} C \\ + \end{array}\right\} R \left\{\begin{array}{c} C \\ + \end{array}\right.$$

where C is any consonant except a semivowel and R is any resonant. Common pronunciations of *happens* /hǽpnz/, *bottles* /bɔ́tlz/, *mountain* /máwntn/, *church* /tšrtš/, *working* /wŕkiŋ/, *irksome* /ŕksəm/, *enclosed* /ŋklɔ́:zd/, and *ellipse* /llíps/ illustrate this. In some cases, of course, variants with a vowel may occur; I can say /hǽpənz/, /en+klɔ́:zd/, and /ilíps/, especially in more deliberate speech.

If one or both of the consonants on either side of a consonantal resonant are also consonantal resonants, the situation is more complicated. It is necessary to recognize a hierarchy of resonants. Vowels, the most open, rank highest; /r/, the most open of the consonants, comes next; then /l/, and finally the nasals. The rule now is that a resonant is syllabic if it is of rank equal to or higher than that of the consonants on either side of it.[8] If we adopt the further convention, quite justified in phonemic practice, that a phonetically long resonant is phonemically double, the contrast between such pairs as *Hitler* and *littler* is accounted for as /hítlr/ and /lítllr/ respectively. The first /l/ of the final sequence in *littler* is syllabic since it is of higher rank than the preceding /t/ and equal in rank to the following /l/. The second /l/ is not syllabic, since it is of lower rank than the following /r/. The final /r/ in both words is syllabic, since it comes between the lower-ranking /l/ and the following open transition. Similarly the /m/ of *calm*, for those who pronounce the /l/, will not be syllabic, since the preceding /l/ outranks it, but the /l/ of *camel* /kǽml/, sandwiched between the lower-ranking /m/ and the open transition, must be syllabic.

Some other pairs illustrating the contrast between syllabic and non-syllabic resonants are *collapse* /kllǽps/ and *claps* /klæps/, *some miles* /smmáylz/ or /sm máylz/ and *smiles* /smaylz/. A four-way contrast is illustrated by the following set:

prayed	/pre:d/
parade	/prré:d/
per aide	/pr é:d/
per raid	/pr ré:d/

---

[8] I am grateful for the assistance of my colleagues W. Freeman Twaddell and Henry Kučera in working out this rule.

Some of the most elaborate sequences appear in words like *armorer* /ármrr/, where the rules call for both of the last two /r/'s to be syllabic, as indeed they are, or *charneler* (as I suppose we should have to call the keeper of a charnel house) /tšárnllr/, where out of the sequence of five consecutive resonants, the rules neatly sort out the first /l/ and the last /r/ as syllabic.

The Trager-Smith suprasegmental phonemes, as I said above, seem to me much more logically handled as tactical features. We have already dealt with open transition above. The three terminals — rising, level, and fading — combine the qualities of open transition with pitch phenomena over the last voiced phone before the end of the utterance or major break in it; they need no further discussion beyond their transfer from inventory to tactics. Pitch, I believe, is best handled by assuming a normal pitch level — pitch /2/ in the Trager-Smith treatment — and the tactical features of raising and lowering, which account for /3/ and /1/. Pitch /4/, as we shall see, is related to accent; it is a raising of an already raised pitch by means of a second accent indicating contrast or special emphasis.

Stress presents more problems, and I cannot claim to have solved them all. Tentatively, I believe it should be split into two features, *stress* proper and *accent*. The first of these, stress, is a feature of the phonemic word, defined as one or more consecutive syllables bounded by open transitions (including, of course, utterance beginnings and the three terminals). It would be neat to find that every phonemic word has one and only one stress, but it doesn't work out that way; at least there are some phonemic words that have no stress at all. But I think that we need only one grade of stress, contrasting simply with absence of stress, and that there is never more than one stress in a phonemic word. Stress is marked /'/.

Accent, marked by boldface type, is a feature of the *phonemic phrase*, which is a sequence of one or more phonemic words bounded by terminals (including utterance beginning). Every phonemic phrase has one and only one accent. Its normal position is on the last stressed syllable of the phrase, and its principal phonetic realization is a raising — or sometimes a lowering — of pitch on that syllable, often accompanied by more forceful articulation. This combination of stress and accent produces the primary stress of the Trager-Smith analysis. But the position of accent is not wholly predictable; if it were we could disregard it altogether as a phonological feature. In order to signal some special grammatical or semantic point, the accent may appear on any stressed syllable; thus **Í**'m *cóming* contrasts with the normal *Í'm* **cóming**. A doubled accent may also appear, which produces a second raising of pitch (to Trager-Smith /4/), as in **Í'm cóming**! This doubled accent may fall on a normally unstressed syllable, as in **Í CAN** *cóme*! /áy kæn kə́m↘/ contrasted with /áykŋ kə́m↘/. Placing of the accent on the unstressed auxiliary requires that it have the full form /kæn/ rather than the form with syllabic /ŋ/, since /r/ is the only syllabic resonant that can be stressed. Since accent requires either raising or lowering of the pitch, and since raising is much more common than lowering, raising need not be marked. When accent produces lowering, as in *I could go* spoken in a tentative way, it can be indicated by a downward-pointing arrow; otherwise pitch raising will be assumed at the accented syllable; thus /áy↓kúd gó:↗/ contrasts with both /áy kúd gó:↘/ and /áykəd gó:↘/.

This is admittedly a rather sketchy treatment of such a complex matter as the phonology of an idiolect. Furthermore, the analysis which works with this dialect certainly will not work with all others. It is put forward with two objectives: to suggest a way of avoiding persistent trouble spots in transcription, and to urge that the straitjacket of the Trager-Smith overall pattern should not be allowed to force analyses of individual dialects into distorted or unsymmetrical shapes. The problem of devising an overall pattern which is not a straitjacket still remains unsolved.

Brown University

THE GEORGETOWN-IBM EXPERIMENT OF 1954: AN EVALUATION IN RETROSPECT*

PAUL L. GARVIN

Enough time has elapsed and sufficient other work has been attempted in machine translation since 1954 to allow an appraisal of this much-talked-about demonstration in the light of the experience since gained.

Whatever its implications may have been in terms of publicizing and stirring up interest in the problem, from a research standpoint the purpose of the verbal program underlying the Georgetown-IBM experiment of 7 January 1954 was to test the feasibility of machine translation by devising a maximally simple but realistic set of translation rules that were also programmable. The actual execution of the program on the 701 computer turned out to be an interesting exercise in nonmathematical programming, but showed nothing about translation beyond what was already contained in the verbal rules.

The verbal program was simple because the translation algorithm consisted of a few severely limited rules, each containing a simple recognition routine with one or two simple commands. It was realistic because the rules dealt with genuine decision problems, based on the identification of the two fundamental types of translation decisions: selection decisions and arrangement decisions.

The limitations of the translation algorithm were dual: the search span of the recognition routine was restricted to the immediately adjacent item[1] to the left or right; the command routine was restricted, for selection decisions, to a choice from among two equivalents, for arrangement decisions, to a rearrangement of the translations of two immediately adjacent items.

The translation program was applied to one Russian sentence at a time: the lookup would bring the glossary entries corresponding to the items of the sentence into the working storage, where the algorithm would go into effect.[2]

The requirements of simplicity and realism were reconciled on the basis of an analy-

---

* Work on this paper was done under the sponsorship of the AF Office of Scientific Research of the Office of Aerospace Research under Contract No. AF 49 (638) – 1128.

[1] The term "item was introduced to designate Russian words or word partials, as opposed to the term "word" which was reserved for computer words. The term "decision point" was introduced to designate an item for which the program has to make a translation decision, the term "decision cue" (or "cue") to designate an item which is considered the relevant condition for making a certain decision.

[2] A statement of the verbal program, the transliteration table, an excerpt from the machine glossary, as well as a selection from the original test sentences, are contained in the Appendix.

sis of the logical structure of a few translation problems. The different variables entering into each problem were isolated, and the rules were then designed to deal each with one particular variable, leaving the remaining aspects of the problem unsolved, or giving an arbitrary solution. In a number of cases, for instance, where the correct choice would have required the operation of rules which were not included in this simple program, a translation appropriate to the input sentences was arbitrarily placed into the glossary. The underlying assumption was that additional rules covering this residue could be written later, without invalidating the rules included in the experiment.

Thus, the translation of Russian case suffixes was analyzed into two decision steps: a first-order decision to determine whether or not to translate the suffix by a preposition, and a second-order decision to choose the particular preposition where one is required. In the experiment, only the first-order decision was implemented, and for only a few suffixes; the second-order decision was ignored by arbitrarily assigning a simple English prepositional translation to each suffix (namely, that which impressionistically seemed the most frequent). This was done by applying rule 3: case suffixes with other than accusatival function were translated by zero whenever a Russian preposition or adjectival suffix preceded the item in question, they were translated by a preposition when this condition did not apply, and in the latter instance, the order of the translations of stem and suffix (the English noun or adjective, and preposition, respectively) was then inverted.

The same rule was used to effect the translation decision for first-person plural forms of verbs, which is analogous to the first-order decision for case suffixes: the verb form was translated without using a pronoun in English whenever a pronoun was present in the Russian text (sentence 32).

Another method of simplifying the translation decision was to limit the cue distance (i.e., the distance between decision cue and decision point) and cue location arbitrarily to conform to the one-word search span, while realistically defining the decision cue in terms of grammatical conditions. An instance of this was the application of rule 3 to the translation of the case suffixes -а, -я. For the appropriate nouns these were interpreted as animate accusatives and translated by zero, whenever they were preceded by a transitive verb form (sentence 40).

A further simplification of certain selection decisions affecting the translation of prepositions, verbs, and nouns, was brought about by not only restricting the cue distance but also limiting the scope of the decision itself to a choice between two equivalents.

Thus, the translation of the preposition к was effected by rule 2 as determined by certain governed nouns, and other aspects of the translation decision were ignored (sentences 4, 19, 40). Conversely, rule 3 was used to translate a noun as determined by the immediately preceding governing verb (sentence 31), or by a modifying adjective (sentences 15-17). The definite article was selected by rule 5 in a few cases in which the Russian noun in question preceded a noun in the genetive, corresponding to the English construction *N of N*, in which an article is frequently required for the first of the two nouns (sentences 19, 20, 27-29).[3]

One arrangement decision in addition to that required for case suffix translation was made: rule 1 was used to invert the order of the translations of a verb and its immediately following subject (sentences 2, 7, 11, 13, 33-34, 45).

Finally, one idiom translation was attempted: rules 3 and 5 were used to translate a three-word Russian idiom by its two-word English equivalent (sentence 26). This was done by choosing the second English word as the equivalent of the second Russian word by rule 5, with the third Russian word considered the cue, and by choosing zero as the equivalent of the third Russian word by rule 3, with the second Russian word considered the cue (for the term "cue", see fn. 2).

The program utilized a dictionary lookup for calling the translation algorithm in the following manner:

The suffixes for which translation decisions were made, and the stems from which they had to be detached, were each entered in the glossary separately. A stem-suffix splitting subroutine, called the "hyphen rule", was included in the lookup. It was applied only to the so-called subdivided items, i.e., the items involved in the above suffix-translation decisions; all other glossary items were entered undivided.

All entries, whether they represented undivided items or the portions of subdivided items, were listed in a single alphabetic sequence.

The five rules of the translation algorithm were operated by a set of two-digit and three-digit numerical code symbols, called diacritics, attached to the glossary entries. The first of the digits was used to indicate whether the diacritic was assigned to a decision-point entry or a decision-cue entry. The second digit indicated the number of the rule to be applied, and the third digit, used only for some decision-cue diacritics, marked which of two choices was to be made (for terms, see fn. 2).

One limitation was imposed by the convenience of the computer program, namely that a particular glossary entry was allowed to contain no more than two three-digit diacritics and one two-digit diacritic.

The general characteristics of the 1954 experiment can be summarized as follows:

(1) The scope of the translation program was clearly specified. Any sentence meeting its narrow specifications could be translated, provided the required entries were present in the glossary. The glossary could be expanded without difficulty and the program made to operate on it, provided the new entries were limited to items to which the previously established code diacritics could be assigned.

(2) The lookup routine was designed for maximum efficiency of the translation algorithm, in that the splitting subroutine was applied only to those cases where it would serve to simplify the operation of the rules, and not to all grammatically possible cases.

(3) The translation algorithm was based on the collocation of decision points and

[3] This solution was suggested by A. A. Hill.

decision cues, rather than directly on the linguistic factors involved, although the decision points and cues themselves were established by linguistic analysis. The same rule was thus used to solve problems of different linguistic structure, but with similar decision structure; rule 3, for instance, was used to translate case suffixes, to choose the translation of nouns on the basis of the verbs governing them, to translate verbs with or without pronouns, and was also utilized in the one idiom translation.

(4) The word length of a sentence turned out to be operationally trivial, since the rules allowed the translation of consecutive strings of similar constructions, provided they were within the specifications of the algorithm.

(5) Selection and arrangement were confirmed as the basic algorithmic operations. "Omission" and "insertion" emerged as simple variants of the selection problem: omission amounted to the choice of a zero equivalent; insertion to the choice of a two-or-more word equivalent for a single input word.

The importance of the 1954 experiment lies in the fact that it formed a significant first step in a continuing research process which is first now nearing completion. This first step consisted in providing an essentially correct formulation of the problem of machine translation which can be succinctly stated as follows:

(1) The machine translation problem is basically a decision problem.

(2) The two fundamental types of decisions are selection decisions and arrangement decisions.

(3) For the automatic implementation of a translation decision, the algorithm has to have the capability for recognizing the decision points and the appropriate decision cues.

The research derived from this formulation has therefore been focused on the detection of the recognition criteria needed for the identification of the decision points and decision cues. This approach to the decision problem is based on an understanding of syntactic and semantic structure which increases as our empirical treatment of it develops.

The Bunker-Ramo Corporation

APPENDIX: DOCUMENTATION OF THE 1954 EXPERIMENT

1. *Verbal Program*

LOOKUP

Match each item of the input sentence consecutively against items stored at the head of glossary entries. Apply hyphen rule whenever necessary.

Hyphen rule. If the lookup does not find a match for all the letters of an input item with a complete item in the glossary, try first for a match of the initial letters with a left partial (stem, as indicated in the glossary by a following hyphen), then try for a match of the remaining letters with a right partial (suffix, as indicated in the glossary by a preceding hyphen).

Bring matched glossary entries into working storage in the order of the input.

ALGORITHM

Calling the rules. Scan the diacritic field of the dictionary entries in working storage consecutively from left to right until you find the first decision-point diacritic, as indicated by a numeral 1 in the first digit position, and operate the rule indicated by the second digit of the diacritic. Then return to scanning for diacritics, beginning with the entry immediately to the right of where you left off.

Rule 1. Look for cue diacritic 21 in the diacritic part of a complete-item entry immediately to the left of the decision point.

Yes — invert the order of the translations of the items concerned.

No — retain order.

Rule 2. If the decision point is a complete item, look for cue diacritics 221 or 222 in the diacritic field of a complete-item entry, or of either partial entry for a subdivided item, immediately to the right of the decision point. If the decision point is a left partial, look for cue diacritics in the corresponding right-partial entry. Select as follows:

221 — choose the first equivalent of the decision-point entry.

222 — choose the second equivalent of the decision-point entry.

Rule 3. If the decision point is a left partial, look for cue diacritic 23 in the diacritic field of a complete-item entry, or of either partial entry for a subdivided item, immediately to the left of the decision point. If the decision point is a right partial, look for cue diacritic 23 in the diacritic field of a corresponding left-partial entry.

Yes — choose the second equivalent of the decision-point entry.

No — choose the first equivalent of the decision-point entry, then invert order as follows: if the decision point is a complete item or a left partial, place its translation before that of the item immediately to the left of it; if the decision point is a right partial, invert the order of the translations of the right and left partials.

Rule 4. Look for cue diacritics 241 or 242 in the diacritic field of a complete-item entry or of either partial entry for a subdivided item, immediately to the left of the decision point. Select as follows:

241 — choose the first equivalent of the decision-point entry.

242 — choose the second equivalent of the decision-point entry.

Rule 5. Look for cue diacritic 25 in the diacritic field of a complete-item entry, or of either partial entry for a subdivided item, immediately to the right of the decision point.

Yes — choose the second equivalent of the decision-point entry.

No — choose the first equivalent of the decision-point entry.

2. *Transliteration table*

А	A		Ж	ZH		М	M		С	S		Ц	TS		Ь	J
Б	B		З	Z		Н	N		Т	T		Ч	CH		Э	E
В	V		И	YI		О	O		У	U		Ш	SH		Ю	YU
Г	G		Й	Y		П	P		Ф	F		Щ	SHCH		Я	YA
Д	D		К	K		Р	R		Х	X		Ы	I		Ъ	W
Е	YE		Л	L												

3. *Excerpt From Glossary*

ENTRY	EQUIVALENTS	CODES		
-A	OF	131	222	25
	--	132	222	25
-AMYI	BY	131	222	
	--	132	222	
BO-	BATTLE	222		
BOLJSH-	A LARGE			
	LARGE			
BOYETS	FIGHTER	242		
BYENZYIN	GASOLINE	241	21	
BYETON-	CONCRETE			
DLYIN-	LENGTH			
DOBIVAYUT	THEY OBTAIN	110		
DOMA	AT HOME	151	241	
	HOUSES	152	241	
DOROGI	ROADS	241		
DUG-	ARC			
DYINAMYIT	DYNAMITE	241	21	
FAKTOR-	FACTOR			
FYEDYERATSYIYA	A FEDERATION			
	THE FEDERATION			
GRAZHDANSK-	CIVIL			
-I	OF	131	25	
	--	132	25	
-IM	BY	131	23	
	--	132	23	
-IMYI	BY	131	222	23
	--	132	222	23
-IX	OF	131	222	23

ENTRY	EQUIVALENTS	CODES		
	--	132	222	23
-IY	--			
-IYE	--	222		
-JYU	BY	131		
	--	132		
K	TO	121	23	
	FOR	122	23	
KACHYESTVO	QUALITY	151	222	
	THE QUALITY	152	222	
KALORYIYNOST-	CALORY CONTENT			
KALORYIYNOSTJ	CALORY CONTENT			
KAMN-	STONE			
KAMYENN-	STONY	151		
	--	152		
KARTOFYEL-	POTATOES			
KLYINOM	BY A WEDGE	131		
	IN WEDGE FORMATION	132		
KRAXMAL	STARCH	21		
KYIRPYICH-	BRICK			
KYISLORODN-	OXYGEN			
LYISHYENYI-	DEPRIVAL	221		
MATYERYIAL-	MATERIAL			
MI	WE	23		
MISLYI	THOUGHTS			
MNOG-	MANY			
MYEDJ	COPPER	21		
MYEST-	PLACE	151	23	
	SITE	152	23	
MYEXANYICHESK-	MECHANICAL	242		
MYEZHDUNARODN-	INTERNATIONAL			
NYIVYELYIROVANYI-	REVELING			
NA	ON	121	23	
	FOR	122	23	
NAUKA	A SCIENCE	242		
	THE SCIENCE	242		
NYEFT-	CRUDE OIL			
NYITROGLYITSYERYIN-	NITROGLYCERINE			
NYIVYELYIROVAHYI-	LEVELING			
O	ABOUT	141	23	
	OF	142	23	
OBRABOTKA	PROCESSING			
-OGO	OF	131	23	
	--	132	23	
-OM	BY	131		
	--	132		
OPRYEDYELYAYET	DETERMINES			
OPRYEDYELYAYETSYA	IS DETERMINED			
OPTYICHYESK-	OPTICAL			
OTDYEL-	SECTION			

THE GEORGETOWN — IBM EXPERIMENT OF 1954

ENTRY	EQUIVALENTS	CODES	
OTDYELYENYIYE	DIVISION	121	242
	SQUAD	122	242
OTNOSHYENYI-	RELATION	151	
	THE RELATION	152	
-OV	OF	131	222
	--	132	222
-OYE	--		
POGOD-	WEATHER		
POLUCHAYET	GETS		
POLYITYICHYESK-	POLITICAL		
PONYIMANYIYE	UNDERSTANDING	242	
POSLYEDN-	LAST		
	LATEST		
POSRYEDSTVOM	BY MEANS OF	23	
POVISHAYET	INCREASES	121	
	IMPROVES	122	
POZDNO	LATE		
PRAV	OF RIGHTS	131	
	RIGHTS	132	
PRAVO	RIGHT	141	242
	LAW	142	242
PROTSYESS-	PROCESS		
PRYI	AT	121	23
	IN	122	23
PRYIGOTOVLYAYETSYA	IS PREPARED	141	
	PREPARES SELF	142	
PRYIGOTOVLYAYUT	THEY PREPARE	110	
PRYIGOVORYIL	SENTENCED	23	
PRYIMYES-	ADMIXTURE		
PSHYENYITS-	WHEAT		
PUT-	PATH	141	
	METHOD	142	
PYERYEDAYEM	WE TRANSMIT	131	
	TRANSMIT	132	
PYERYEDAYET	TRANSMITS		
PYERYEGOVORI	NEGOTIATIONS	110	241
PYERYEMYIRYI-	AN ARMISTICE		
	THE ARMISTICE		
RABOT-	WORK	222	
RADYIOSTANTSYIYA	A RADIO STATION		
	THE RADIO STATION		
RADYIUS-	RADIUS	221	
RINK-	THE MARKET		
RUD-	ORE		
RYECH-	SPEECH		
RYESHYENYI-	SOLUTION	121	221
	DECISION	122	221
S	WITH	23	

ENTRY	EQUIVALENTS	CODES		
SHTAT-	STATE	121		
	STATES	122		
SOOBSHCHYENYIYA	COMMUNICATIONS	241		
SOSTOYIT	CONSISTS			
SOYEDYINYENYI-	COMPOUND	121	242	
	COMPOUNDS	122	242	
SPROS-	THE DEMAND			
SPYIRT	ALCOHOL	21		
STROYATSYA	ARE CONSTRUCTED	141	242	25
	LINE UP	142	242	25
STROYITSYA	IS CONSTRUCTED	141	222	23
	LINES UP	142	222	23
SYELITR-	SALTPETER			
SYERZHANT-	A SERGEANT			
	THE SERGEANT			
TOL	T.N.T.	241	21	
TSYEL-	TARGET	131	25	
	--	132	25	
TSYENA	PRICE	151		
	THE PRICE	152		
-U	TO	131		
	--	132		
UGL-	COAL	121	25	
	ANGLE	122	25	
UGOL	ANGLE			
UGOLOVN-	PENAL	242		
UTROM	IN THE MORNING			
V	IN	122	23	
	TO	122	23	
VAZHN-	AN IMPORTANT			
	IMPORTANT			
VIRABATIVAYETSYA	IS PRODUCED			
VIRABATIVAYUT	THEY PRODUCE	110		
VLADYIMYIR	VLADIMIR	241		
VOPROS-	QUESTION	121		
	QUESTIONS	122		
VOYSKA	TROOPS	242		
VOZVISHYENYIYE	ELEVATION			
VYEDUTSYA	ARE CONDUCTED	21		
VYELYICHYINA	MAGNITUDE			
XYIMYI-	CHEMISTRY			
XYIMYICHYESK-	CHEMICAL	242		
-Y	OF	131	222	
	--	132	222	
-YA	OF	131	221	25
	--	132	221	25
YAVLYAYETSYA	APPEARS	141	23	
	CONSTITUTES	142	23	
-YAX	----	222		

ENTRYE	QÙIVALENTS	CODES		
-YE	TO	131	221	
	--	132	221	
-YEM	BY	131		
	--	132		
-YI	OF	131	25	
	--	132	25	
-YIM	BY	131	23	
	--	132	23	
-YIX	OF	131	222	23
	--	132	222	23
-YIYE	---	222		
YIZ	OUT OF	23		
YIZMYERYENYI-	MEASUREMENT			
YIZVYESTYIYA	BULLETINS			
-YU	TO	131		
	--	132		
ZAKONODATYELJSTV-	LEGISLATION			
ZHALOVANYIYE	SALARY			
ZHYELYEZO	IRON	21		

4. *Selected Test Sentences*

1. PRYIGOTOVLYAYUT TOL
2. TOL PRYIGOTOVLYAYUT YIZ* UGLYA
3. TOL PRYIGOTOVLYAYETSYA YIZ UGLYA
4. BOYETS PRYIGOTOVLYAYETSYA K BOYU
5. KACHYESTVO UGLYA OPRYEDYELYAYETSYA KALORYIYNOSTJYU
6. TOL PRYIGOTOVLYAYETSYA YIZ KAMYENNOGO UGLYA
7. BYENZYIN DOBIVAYUT YIZ NYEFTYI
8. BYENZYIN DOBIVAYETSYA YIZ NYEFTYI
9. AMMONYIT PRYIGOTOVLYAYUT YIZ SYELYITRI
10. AMMONYIT PRYIGOTOVLYAYETSYA YIZ SYELYITRI
11. SPYIRT VIRABATIVAYUT YIZ KARTOFYELYA
12. SPYIRT VIRABATIVAYETSYA YIZ KARTOFYELYA
13. KRAXMAL VIRABATIVAYUT YIZ KARTOFYELYA
14. KRAXMAL VIRABATIVAYETSYA YIZ KARTOFYELYA
15. TOL PRYIGOTOVLYAYETSYA XYIMYICHYESKYIM PUTYEM YIZ KAMYENNOGO UGLYA
16. AMMONYIT PRYIGOTOVLYAYETSYA XYIMYICHYESKYIM PUTYEM YIZ SYELYITRI
17. KRAXMAL VIRABATIVAYETSYA MYEXANYICHYESKYIM PUTYEM YIZ KARTOFYELYA
18. TSYENA KARTOFYELYA OPRYEDYELYAYETSYA RINKOM
19. VYELYICHYINA UGLA OPRYEDYELYAYETSYA OTNOSHYENYIYEM DLYINI DUGI K RADYIUSU
20. KALORYIYNOSTJ OPRYEDYELYAYET KACHYESTVO UGLYA
21. OBRABOTKA POVISHAYET KACHYESTVO NYEFTYI

22. ZHYELYEZO DOBIVAYETSYA YIZ RUDI
23. MYEDJ DOBIVAYETSYA YIZ RUDI
24. DYINAMYIT PRYIGOTOVLYAYETSYA YIZ NYTROGLYITSYERINA S PRYIMYESJYU YINYERTNOGO MATERYIALA
25. VOZVISHYENYIYE OPRYEDYELYAYETSYA NYIVYELYIROVANYIYEM
26. UGOL MYESTA TSYELYI OPRYEDYELYAYETSYA OPTYICHYESKYIM YIZMYERYENYIYEM
27. TSYENA PSHYENYITSI OPRYEDYELYAYETSYA RINKOM
28. TSYENA PSHYENYITSI OPRYEDYELYAYETSYA SPROSOM
29. TSYENA KARTOFYELYA OPRYEDYELYAYETSYA SPROSOM
30. DOROGI STROYATSYA YIZ KAMNYA
31. VOYSKA STROYATSYA KLYINOM
32. MI PYERYEDAYEM MISLYIPOSRYEDSTVOM RYECHYI
33. ZHYELYEZO DOBIVAYUT YIZ RUDI
34. MYEDJ DOBIVAYUT YIZ RUDI
35. ZHYELYEZO DOBIVAYETSYA YIZ RUDI XYIMYICHESKYIM PROTSYESSOM
36. MYEDJ DOBIVAYETSYA YIZ RUDI XYIMYICHYESKYIM PROTSYESSOM
37. DYINAMYIT PRYIGOTOVLYAYETSYA XYIMYICHYESKYIM PUTYEM YIZ NYITROGLYITSYERYINA S PRYIMYESJYU YINYERTNOGO MATYERYIALA
38. DOMA STROYATSYA YIZ KYIRPYICHA
39. DOMA STROYATSYA YIZ BYETONA
40. VOYENNIY SUD PRYIGOVORYIL SYERZHANTA K LYISHYENYIYU GRAZHDANSKYIX PRAV
41. UGOLOVNOYE PRAVO YAVLYAYETSYA VAZHNIM OTDYELOM ZAKONODATYELJSTVA
42. NAUKA O KYISLORODNIX SOYEDYINYENYIYAX YAVLYAYETSYA VAZHNIM OTDYELOM XYIMYIYI
43. VLADYIMYIR YAVLYAYETSYA NA RABOTU POZDNO UTROM
44. MYEZHDUNARODNOYE PONYIMANYIYE YAVLYAYETSYA VAZHNIM FAKTOROM V RYESHYENYIYI POLYITYICHYESKYIX VOPROSOV
45. VYEDUTSYA PYEREGOVORI O PYERYEMYIRYIYI
46. FYEDYERATSYIYA SOSTOYIT YIZ MNOGYIX SHTATOV
47. RADYIOSTANTSYIYA PYERYEDAYET POSLYEDNYIYE SOOBSHCHYENYIYA O POGODYE
48. RADYIOSTANTSYIYA PYERYEDAYET POSLYEDNYIYE POLYITYICHYESKYIYE YIZVYESTYIYA
49. VLADYIMYIR POLUCHAYET BOLJSHOYE ZHALOVANYIYE

EXPERIMENTAL MACHINE TRANSLATION

BOZENA HENISZ-DOSTERT

This paper falls into two parts:

PART I: The presentation of examples demonstrating the validity of the cyclic procedure of output improvement,

PART II: The presentation of an example of linguistic formulations based on output investigation and aimed at output improvement.

All of the research leading to the present paper is based on the author's nine months of work at the EURATOM Research Center in Ispra, Italy (November 1963-July 1964)

PART I: INTRODUCTION

Fifteen years ago the words "machine translation" would have been "grammatically correct", but as nonsensical as anything that is not within the sphere of human perception. Ten years ago, they would have already referred to an actual occurrence (highly advertised at the time), but would have to be meant largely in terms of the future. Today, they refer to a complex past, to a definite present, and to a promising future.

Those who have had an interest in MT the past several years have the historical facts well in their minds; and those who at this time may be developing an interest in the field may find them in numerous publications put out by research centers which have been mushrooming all over this country as well as abroad in the past few years.

One of the procedures followed by MT researchers has been that of gradual, "cyclic" improvement, based on repeated attempts at formulating the linguistic data in the most rigorous way possible, and on testing them in repeated machine translation runs.

One of the early, and consistent, advocators of this procedure was Dr. Léon Dostert. (See "The Georgetown-I.B.M. Experiment", Locke, W. N. and A. D. Booth, *Eds.*, *Machine Translation of Languages* (M.I.T. and Wiley, 1955), pp. 124-135, "Machine

Translation and Information Retrieval", *Vistas in Information Handling* (Spartan Books, Washington, 1963), Chapter 5, and *General Report* (Georgetown University Machine Translation Research Project, Washington, 1963), Preface).

Some of the results of many years spent by numerous researchers in the application of this procedure are presented here on the basis of examples coming from cyclic translation runs.

Three outputs have been examined from the point of view of this study: those of October, 1963, February, 1964 and June 1964. The examples quoted are consequently marked as "Oct. 63", "Feb. 64" and "June 64".

In general, the linguistic formulations resulting in the improved versions are not discussed. In some cases, some of the linguistic formulations are quoted.

Naturally, the outputs quoted above, as any previous ones, have been studied in detail by the investigators whose linguistic and programming formulations led to them. But as an innovation in evaluation a procedure was launched in December 1963 which was aimed at obtaining the comments of the users of the translations. A questionnaire was devised to facilitate for the scientists the task of output evaluation. The results obtained by the distribution of this questionnaire, and their analysis by one of the members of the EURATOM staff are presented in APPENDIX II[1].

The examples which are given below are actual representations of machine-produced output. No pre-editing or post-editing was involved in the process. The examples come from texts in physics, chemistry, mathematics, and cybernetics. All the translations were made with the SLC Programming System developed by Dr. A. F. R. Brown. They were made on the 7090 computer at the EURATOM Research Center in Ispra, Italy.

The examples quoted below represent different areas of linguistic research. Consequently, they are marked according to the sub-divisions.

1) *Article Handling*

Experiments with scientific texts from which the articles were eliminated, and which were distributed to native speakers of English specializing in the given scientific disciplines, showed that the elimination of articles did not hinder the readability of the texts. Subsequently the indefinite article was suppressed in the outputs. The definite article was maintained mainly for the purpose of the delimitation of syntagmatic constructions.

The suppression of the indefinite article resulted in numerous improvements. Due to the limitations of space only a few examples are quoted.

---

[1] It should be mentioned that mechanical translations have been made over the past three years at the request of scientists in the EURATOM Research Center. The average rate has been one article a week.

a) *The indefinite article*

... ISSLEDOVANI4 3NERGETICESKO1 ZAVISIMOSTI SECENI4 ZAXVATA
NE1TRONOV ...

Oct. 63 ... the investigations of *an* energy relation of cross-sections of *a* capture of neutrons ...

Feb. 64 ... the investigations of energy relation of cross-sections of capture of neutrons ...

ZNANIE XIMICESKIX SVO1STV INDIVIDUAL6NYX SVOBODNYX RADIKALOV
CREZVYCA1NO VAJNO ...

Oct. 63 *A* knowledge of chemical properties of individual free radicals is extremely important ...

Feb. 64 Knowledge of chemical properties of individual free radicals is extremely important ...

OB5A4 TEORI4, KOTORA4 RAZVIVAETS4 V GLAVE 5$, VKLHCAET V
SEB4 V PERERABOTANNOM VIDE OSNOVNYE REZUL6TATY RABOT ...

Oct. 63 *A* general theory, which develops in *a* chapter 5, includes in *a* processed form the main results of works ...

Feb. 64 General theory, which is developed in chapter 5, includes in processed form the main results of works ...

ALGORITM PEREVODA S FRANQUZSKOGO 4ZYKA NA RUSSKI1,
Oct. 63 The algotithm of *a* translation from *a* French tongue on Russian,
Feb. 64 The algorithm of   translation from   French language on Russian,

b) *The definite article*

The insertion of the definite article has been somewhat improved in the February run and more substantially so in the June run.

TRUDY VTORO1 MEJDUNARODNO1 KONFERENQII ...
Oct. 63   Labors second an international conference ...
Feb. 64 *The* labors of *the* second international conference ...

... ZNACENI4 A$ U PERVYX V P4T6 RAZ MEN6WE, CEM U VTORYX.
Oct. 63 ... values A at first in five times less, than at second.
Feb. 64 ... values (algebraic formula) at *the* first in five times less, than at *the* second.

PRI INIQIIROVANNOM RASPADE PROPRIONATA RTUTI ...
Feb. 64 Upon initiated the decay of propionate of mercury ...
June 64 Upon the initiated decomposition of *the* propionate of mercury ...

ANALOGICNO I PRI REAKQII S SERO1 FENIL-RADIKALY PEREXODILI NA SERU,

Feb. 64 Analogously and also upon reaction with gray phenyl-radicals went over on sulphur,

June 64 Analogously and upon reaction with gray *the* phenyl-radicals went over on sulphur,

2) *The Genitive Case*

Frequently, the genitive case was either not recognized or incorrectly interpreted (as for example plural, see example 4).

3TO VLI4NIE SKAZYVAETS4 NA UVELICENII 3LEKTRONNO1 PLOTNOSTI ...

Oct. 63 This influence affects an increase the electronic density ...
Feb. 64 This influence affects   increase *of* electronic density ...

, V SLUCAE TAKO1 OWIBKI ...
Feb. 64 , in a case such an errors ...
June 64 , in the case *of* such an error ...

IZUCENIE FOTOREAKQI1 DIFENILRTUTI ...
Feb. 64 The study of the photoreactions   diphenylmercuries ...
June 64 The study *of* the photoreactions *of* diphenylmercur*y* ...

... LIW6 ODIN PRIMER TAKO1 REAKQII ...
Oct. 63 ... only one example   such reactions ...
Feb. 64 ... only one example *of* such a reaction ...

IZ-ZA SVOE1 OTNOSITEL6NO BOL6WE1 STABIL6NOSTI ...
Feb. 64 Because of its/their relatively greater *to* stability ...
June 64 Because of its/their relatively greater   stability ...

3) *The Dative Case*

Earlier outputs showed either the lack of the recognition of the forms in the dative case, and consequently no insertions, or wrong insertions.

... I PODOBNYX EMU RADIKALOV ...
Oct. 63 ... and similar   it radicals
Feb. 64 ... and similar *to* it radicals ...

```
... I PO UROVN4M SEREBRA.
```
Oct. 63 ... and according to *to* the levels of silver.
Feb. 64 ... and according to   the levels of silver.

```
OTNOSITEL6NO REAKQI1 RAZLOJENI4 ...
```
Oct. 63 The relatively reactions of decomposition ...
Feb. 64 Relatively *to* the reactions of decomposition ...

4) *The Instrumental Case*

Earlier outputs showed indiscriminate insertion of 'by' whenever a word or a string of words in the instrumental case occurred in Russian.

```
, SOVPADAET S REZUL6TATAMI RABOT ...
```
Oct. 63 , coincides with *by* the results of works ...
Feb. 64 , coincides with   the results of works ...

```
3TO POSLUJILO OSNOVANIEM ...
```
Oct. 63 This served *by* a basis ...
Feb. 64 This served *as* a basis ...

```
... 3NERGI4 SV4ZI MEJDU VODORODOM I UGLERODOM ...
```
Oct. 63 ... the energy of bond between *by* hydrogen and *by* carbon ...
Feb. 64 ... the energy of the bond between   hydrogen and   carbon ...

```
... OBLADAHT RAZNO1 3NERGIE1 ...
```
Oct. 63 ... possess different *by* energy ...
Feb. 64 ... possess different   energy ...

5) *Reflexive Verbs*

Considerable improvement was achieved in the translation of reflexive verbs which were usually translated before as the corresponding non-reflexive verbs. The most recent translations made in Oak Ridge, Tenn. in August 1964 showed the general character of this improvement, since reflexive verbs were correctly transferred also in these random translation runs. (See APPENDIX III).

```
3TA RAZNIQA VVODILAS6 KAK POPRAVKA V NORMIROVKE ...
```
Oct. 63 This difference *introduced*   as correction to a normalization.
Feb. 64 This difference *was introduced* as correction to normalization. ...

```
, NE DISPROPORTIONIZUETS4 I NE DIMERIZUETS4 ...
```
Oct. 63 , does not dispnoportunate and does not it *dimerize*.
Feb. 64 , *is* not *disproportionated* and *is* not *dimerized*.

V 3TOM PARAGRAFE IZLAGAHTS4 REZUL6TATY,
Oct. 63 In this paragraph there   *present* results,
Feb. 64 In this paragraph there *are presented* results,

... MATERIAL VVODITS4 V MACHINU NA PERFOKARTAX,
Oct. 63 ... material it *introduces* into a machine on punched cards,
Feb. 64 ... material *is introduced* into machine on punched cards,

6) *Impersonal Structures*

Definite progress is evident particularly in a) the treatment of structures with such predicate words as MOJNO, NEOBXODIMO, VOZMOJNO, IZVESTNO, and other "O-forms" (short neuter predicates), and b) structures following ESLI.

It was decided with regard to a) that the insertion of 'it is' will suit most transfer situations for the present time, although some of the translations may be awkward. However, only rearrangement routines are necessary to obtain correct output sequences. For this reason it was considered preferable to have all the "building blocks" in correct form even if the ordering is not correct as yet, rather than to write rules which would be applicable only to very specific situations, and would be rather complicated. Thus, example a) 2 could be translated as 'The same can be observed...', but since the future general arrangement routine is going to call for any predicate to be followed by its object, it is preferable to maintain the present translation.

a)
TEOREMU 6.2 MOJNO RASSMATRIVAT6 KAK NEKOTOROE OBOB5ENIE TEOREMY 2.1 ...
Oct. 63 The theorem 6.2 is possible to consider as a certain generalization of the theorem 2.1...
Feb. 64 The theorem 6.2 *it* is possible to consider as certain generalization of theorem 2.1...

3TO JE MOJNO NABLHDAT6 ...
Oct. 63 This however is possible to observe ...
Feb. 64 The same *it* is possible to observe ...

PRINIMA4 VO VNIMANIE 3TO POLOJENIE, NEOBXODIMO DOPUSTIT6 ...
Oct. 63 Assuming into attention this position, necessary to permit ...
Feb. 64 Assuming into attention this position *is* necessary to permit ...

... NEOBXODIMO ZNAT6 SECENI4 ...
Feb. 64 ... necessary to know the cross-sections ...
June 64 ... *it is* necessary to know the cross-sections ...

V DAL6NE1WEM VOZMOJNO DISPROPORQIONIROVANIE ...
Feb. 64 Into subsequently possible disproportionation ...
June 64 Subsequently *is* possible disproportonation ...

KAK IZVESTNO IZ LITERATURNYX DANNYX,
Feb. 64 As known from the literature given,
June 64 As *is* known from the literature data,

, KOTORUH LEGKO PODSCITAT6,
Feb. 64 , which easily to calculate,
June 64 , which *it is* easy to calculate,

... INTERESNO IZMERIT6 ...
Feb. 64 ... interesting to measure ...
June 64 ... *it is* interesting to measure ...

IZ RIS 4. VIDNO, CTO ...
Feb. 64 From Fig. 4. apparent, that ...
June 64 From Fig. 4. it is apparent, that ...

b)

ESLI DOBAVL4T6 K REAKQIONNO1 MASSE ...
Oct. 63 If it is added to the reaction mass ...
Feb. 64 If *one adds* to the reaction mass ...

, ESLI PONIMAT6 STROGUH MARKOVOST6 V BOLEE JESTKOM SMYSLE RABOTY ...
Oct. 63 , if it is understood strict MARKOVOST6 in the more stiff sense of work ...
Feb. 64 , if *one understands* strict MARKOVOST6 in the more stiff sense of work ...

7) *Copula Insertion*

This improvement is particularly noticeable in connection with predicates in the short neuter form (sometimes referred to as "O-forms"), and other short form predicates.

, TO ZNANIE IX SVO1STV I REAKQI1 OSOBENNO VAJNO.
Oct. 63 , this knowledge of their properties and also reactions especially important.
Feb. 64 , this knowledge of their properties and also reactions *is* especially important.

... I OQENENY IX PARAMETRY.
Feb. 64 ... and   evaluated their parameters.
June 64 ... and *were* evaluated their parameters.

AVTORY PRIZNATEL6NY ...
Feb. 64 The authors   grateful ...
June 64 The authors *are* grateful ...

, KOTOROE NE POME5ENO V SLOVAR ...
Oct. 63 , which   not placed into a dictionary ...
Feb. 64 , which *was* not placed into dictionary ...

POSLE TOGO KAK VSE SLOVA FRAZY OBRABOTANY OPISANNOM
SPOSOBOM,
Oct. 63 After this as all of the words of the phrase treated with described method,
Feb. 64 After this as all of the words of the phrase *were* treated with described method,

OSOBENNO OPASNY V 3TOM OTNOWENII KOROTKIE OSNOVY ...
Oct. 63 Especially dangerous in this relation short bases ...
Feb. 64 *Are* especially dangerous in this relation short bases ...

8) *The Lexical Area*

Improvements in this area fall into two groups: a) filling in lexical gaps, i.e. words which were not in the dictionary and consequently were not translated but just printed out the way they are in Russian, and b) semantic substitutions aiming at a more accurate or generally applicable equivalent.

a)

VSLEDSTVIE 3TOGO ...
Feb. 64 VSLEDSTVIE this ...
June 64 *As a result* of this ...

VO VSEX BEZ ISKLHCENI4 ...
Feb. 64 In VSEX without exception ...
June 64 In *all* without exception ...

b)

NE VSE REAKQII, IMEH5IE MESTO S DRUGIMI ALKIL6NYMI
RADIKALAMI,
Feb. 64 Not all of the reactions, which *have place* with other alkyl radicals,
June 64 Not all of the reactions, which *occur* with other alkyl radicals,

3TOT RADIKAL XOROWO IZUCEN ...
Feb. 64 This radical was *readily* studied ...
June 64 This radical was *well* studied ...

9) *Prepositions*

Various changes were made in the translation of prepositions based on the study of their contextual distribution.

V TO JE VREM4 ...
Oct. 63 *In* the same time ...
Feb. 64 *At* the same time ...

... V 1959 G.
Oct. 63 ... *into* 1959 G.
Feb. 64 ... *in* 1959.

POSTUPILA V REDAKQIH ...
Feb. 64 Was received *into* editorial office ...
June 64 Was received *in* editorial office ...

, I POME5AHTS4 V SPECIAL6NO OTVEDENNOE MESTO PAM4TI.
Oct. 63 , and are placed *in* special the assigned place of memory.
Feb. 64 , and are placed *into* the specially assigned place of memory.

IZ-ZA MALOGO TEPLOVOGO SECENI4 ...
Oct. 63 *From-for* a small thermal cross-section ...
Feb. 64 *Because of* small thermal cross-section ...

10) *Homographs*

The following example shows partial improvement: the formulations worked for one context in which the homographic form was found, and did not work for the other.

... NAWI DANNYE XOROWO SOGLASOVALIS6 S DANNYMI RABOT ...
Oct. 63 ... our *given* good conformed from *given* works ...
Feb. 64 ... our *given* readily conformed with the *data* of works ...

11) *Syntagmatic Strings*

Strings of words which are in morphosyntactic agreement were in some cases not recognized as such, and consequently erroneously translated, especially with regard to prepositions and articles preceding them.

, PRINADLEJA5IE DRUGIM IZOTOPAM.
Oct. 63 , which belong *the other to isotopes.*
Feb. 64 , which belong *to the other isotopes.*

... SOOTVETSTVUET PROQENTNYM SODERJANI4M ...
Oct. 63 corresponds *the percentage to contents* ...
Feb. 64 correspond *to the percentage contents* ...

, NAXOD45IES4 V ORTO-POLOJENII K TREXVALENTNOMU ATOMU UGLERODA.
Oct. 63 , which are found in an ortho-position *K a trivalent to atom* of carbon.
Feb. 64 , which are found in ortho-position *to trivalent atom* of carbon.

, SOOTVETSTVUH5EM ALFAVITNOMU POR4DKU SLOV,
Oct, 63 , corresponding *the alphabetic to order* of words,
Feb. 64 , corresponding *to the alphabetic order* of words,
OBRAZOVANIE OTNOSITEL6NO NEBOL6WIX KOLICESTV RTUTI ...
Feb. 64 Formation *relatively to small amounts* of mercury ...
June 64 The formation *of relatively small quantities* of mercury ...
, OBRAZUH5EGOS4 PRI TERMICESKOM RASPADE PEREKISI ...
Feb. 64 , formed upon *thermal the decay* of peroxide ...
June 64 , formed upon *the thermal decomposition* of peroxide ...

12) *The Subject Routine*

The most noticeable improvement is the elimination of 'it' and 'they' which used to be inserted if the subject was not recognized. This improvement was achieved fully in the February runs and there are no such errors in the June translations.

... NESKOL6KO POSLEDNIX STROK MOGUT BYT6 PUSTYMI.
Oct. 63 ... somewhat of the last lines *they* can be empty.
Feb. 64 ... several last lines can be empty.
... I POKAZAT6, CTO 3TOT 3FEKT OTSUTSTVUET ...
Oct. 63 ... and to show , that this effect *it* is absent ...
Feb. 64 ... and to show, that this affect is absent ...
CA5E VSEGO OWIBKI SV4ZANY S ABSOLHTNO1 NORMIROVKO1 ...
Oct. 63 Mostly in all errors *they* are connected with the absolute normalization ...
Feb. 64 Mostly in all errors are connected with the absolute normali**z**ation ...
V R4DU SOEDINENI1, SODERJA5IX GALOID CETYREXLORISTY1 UGLEROD ZANIMAET OSOBOE MESTO,
Oct. 63 In the series of compounds, which contain a haloid, tetrachloride carbon *it* occupies a special place ,
Feb. 64 In series of compounds, which contain haloid, carbon tetrachloride occupies special place,

13) *Sentences with the Subject Following the Predicate*

The problem here is the insertion or non-insertion of 'there'. Some progress has been achieved in this area, especially in the June runs.

V KAJDO1 STROKE ZAPISYVAHTS4 7 BUKV,
Feb. 64 In each line *there* are recorded 7 letters,
June 64 In each line   are recorded 7 letters,

, PROVER4HT, NAXODIT6S4 LI V NE1 PERVOE SLOVO,

Feb. 64 ,test, whether is in it the first word,
June 64 ,test , whether *there* is in it the first word,

3TOT RADIKAL XOROWO IZUCEN, I, KAK POKAZANO V LITERATURE, RASPADAETS4 NA AQETON ...

Feb. 64 This radical was readily studied , and, as was showed in the literature, *there* decomposes on acetone ...

June 64 This radical was well studied, and , as was showed in the literature, decomposes on acetone ...

... U NIX EST6 RASXOJDIE ...

Feb. 64 at them is derivation ...
June 64 at them *there* is derivation ...

14) *The LI Routine*

An example is given here of linguistic formulations which resulted in output improvement.

First, some examples of incorrect transfer are quoted from earlier outputs. The errors were due to the indiscriminate translation of LI as 'whether'.

Next, some of the formulations are quoted.

Finally, examples of improved output are given.

The formulations referred to have been published as *The Transfer of Russian LI into English* by Bozena Henisz, Georgetown University Machine Translation Research Project, Paper No. 32, June 1963.

OZNACAET LI 3TO, CTO MAWINA MYSLIT?
Signifies whether this, that a machine thinks?

NE MOGUT LI MAWINY OBLEGCIT6 ...?
Cannot whether automatic devices facilitate ...?

Formulations

	Y	N	A
B. *LI*: *Direct Question Particle*			
1. Transfer i as zero.	—	—	2
2. Mark the sentence for interrogative rearrangements and insertions.	—	—	99

Signifies this, that a machine thinks?
Cannot automatic devices facilitate ...?

ODIN CELOVEK VR4D LI MOG BY UPRAVL4T DVIJENIEM ...
One man it is doubtful whether whether could mangage by the movement. ...

Formulations

C. *LI*: *Emphatic Particle*

	Y	N	A
1. Is i-l VR4D or EDVA?	2	D	—
2. Transfer i as zero.	—	—	99

One man hardly could control the movement ...

BUDUT LI 3TO KVADRATICNYE FORMY, VODA, JURAVLI ILI ...
will be whether this quadratic forms, water, cranes or ...

Formulations

D. *LI*: *Conjunction for Indirect Questions*

	Y	N	A
1. Is there a word LI i+n?	2	6	—
2. Does i+n begin with a capital letter?	6	3	—
3. Is there a comma i+m between i and i+n?	4	Ø	—
4. Transfer i+n as 'or whether'.	—	—	5
5. Place 'or whether' immediately after i+m.	—	—	6
6. Transfer i as 'whether'.			
7. Is there a comma or a conjunction, or such a clause introducer as T.E. ('that is') i—n?	8	9	—
8. Place 'whether' immediately after the comma, conjunction, or T.E.. If a conjunction or T.E. follows the comma, place 'whether' after the conjunction or T.E..	—	—	9
9. Place 'whether' as the first word in the sentence.			99

The desirable translation of the example preceding these formulations has not been obtained due to the partial rerun of the text. It is:
whether this will be quadratic forms, water, cranes or. ...

The above examples are from the translation of a book on cybernetics : MAWINA I MYSL6 by Z. Rovenski, A. Uemov, E. Uemov. The following examples are from the translations made in Ispra which were mentioned above.

PRI IZUCENII POVEDENI4 3TOGO RADIKALA NAS INTERESOVAL
VOPROS, BUDET LI IMET MESTO REAKQI4 ...

Oct. 63 Whether upon the study of behavior of this radical us interested a question, is take the reaction ...

Feb. 64 Upon the study of this radical us interested the question, *whether* will occur the reaction ...

PO OKONCANII POISKA PERVOGO SLOVA PROVERAHT, NE SODERJITS4
3TO SLOVO ...

Oct. 63 Whether according to the completion of the search of the first word test, is not contained this word ...

Feb. 64 According to the completion of the search of the first word test, *whether* is not contained this word ...

PROVERAHT, 4VL4ETS4 LI OBOROT QELYM ...
Oct. 63 Whether they test, is the revolution whole.
Feb. 64 Test, whether is the revolution whole.

15) *Multiple Negatives*

The presentation here is very much the same as for the LI routine.

The errors in the former outputs were due to the fact that whenever the Russian text contained more than one negative word, all of them were translated as negative, while English (at least standard English) tolerates only single negatives for the negative value. Double negatives result in a positive in modern Standard English.

Russian negative forms were grouped into Class I negatives and Class II negatives.

Class I negatives are always logically negative:

NE   : 'not'
NET   : 'there is not'
NEL6Z4 : 'it is not possible'

Class II negatives are either logically negative or insignificant with respect to logical negation. Class II negatives were supplied with two translations. Some Class II negatives are:

	First Translation	Second Translation
NIKTO	no one	anyone
NICTO	nothing	anything
NIKOGDA	never	ever
NIGDE	nowhere	anywhere
NIKAK01	no	any

The first five examples that follow of incorrect and improved translation are from the book on cybernetics mentioned above (MAWINA I MYSL6).

ON NIKOGDA NE DUMAL ...
It *never did not* think ...
It *never* thought ...

... IX NIKTO NE NAZOVET AVTOMATICESKIMI.
... them *anybody does not* call automatic.
... them *nobody* calls automatic.

... NE IME4 OBYCNO NICEGO OB5EGO S NIM ...
... *not* having usual *nothing* general S it ...
... having usual *nothing* general with it ...

... XOT4 SOZNANI4 V PRIRODE NET ...
... although consciousness in nature *not* ...
... although *there is no* consciousness in nature ...

NEL6Z4 LI AVTOMATIZIROVAT6 ...?
Is *impossible* whether to automatize ...
It is not possible to automatize ...?

Formulations

It is impossible to quote all the formulations pertinent to the improvements shown by the examples because of the comprehensiveness of the formulations. The formulations were published as *The Transfer of Multiple Negatives in Russian into English* by R. Ross Macdonald with Bozena Henisz, Georgetown University Machine Translation Research Project, Paper No. 33, June 1963.
The following formulations are intended as an illustration.

D. *Class II negatives, conjunct and disjunct*

	Y	N	A
1. Is there a Class II negative i—n?	3	2	—
2. Translate i by means of the first meaning.	—	—	Z
3. Translate i by means of the second meaning.	—	—	Z

F. *NE*
d.

	Y	N	A
1. Does NE modify the predicate?	2	4	—
2. Is there a Class II negative in the segment?	3	5	—
3. Translate NE : Ø .	—	—	99
4. Translate NE : 'not' .	—	—	99
5. Use the existing routines for NE.	—	—	99

The following examples come form the translations runs made in Ispra.

V TERMICESKIX REAKQI4X NIKOGDA NE NABLHDALOS6 DIMERIZAQII
...
Feb. 64 In thermal reactions *never* was *not* observed the dimerization. ...
June 64 In thermal reactions *never* was observed the dimerizations. ...

, MY NICEGO NE TER4EM ...
Feb. 64 , we *nothing do not* lose ...
June 64 , we *nothing lose* ...

PO3TOMU NIKAKIX POPRAVOK NE VVODILOS6.
Feb. 64 Therefore *no* corrections was *not* introduced.
June 64 Therefore *no* corrections was introduced,

, CTO NIKOGDA NE OTMECALOS6 V LITERATURE I NE NABLHDALOS6 V NAWIX OPYTAX.

Feb. 64 , that *never* was *not* noted in the literature and was not observed in our experiments.

June 64 , that *never* was noted in the literature and was not observed in our experiments,

, CTO ONI NE IZVESTNY DL4 METIL-RADIKALA.

Oct. 63 , that they *not are known* for a methyl-radical.

Feb. 64 , that they *are not known* for methyl-radical.

PART II

The following is a presentation of linguistic formulations aimed at output improvement, which, however, have not been programmed yet, and consequently have not been tested in translation runs.

These formulations are the result of the present author's examination of translation outputs and concordances. The results of the investigation were written as a complete paper and are presented in their entirety.

The Transfer of Russian I into English

The research which led to this paper was made possible by grants from The Atomic Energy Commission and from EURATOM, which are gratefully acknowledged.

0. *Abstract*

This paper is concerned with the transfer of the Russian item *I* into English for machine translation purposes.

The problems connected with the existing rules are briefly discussed and are exemplified by some unacceptable translations.

A new set of transfer formulations is established.

1. *Objective*

The objective of this study was the establishment of a linguistic program for a more acceptable transfer of the Russian item *I* into English. The formulations were intended for inclusion in the Russian-to-English machine translation program.

2. *The Problem*

The transfer of homographic "isolated letters", of which *I* is one, is among the most complicated problems in MT on account of the multiple structural and semantic functions of these items and the lack, on the whole, of simple environmental clues for the resolution of the ambiguities. The procedure of Lexical Choice has been used until now for the resolution of the ambiguities and for the choice of English equivalents. (See the *General Report*, Georgetown University Machine Translation Research Project, Paper No. 30; and *Lexical Choice*, Occasional Paper No. 15). It has been effective to a certain extent, but in many cases the rules were based on broad environmental criteria such as subjects and predicates, or agreement and government strings. These criteria are perfectly valid, and often the only ones that can be employed, but solutions based on them obviously assume the correct identification of what is usually most difficult to identify and thus they are open to the risk of a high percentage of failures.

The research leading to this paper flowed out of the work on clause separators undertaken as part of a new correction and improvement procedure aiming at the simplification and condensation of the existing routines. The procedure was applied to two areas: to nouns exhibiting morphological ambiguities, especially in connection with subject recognition (nouns which have the same morphological form in the genitive singular and in the nominative and accusative plural), and to clause separators. The new aspect of the procedure consisted in providing a model of correct solutions and including it in the material to be run. As a result, machine-produced sentence diagrams were obtained which showed both the correct solutions and the analysis performed by the machine on the basis of the programmed formulations. This facilitated very considerably the identification of errors and, consequently, the correction and improvement work. One of the problems connected with clause separators is the transfer of *I* and, in particular, the determination of its function as a clause separator as against its other functions. This naturally necessitated the examination of all the functions of *I*, and the research led to the formulation of the linguistic transfer rules which are presented below.

A few examples will illustrate some incorrect transfers of *I*. These examples are from the translations made with the program as it was in February 1964. The desirable translation is indicated in parentheses.

G$A- I G$B-NAFTIL-RADIKALY, ..., IMELI I SXODSTVO I RAZLICIE
S FENIL-RADIKALOM.
A*i* beta-naphthyl -radicals, ..., had *and* congruity and difference with phenyl-radical.
('and', 'both')

ANALOGICNO PROXODIL I OTRYV VODORODA OT XLOROFORMA.
Analogously passed *and* the breaking away of hydrogen from chloroform. ('also')

OBRAZOVANIE DIBENZILA IZ BENZIL-RADIKALOV OPISANO TAKJE <u>I</u> DL4 GAZOVO1 FAZY.

The formation of benzyl from benzyl-radicals was described *and also* for gaseous phase. ('also')

KROME METIL- I 3TIL-RADIKALOV NAMI ISSLEDOVALIS6 <u>I</u> NEKOTORYE DRUGIE ALKIL6NYE RADIKALY,

Besides methyl- and ethyl-radicals by us there were studied *and* other alkyl radicals, ('also')

REAKQII PREDPOCTITEL6NOGO OTRYVA VODORODA PERED XLOROM OTMECALIS6 NAMI NEODNOKRATNO <u>I</u> RANEE.

The reactions of preferable breaking away of hydrogen before chlorine were noted by us repeatedly *and* previously. ('also')

TO JE SAMOE NABLHDALOS6 <u>I</u> V NAWIX OPYTAX ...

The same was observed *and* in our experiments ... ('also')

3TO JE MOJNO NABLHDAT6 <u>I</u> PRI REAKQII ...

The same it is possible to observe *and* by the reaction ... ('also')

ANALOGICNO <u>I</u> PRI REAKQII S SERO1 FENIL-RADIKALY PEREXODILI NA SERU,

Analogously *and also* upon reaction with gray phenyl-radicals went over on sulphur, ('also')

RAZLOJENIE METIL-RADIKALA NA (FBHF) 5 ESLI <u>I</u> MOJET IMET6 MESTO,

The decomposition of the methyl-radical on (long formula) if *also* can occur, (zero)

DAJE <u>I</u> PRI KOMNATNO1 TEMPERATURE IMEET MESTO REAKQI4 ...

Even *also* at room temperature occurs the reaction ... (zero)

3. *Corpus*

The material used for this study consisted of:

a. A concordance in physics based on a text of 83,000 running words,
b. A concordance in cybernetics based on a text of 45,000 running words,
c. Texts in physics, chemistry, mathematics and cybernetics of approximately 14,000 running words.

4. *Procedure*

The research was focused on the establishment of rules of transfer for those occurrences of *I* which call for a translation other than 'and'. Special attention was paid to the cases calling for the English equivalent 'also' and for zeroing *I* in translation. It was found most effective to base a few of the solutions on lists of items occurring in the environment of *I*, although it is fully realized that they may not be exhaustive.

Exhaustiveness was not attempted, and in some cases even deliberately avoided, since some infrequent and untypical occurrences of *I* would have called for numerous formulations based on very broad and unspecific environmental clues.

5. *Structural Analysis*

Among the most frequent functions of *I* are those of:

a. inter-clause coordinating conjunction,
b. coordinating conjunction between single or modified items (strings) showing structural concordance,
c. clause introducer,
d. a non-linguistic symbol (e.g. a mathematical one),
e. an enumerative conjunction,
f. an "additive" particle (this term is used here to refer to some occurrences of *I* which call for the translation 'also'),
g. an "emphatic" particle. (The term "emphatic" is placed in quotation marks, since a detailed analysis of the style of the writer would often be required to determine whether he uses the item *I* with the intention or emphasis of not. In any case, zero transfer is required in the cases to which the above term refers. One frequent occurrence of this type is between the subject and the predicate).

6. *The Linguistic Statement*

The following rules have been formulated for the transfer of *I*. They are presented in the form of a "verbalized flow chart", a description of which may be found in the *General Report*, Georgetown University Machine Translation Research Project, Paper No. 30, p. 68.

$i = I$

A	Y	N	A
1. Is i between quotation marks?	5	2	—
2. Is i+1 an equals sign, or a closing paranthesis?	5	3	—
3. Is there a $ keypunched immediately to the left of i as a prefix to i?	4	6	—
4. Is C keypunched immediately to the left of $?	6	5	—

	Y	N	A
5. Exclude i .	—	—	99
6. Do not exclude i .	—	—	B

B

	Y	N	A
1. Is there an i+n which is also I ?	2	C	—
2. Is there an item between i and i+n which shows morphosyntactic coordination with an item after i+n ?	3	C	—
3. Is there an item to the left of i which shows morphosyntactic coordination with an item to the right of i ?	C	4	—
4. Translate i as 'both'.	—	—	5
5. Is i+n+m also I ?	6	C	—
6. Is there an item between i and i+n which shows morphosyntactic coordination with an item between i+n and i+n+m and with an item after i+n+m ?	7	C	—
7. Is there an item to the left of i which shows morphosyntactic coordination with an item to the right of i ?	C	8	—
8. Zero i .	—	—	99

C

	Y	N	A
1. Is i−n (mostly i−1) a subject, or an adverb, or a noun in the instrumental case?	2	4	—
2. Is there a predicate to the left of i−n or between i−n and i ?	4	3	—
3. Is there a predicate to the right of i ?	7	4	—
4. Is i−n XOT4, or TAKJE, or DAJE?	7	5	—
5. Is i−1 E5E, or UJE?	7	6	—
6. Is i−1 BYL and is i+1 a short form adjective or participle?	7	D	—
7. Zero i .			99

D

	Y	N	A
1. Is there a predicate in i−n (mostly i−1) ?	2	4	—
2. Is there a subject to the left of the predicate (or between the predicate and i) ?	4	3	—
3. Is there a subject (a noun, or an adjective acting as a noun, or a pronoun) in i+n (n usually = 1, may ≦ 5) ?	13	4	—
4. Is i−1 an item from list 1 (see below) ?	13	5	—
5. Are i−1 and i−2 V CASTNOSTI, or A ZATEM, or PRI 3TOM, or ESLI JE, or TAK JE?	13	6	—

		Y	N	A
6. Are i−2 and i−3 A ZNACIT?		13	7	—
7. Are i−1 and i−2 and i−3 V TOM CISLE ?		13	8	—
8. Is i−n SLEDOVATEL6NO, or NO, or KROME, or PRICEM?		13	9	—
9. Are i−n and i−n−1 NE TOL6KO?		13	10	—
10. Are there a subject and a predicate to the right of i ?		E	11	—
11. Is i+1 BEZ ?		13	12	—
12. Is i−1 or i−2 PRI or DL4		13	E	—
13. Translate i as 'also'.				99

List 1

CTO, KAK, TO, OTSHDA, VPROCEM, DA, ODNAKO, ESLI, PO3TOMU, T.E., VED6, TAK.

E

	Y	N	A
1. Is i between two clauses?	4	2	—
2. Is there any item to the left of i showing morphosyntactic coordination with an item to the right of i within a clause ?	4	3	—
3. Is i+1 T.D. or DR. ?	4	A	—
4. Translate i as 'and' .			99

7. Conclusion

The formulations presented above are an attempt at a more systematic procedure for the transfer of single letters with multiple structural functions and with more than one English equivalent.

Further research on single letters is much needed. The problem, in addition to being of general linguistic interest, is one of particular importance for language mechanical data processing.

APPENDIX I: TRANSLITERATION OF RUSSIAN (CYRILLIC) CHARACTERS

Group 1	Group 2	Group 3	
А A О O	В V С S	Б B	Ц Q
Е E Т T	Н N У U	Г G	Ч C
К K Х X	Р R	Д D	Ш W
М M		Ж J	Щ 5
		З Z	Ъ 7
		И I	Ь 6
		Й 1	Ы Y
		Л L	Э 3
		П P	Ю H
		Ф F	Я 4

APPENDIX II: THE QUESTIONNAIRE

The following questionnaire, mentioned before, was distributed to scientists in the EURATOM Research Center in Ispra, Italy in the spring of 1964. Its purpose was to obtain an evaluation of machine translations from actual or potential users of machine translated texts.

This questionnaire was devised by Dr. Dostert.

An analysis of the results of the questionnaire was made by Mr. J. Rousseau of the group of Automatic Linguistics in the EURATOM Center. The statistical analysis given below is quoted after the one made by Mr. Rousseau.

I am grateful to Mr. J. Rousseaux for making his analysis available to me.

An asterisk following the figures denoting the number of answers means that either the question was considered not clear, or the answers were hesitant or divided.

Text	Physics	Chemistry	Mathematics and Cybernetics
Number of questionnaires distributed	23	20	9
Number of questionnaires with answers received	5	9	6

QUESTIONS	ANSWERS		
	Physics	Chemistry	Mathematics and Cybernetics
1. Is your knowledge of English			
fluent	5	8	5
fair	0	1	1
2. Do you have competence in reading Russian?			
yes	2	2	0
no	5	7	6
3. Are the difficulties presented by the translation such as to preclude the general understanding of the article?			
yes	1*	1*	2
no	4	8	4
4. In what degree of accuracy is the *information* transferred?			
adequate	3	7	0
sufficient	0	0	2, 1*
inadequate	2	2*	2
5. To make the translation available, do you consider that revision is:			
superfluous	1, 1*	1, 1*	
desirable	7	1	2
indispensable	0	2	4
6. The ameliorations that you principally wish the translation would aim at:			
General vocabulary	1	1	
Technical vocabulary	5	9	3
Grammar	3	1	5
Style	0	1	3
General presentation	1	0	3
Other	titles	titles	

QUESTIONS	ANSWERS		
	Physics	Chemistry	Mathematics and Cybernetics
7. Does the reading of the translation require an excessive amount of time, bearing in mind its length?			
yes	3	2, 2*	4
no	5	2	2
If yes, is this attributable			
a) to the subject matter	0	4* both	2* both
b) to the form of the translation	3	1	2
8. Are the last pages of any of the articles more easily and rapidly read than the first?			
yes	1	4, 1*	2
no	3	4	4
To what extent?		30% 50%	substantial
9. Have you had occasion to use texts translated on this system before?			
yes	1	4	0
no	4	5	6
If yes, do you consider the quality of the translations submitted for this evaluation really higher than those you have read before?			
yes	1	3	0
no	0	1	0
10. Could the speed of access to information compensate, in your judgement, for possible inadequacies of the mechanical translation?			
yes	3, 2*	7, 1*	4, 2*
no	0	1	0

QUESTIONS	ANSWERS		
	Physics	Chemistsy	Mathematics and Cybernetics
What is the maximum lapse of time in machine translation processing which you consider acceptable?	1 week — 3 persons 2 weeks — 2 persons 1 month — 3 persons		
11. Have you any suggestion or comment which could assist in evaluation of MT output?	0	0	0

Summation

Question 1: generally good
Question 2: generally no
Questions 3; 4, 5 — see following detailed analysis
Question 3: usually understandable
Question 4: generally satisfactory
Question 5: the answers differ according to the text, in the order from better to worse: chemistry, physics, mathematics and cybernetics.
Question 6: technical vocabulary
Question 7: mixed
Question 8: mixed
Question 9: generally no

Analysis of answers to questions 3, 4, 5*

Liste des réponses aux questions 3, 4, 5

Question 3: sens général de l'article (general meaning of the article)
Question 4: précision de l'information transmie (accuracy of the transmitted information)
Question 5: nécessité d'une révision (need for revision)

* This table is an exact reproduction of Mr. Rousseau's analysis.

La réponse est symbolisée par " + " si c'est la plus favorable, par " — " si c'est la plus défavorable, par " . " si c'est la moyenne. " + . " vent dire intermédiaire entre meilleure et moyenne, etc. (An answer is marked " + " if it is very favorable, as " — " if it is very unfavorable, as " . " if it is average. " + . " indicates intermediate between very good and average, etc.)

		QUESTIONS		
		3	4	5
ARTICLE	Chimie	+	+	.
		—	+	.
		+	+	.
		+	.	.
		+	+	+
		+	+	.
		+	+	.
		+	+	+.
		+	.	.
	Physique	.	—	—
		+	+	+
		+	+	.—
		+	+.	.
		+	—	—
	Math. — Cyb.	+	—	—
		—	.	—
		+	.	—
		+	—	—
		+	.	.
		—	.	.

APPENDIX III

This appendix contains exact reproductions of machine-translated texts. Samples of four translatios are presented here.

All of the translations were made on the 7090 computer with the SLC Programming System.

First, the first four paragraphs of the article on cybernetics, from which examples were quoted in this paper, are presented. The article is: CONCERNING MACHINE TRANSLATION FROM FRENCH LANGUAGE ON RUSSIAN (this title is machine-translated) by G. V. VAKULOVSKAYA and O. S. KULAGINA.

There are five parts in this presentation:
1) The Russian text
2) The translation of October 1963
3) The translation of February 1964
4) The translation of June 1964

Second, a sample of a text in physics is presented. This text was chosen by scientists in Union Carbide Nuclear, Oak Ridge, Tenn. The translation was a random run (i.e. the text had never been seen or examined by MT researchers).

One page of this translation is presented, preceded by the Russian text.

The translation was made in Union Carbide Nuclear at Oak Ridge, Tenn. in August 1964.

1. *The Russian Text*

(The transliteration System is given in APPENDIX I).

```
$P  1$  *
P* ALGORITM PEREVODA S FRANQUZSKOGO 4ZYKA NA RUSSKI1 ,
PRIVEDENNY1 V (/ 2$/) , REALIZOVAN NA MAWINE (( C$STRELA
)) PRI POMO5I 17$ PROGRAMM , OB5I1 OB7EM KOTORYX OKOLO
8500$ PRIKAZOV , I OKOLO 2000$ 4CEEK ZANIMAET TABLIQY I
KONSTANTY *
$P  2$  *
P* OPIWEM POR4DOK RABOTY 3TIX PROGRAMM I KAJDUH IZ NIX   *
$P  3$
P*  PERVA4 PROGRAMMA  -   PROGRAMMA POISKA SLOV V SLOVARE   *
3TA PROGRAMMA VVODIT V MAWINU OCEREDNUH FRAZU , PRICEM V
NAST045EE VREM4 , POKA NET AVTOMATICESKOGO CTENI4 S KNIGI
I MATERIAL VVODITS4 V MAWINU NA PERFOKARTAX ,
PREDPOLAGAETS4 , CTO KAJDA4 FRAZA NACINAETS4 S NOVO1
PERFOKARTY I ZANIMAET QELOE CISLO PERFOKART ( NESKOL6KO
POSLEDNIX STROK MOGUT BYT6 PUSTYMI )   *
POSLE POSLEDNEGO SLOVA FRAZY STAVITS4 TOCKA ,
ZAKODIROVANNA4 V VIDE DVUX STROK .. (FBHF)  10  *
KAJDOE SLOVO NACINAETS4 S NOVO1 STROKI PERFOKARTY  *
V KAJDO1 STROKE ZAPISYVAHTS4 7$ BUKV , PRIVEM 6$ BUKV
PIWUTS4 V RAZR4DAX ADRESOV ( PO DVE BUKVY V KAJDOM ADRESE
) , A 7$ - 4 - V RAZR4DAX KODA OPERAQII   *
ESLI SLOVO ZANIMAET NESKOL6KO STROK , TO VO VSEX STROKAX ,
```

KROME POSLEDNE1 , STAVITS4 ZNAK PERENOSA (1$ V
KONTROL6NOM SIGNALE) *
TAKOE RAZME5ENIE BUKV OKAZYVAETS4 UDOBNYM PRI KODIROVKE
FRAZY , NO ONO NE SOVPADAET S TEM , KOTOROE PRIN4TO V
SLOVARE , GDE VSE BUKVY STO4T PODR4D , A ZNAK PERENOSA
STAVITS4 V POSLEDNEM RAZR4DE 4CE1KI (ZNAK PERENOSA V
KONTROL6NOM SIGNALE MEWAL BY SRAVNENIH SLOV) *
PO3TOMU PERVA4 PROGRAMMA NACINAET SVOH RABOTU S TOGO , CTO
IZMEN4ET KODIROVKU FRAZY , ZAPISYVA4 SLOVO TAK , KAK 3TO
SDELANO V SLOVARE *
ZATEM MAWINA OBRABATYVAET SLITNYE ARTIKLI , RAZBIVA4
KAJDY1 IZ NIX NA DVA SLOVA , TAK , NAPRIMER , L$AU
PREVRA5AETS4 V L$A L$LE , L$DUQUEL V L$DE L$LEQUEL I T. D.
*
3TO IZBAVL4ET OT NEOBXODIMOSTI OBRABATYVAT6 3TI SLOVA
SPEQIAL6NYM OBRAZOM (KAK ARTIKL6 - PREDLOG) *
$P 4$ *
P* POSLE 3TOGO NACINAETS4 PERESTANOVKA SLOV FRAZY V
ALFAVITNOM POR4DKE, T. E. UPOR4DOCENIE SLOV PO
VOZRASTANIH VELICIN IX KODOV , PRICEM V MOMENT SRAVNENI4
KODOV DVUX SLOV K KAJDOMU IZ NIX POSLE KODA POSLEDNE1
BUKVY PRIPISANO CISLO 77$ (VOS6MERICNA4 SISTEMA) DL4
TOGO , CTOBY KOROTKA4 OSNOVA OKAZALAS6 POZADI DLINNO1 , V
KOTORUH ONA VXODIT , KAK 3TO IMEET MESTO V SLOVARE (SM.
(/ 1$ /) *
PRI PERESTANOVKE SLOV DL4 ZAPOMINANI4 IX PERVONACAL6NOGO
POR4DKA VO FRAZE STROITS4 TABLIQA SOOTVETSTVI1 (T. C.),
KOTORA4 IMEET SLEDUH5I1 VID *
KAJDOMU SLOVU FRAZY SOOTVETSTVUET ODNA STROKA T. S. *
STROKI RASPOLOJENY V TOM POR4DKE , V KAKOM IDUT SLOVA VO
FRAZE (T. E. 1$ - 4 STROKA T. S. SOOTVETSTVUET PERVOMU
SLOVU FRAZY , 2$ - 4 - VTOROMU , I T. D.) *
(PAGE) AD246$ *
V STROKE ZAPOMINAETS4 ADRES 3TOGO SLOVA V ZAPISI V
ALFAVITNOM POR4DKE *
ESLI KAKOE-TO SLOVO PRISUTSTVUET VO FRAZE NESKOL6KO RAZ (
IMEHTS4 V VIDU SLOVA , SOVPADAH5IE QELIKOM , VKLHCA4
OKONCANI4) , TO V ALFAVITNO1 RASSTANOVKE SLOV ONO
FIGURIRUET ODIN RAZ *
V T. S. DL4 NEGO OTVEDENO STOL6KO STROK , SKOL6KO RAZ ONO
PRISUTSTVUET VO FRAZE , I VO VSEX 3TIX STROKAX STOIT ODIN
I TOT JE ADRES *

2. *The October 1963 Translation*

PGPH. 1 .
    THE ALGORITHM OF A TRANSLATION FROM A FRENCH TONGUE
ON RUSSIAN , GIVEN IN (/ 2 /) , REALIZED ON A MAW

INE ((A //ARROW)) WITH 17 THE PROGRAMS, THE GENERAL VOLUME OF WHICH ABOUT 8500 ORDERS , AND ABOUT 2000 CELLS OCCUPY TABLES AND CONSTANTS .
PGPH. 2 .
    WE DESCRIBE THE ORDER OF WORK OF THESE PROGRAMS AND EACH FROM THEM .
PGPH. 3 .
    THE FIRST PROGRAM - THE PROGRAM OF A SEARCH OF WORDS IN A DICTIONARY .
THIS PROGRAM INTRODUCES INTO A MACHINE THE NEXT PHRASE , YET AT PRESENT , MEANWHILE NOT OF AUTOMATIC READING FROM A BOOK AND MATERIAL IT INTRODUCES INTO A MACHINE ON PUNCHED CARDS , SUPPOSES , THAT EACH PHRASE BEGINS FROM THE NEW PUNCHED CARD AND OCCUPIES THE WHOLE NUMBER OF THE PUNCHED CARDS (SOMEWHAT OF THE LAST LINES THEY CAN BE EMPTY) .
AFTER THE LAST WORD OF THE PHRASE PUTS A POINT , ZAKODIROVANNA4 IN THE FORM OF TWO LINES .. (FBHF) 10 .
EACH WORD BEGINS FROM THE NEW LINE OF A PUNCHED CARD .
IN EACH LINE RECORD 7 LETTERS , YET 6 LETTERS ARE WRITTEN IN THE DISCHARGES OF THE ADDRESSES (ACCORDING TO TWO LETTERS IN EACH ADDRESS) , AND 7 - 4 - IN THE DISCHARGES OF A CODE OF THE OPERATION .
IF A WORD OCCUPIES SOMEWHAT LINES , THEN IN ALL LINES , BESIDES THE LATTER , PUTS THE SYMBOL OF CARRYING OVER (1 IN A CONTROL SIGNAL) .
SUCH A DISPOSITION OF LETTERS TURNS OUT TO BE CONVENIENT UPON KODIROVKE THE PHRASE , BUT IT DOES NOT COINCIDE S BY THIS , WHICH TAKEN IN A DICTIONARY , WHERE ALL OF THE LETTERS THEY ARE IN SUCCESSION , AND THE SYMBOL CF CARRYING OVER IT PUTS IN THE LAST DISCHARGE OF THE CELL (THE SYMBOL OF CARRYING OVER IN A CONTROL SIGNAL IT WOULD MIX TO THE COMPARISON OF WORDS) .
THEREFORE THE FIRST PROGRAM BEGINS ITS WORK S THAT CHANGES KODIROVKU THE PHRASES , RECORDING A WORD AS THIS MADE IN A DICTIONARY .
A THEN MACHINE TREATS SLITNYE ARTICLES , BREAKING EACH FROM THEM ON TWO WORDS , SO , FOR EXAMPLE , AV IT IS TRANSFORMED IN A LE , DUQUEL IN DE LEQUEL ETC. .
THIS FREES FROM THE NECESSITY TO TREAT THESE WORDS WITH A SPECIAL WAY (AS AN ARTICLE - THE PRETEXT) .
PGPH. 4 .
    AFTER THIS BEGINS THE REARRANGEMENT OF WORDS OF THE PHRASE IN AN ALPHABETIC ORDER, I.E. REGULATING OF WORDS ACCORDING TO TO AN INCREASE OF MAGNITUDES OF THEIR CODES , YET IN THE MOMENT OF COMPARISON OF CODES OF TWO WORDS K EACH FROM THEM AFTER THE CODE OF THE LATTER LETTER ASSIGNED A NUMBER 77 (A VOS6MERICNA4 SYSTEM) FOR THIS , A SHORT BASIS TURNED OUT TO BE BEHIND LONG , IN WHICH IT ENTERS , AS THIS TAKE IN A DICTIONA

RY (CF. (/ 1 /) .
UPON THE REARRANGEMENT OF WORDS FOR THE MEMORIZING OF
THEIR INITIAL ORDER IN THE PHRASE BUILDS THE TABLE OF
AGREEMENTS (T. CH.) , WHICH IT HAS A FOLLOWING FORM
.
TO EACH WORD OF THE PHRASE CORRESPONDS AN ONE LINE T.
S. .
LINES LOCATED IN THIS ORDER , IN WHICH GO WORDS IN THE
PHRASE (I.E. 1 - 4 A LINE T. S. CORRESPONDS THE FIR
ST TO WORD OF THE PHRASE , 2 - 4 - SECOND , ETC.) .
(0)-(0)-(0)-PAGE AD246 (0)-(0)-(0)-(0) .
IN A LINE MEMORIZES THE ADDRESS OF THIS WORD IN A RECO
RDING IN AN ALPHABETIC ORDER .
IF WHICH - THIS WORD IS PRESENT IN THE PHRASE SOMEWHAT
OF TIMES (THEY THERE IS IN TO THE FORM OF A WORD , A
GREEING WHOLLY , INCLUDING COMPLETIONS) , THEN IN ALP
HABETIC DISPOSITION OF WORDS IT FIGURES ONE TIME .
IN T. S. FOR IT ASSIGNED SO MANY LINES , HOW MANY A TI
ME IT IS PRESENT IN THE PHRASE , AND IN ALL THESE LINE
S IS ONE AND THE SAME ADDRESS.

3. *The Translation of February 1964*

// . $ //PGPH. 1 .
.$ //THE ALGORITHM OF TRANSLATION FROM FRENCH LANGUAGE
ON RUSSIAN , GIVEN IN (/ 2 /) , REALIZED ON MACHINE (((//ARROW
)) WITH 17 THE PROGRAMS , THE GENERAL VOLUME OF WHICH ABOUT
8500 ORDERS , AND ALSO ABOUT 2000 CELLS OCCUPY TABLES AND
CONSTANTS .
//.$ //PGPH. 2 .
.$ //WE DESCRIBE THE ORDER OF WORK OF THESE PROGRAMS AND
EACH OF THEM .
//.$ //PGPH. 3 .
        //THE FIRST PROGRAM - THE PROGRAM OF SEARCH OF WORDS
IN DICTIONARY .
//THIS PROGRAM INTRODUCES INTO MACHINE THE NEXT PHRASE , YET
AT PRESENT , MEANWHILE NOT AUTOMATIC READING FROM BOOK AND
MATERIAL IS INTRODUCED INTO MACHINE ON PUNCHED CARDS , IS
SUPPOSED , THAT EACH PHRASE IS BEGUN FROM THE NEW PUNCHED CARD
AND OCCUPIES THE WHOLE NUMBER OF THE PUNCHED CARDS (SEVERAL
LAST LINES CAN BE EMPTY) .
//AFTER THE LAST WORD OF THE PHRASE THERE IS PUT POINT ,
$ZAKODIROVANNA4 $ IN THE FORM OF TWO LINES .. (LONG FORMULA) .
//EACH WORD IS BEGUN FROM THE NEW LINE OF PUNCHED CARD .
// IN EACH LINE THERE ARE RECORDED 7 LETTERS , YET 6 LETTERS
ARE WRITTEN IN THE DISCHARGES OF THE ADDRESSES (ACCORDING TO
TWO LETTERS IN EACH ADDRESS) , AND 7 - $4 $ - IN THE
DISCHARGES OF CODE OF THE OPERATION .
//IF WORD OCCUPIES SEVERAL LINES , THEN IN ALL LINES , BESIDES

THE LATTER , THERE IS PUT THE SYMBOL OF CARRYING OVER (1 IN CONTROL SIGNAL) .
//SUCH A DISPOSITION OF LETTERS TURNS OUT TO BE CONVENIENT UPON $KODIROVKE $ THE PHRASE , BUT IT DOES NOT COINCIDE WITH THIS , WHICH WAS TAKEN IN DICTIONARY , WHERE ALL OF THE LETTERS ARE IN SUCCESSION , BUT THE SYMBOL OF CARRYING OVER IS PUT IN THE LAST DISCHARGE OF THE CELL (THE SYMBOL OF CARRYING OVER IN CONTROL SIGNAL WOULD MIX TO THE COMPARISON OF WORDS) .
//THEREFORE THE FIRST PROGRAM BEGINS ITS/THEIR WORK FROM THE FACT THAT CHANGES $KODIROVKU $ THE PHRASES , RECORDING WORD AS THIS WAS MADE IN DICTIONARY .
//THEN MACHINE TREATS $SLITNYE $ ARTICLES , BREAKING EACH OF THEM ON TWO WORDS , SO , FOR EXAMPLE , AV IS TRANSFORMED IN A LE , DUQUEL IN DE LEQUEL ETC. .
//THIS FREES FROM THE NECESSITY TO TREAT THESE WORDS WITH SPECIAL WAY (AS ARTICLE - THE PRETEXT) .
//.$ //PGPH. 4 .
.$ //AFTER THIS THERE IS BEGUN THE REARRANGEMENT OF WORDS OF THE PHRASE IN ALPHABETIC ORDER , I.E. REGULATING OF WORDS ACCORDING TO INCREASE OF MAGNITUDES OF THEIR CODES , YET AT THE MOMENT OF COMPARISON OF CODES OF TWO WORDS TO EACH OF THEM AFTER THE CODE OF OF THE LATTER LETTER ASSIGNED NUMBER 77 ($VOS6MERICNA4 $ SYSTEM) FOR THIS , THAT SHORT BASIS TURNED OUT TO BE BEHIND LONG , INTO WHICH IT ENTERS , AS THIS OCCURS IN DICTIONARY (CF. (/ 1 /)) .
//UPON THE REARRANGEMENT OF WORDS FOR THE MEMORIZING OF THEIR INITIAL ORDER IN THE PHRASE THERE IS BUILT THE TABLE OF AGREEMENTS (T. CH.) , WHICH HAS FOLLOWING FORM .
//TO EACH WORD OF THE PHRASE CORRESPONDS ONE LINE T. S. .
//LINES LOCATED IN THIS ORDER , IN WHICH GO WORDS IN THE PHRASE (I.E. 1 - $4 $ LINE T. S. CORRESPONDS TO THE FIRST WORD OF THE PHRASE , 2 - $4 $ - TO THE SECOND , ETC.) .
//(0)-(0)-(0)- //PAGE AD246 (0)-(0)-(0)-(0) .
//IN LINE THERE IS MEMORIZED THE ADDRESS OF THIS WORD IN RECORDING IN ALPHABETIC ORDER .
//IF SOME WORD IS PRESENT IN THE PHRASE SEVERAL TIMES (THERE ARE IN THE FORM OF WORD , AGREEING WHOLLY , INCLUDING COMPLETIONS) , THEN IN ALPHABETIC DISPOSITION OF WORDS IT FIGURES ONE TIME .
//IN T. S. FOR IT ASSIGNED AS MANY LINES , AS TIMES IT IS PRESENT IN THE PHRASE , AND IN ALL THESE LINES IS THE SAME ADDRESS .

4. *The Translation of June 1964*

PGPH. 1 .
     THE ALGORITHM OF TRANSLATION FROM //FRENCH LANGUAGE ON RUSSIAN , GIVEN IN (/ 2 /), REALIZED ON MACHINE ((//ARROW))

WITH 17 THE PROGRAMS , THE GENERAL VOLUME OF WHICH ABOUT 8500 ORDERS , AND ABOUT 2000 CELLS OCCUPY TABLES AND ALSO CONSTANTS .
PGPH. 2 .
    WE DESCRIBE THE ORDER OF WORK OF THESE PROGRAMS AND EACH OF THEM .
PGPH. 3 .
    THE FIRST PROGRAM - THE PROGRAM OF SEARCH OF WORDS IN DICTIONARY .
THIS PROGRAM INTRODUCES IN MACHINE THE NEXT PHRASE , YET AT PRESENT , MEANWHILE NOT AUTOMATIC READING FROM BOOK AND MATERIAL IS INTRODUCED IN MACHINE ON PUNCHED CARDS , IS SUPPOSED , THAT EACH PHRASE IS BEGUN FROM THE NEW PUNCHED CARD AND OCCUPIES THE WHOLE NUMBER OF THE PUNCHED CARDS (SEVERAL LAST LINES CAN BE EMPTY) .
AFTER THE LAST WORD OF THE PHRASE THERE IS PUT POINT , ZAKODIROVANNA4 IN THE FORM OF TWO LINES .. (LONG FORMULA) .
IN EACH LINE ARE RECORDED 7 LETTERS , YET 6 LETTERS ARE WRITTEN IN THE DISCHARGES OF THE ADDRESSES (AS FAR AS TWO LETTERS IN EACH ADDRESS) , AND 7 - 4 - IN THE DISCHARGES OF CODE OF THE OPERATION .
IF WORD OCCUPIES SEVERAL LINES , THEN IN ALL LINES , BESIDES THE LATTER , THERE IS PUT THE SYMBOL OF CARRYING OVER (1 IN CONTROL SIGNAL) .
SUCH A DISPOSITION OF LETTERS TURNS OUT TO BE CONVENIENT UPON KODIROVKE THE PHRASES , BUT IT DOES NOT COINCIDE WITH THIS , WHICH WAS TAKEN IN DICTIONARY , WHERE ALL OF THE LETTERS ARE IN SUCCESSION , BUT THE SYMBOL OF CARRYING OVER IS PUT IN THE LAST DISCHARGE OF THE CELL (THE SYMBOL OF CARRYING OVER IN CONTROL SIGNAL WOULD MIX TO THE COMPARISON OF WORDS) .
THEREFORE THE FIRST PROGRAM BEGINS ITS/THEIR WORK FROM THE FACT THAT CHANGES KODIROVKU THE PHRASES , RECORDING WORD AS THIS WAS MADE IN DICTIONARY .
THEN MACHINE TREATS SLITNYE ARTICLES , BREAKING EACH OF THEM ON TWO WORDS , SO , FOR EXAMPLE , AV IS TRANSFORMED IN A LE , DUQUEL IN DE LEQUEL ETC . .
THIS FREES FROM THE NECESSITY TO TREAT THESE WORD WITH SPECIAL WAY (AS ARTICLE - THE PRETEXT) .
PGPH. 4 .
    AFTER THIS THERE IS BEGUN THE REARRANGEMENT OF WORDS OF THE PHRASE IN ALPHABETIC ORDER , I.E. REGULATING OF WORDS ACCORDING TO INCREASE OF MAGNITUDES OF THEIR CODES , YET IN THE COURSE OF THE MOMENT OF COMPARISON OF CODES OF TWO WORDS TO EACH OF THEM AFTER THE CODE OF THE LAST LETTER ASSIGNED NUMBER 77 (VOS6MERICNA4 SYSTEM) , THAT SHORT BASIS TURNED OUT TO BE BEHIND LONG , IN WHICH IT ENTERS , AS THIS OCCURS IN DICTIONARY (CF. (/ 1 /)) .
UPON THE REARRANGEMENT OF WORDS FOR THE MEMORIZING OF THEIR INITIAL ORDER IN THE PHRASE THERE IS BUILT THE TABLE OF AGREEMENTS (T. CH.) , WHICH HAS FOLLOWING FORM .

TO EACH WORD OF THE PHRASE CORRESPONDS ONE LINE T. S. .
LINES WERE LOCATED IN THIS ORDER , IN WHICH GO WORDS IN THE
PHRASE (I.E. 1 - 4 LINE T. S. CORRESPONDS TO THE FIRST WORD
OF THE PHRASE , 2 - 4 - TO THE SECOND , ETC.) .
(0)--(0)--(0)-- PAGE AD246 (0)--(0)--(0)--(0) .
IN LINE THERE IS MEMORIZED THE ADDRESS OF THIS WORD IN
RECORDING IN ALPHABETIC ORDER .
IF SOME WORD IS PRESENT IN THE PHRASE SEVERAL TIMES (THERE
ARE IN THE FORM OF WORD , WHICH COINCIDE WHOLLY , INCLUDING
COMPLETIONS) , THEN IN ALPHABETIC DISPOSITION OF WORDS IT
FIGURES ONE TIME .
IN T. S. FOR IT ASSIGNED AS MANY LINES , AS TIMES IT IS
PRESENT IN THE PHRASE , AND IN ALL THESE LINES IS THE SAME
ADDRESS .

5. *A Random Translation Run of a Text in Physics Made in Oak Ridge, Tenn. in August 1964*

a) The Russian Text

(PAGE) 92 C$3KSPERIMENTAL6NYE C$REZUL6TATY C$I C$IX
C$OBSUJDENIE *
P* C$KONDENSIROVANNYE NA XOLODNUH PODLOJKU SLOI TELLURA
OBLADALI SOPROTIVLENIEM , LEJA5IM V PREDELAX NESKOL6KIX
SOT KILOOM *
P* C$IZMERENIE SOPROTIVLENI4 V BOL6WINSTVE SLUCAEV
PROIZVODILOS6 V VOZDUXE *
C$PR4MO1 I OBRATNY1 XODY TEMPERATURNO1 ZAVISIMOSTI
SOPROTIVLENI4 PRI NAGREVANII I OXLAJDENII NE SOVPADAHT ,
PRICEM POSLE KAJDOGO QIKLA NAGREVANIE - OXLAJDENIE
SOPROTIVLENIE OBRAZQA PRI DANNO1 TEMPERATURE VOZRASTAET (
SM. RIS. 1) *
P* C$DLITEL6NOE NABLHDENIE ZA POVEDENIEM OBRAZQOV TELLURA
, NE PODVERGNUTYX TERMICESKO1 OBRABOTKE I NAXOD45IXS4 PRI
KOMNATNO1 TEMPERATURE , POKAZALO NEOBRATIMOE VOZRASTANIE
SOPROTIVLENI4 SO VREMENEM *
P* C$ZAVISIMOSTI SOPROTIVLENI4 OT TEMPERATURY OBRAZQOV
TELLURA , SKONDENSIROVANNYX NA PODOGRETUH PODLOJKU (150 -
160 DEG. CL$C) , PRIVEDENY NA RIS 2 *
C$I V TOM SLUCAE IMEET MESTO REZKOE VOZRASTANIE
SOPROTIVLENI4 OBRAZQA POSLE PERVOGO QIKLA NAGREVANI4 *
VOSPROIZVODIMOST6 KRIVO1 LOG R # F (1/T) USTANAVLIVAETS4
POSLE 4 - 5 QIKLOV NAGREV - OXLAJDENIE *
RIS. 1 C$ZAVISIMOST6 LOG CL$R # F (1/T) DL4 OBRAZQA
TELLURA , KONDENSIROVANNOGO NA XOLODNUH PODLOJKU *
C$VERXNA4 PR4MA4 OTVECAET USTANOVIVWEMUS4 REJIMU *
RIS. 2 C$ZAVISIMOST6 LOG CL$R # F (1/T) DL4 OBRAZQA
TELLURA , KONDENSIROVANNOGO NA GOR4CUH PODLOJKU *

C$VERXNA4 KRIVA4 OTVECAET USTANOVIVWEMUS4 REJIMU *
P* C$OBRAZQY GERMANI4 , KONDENSIROVANNYE NA XOLODNUH
PODLOJKU , OBLADALI SOPROTIVLENIEM V DES4TKI MEGOM *
C$KONDENSIROVANNYE NA PODLOJKI , NAGRETYE DO 500 - 550
DEG. CL$C , PLENKI GERMANI4 IMELI SOPROTIVLENIE , LEJA5EE
V PREDELAX OT 7 DO 30 KOM, (BOL6WINSTVO 10 - 16 KOM,) *
C$V 3TOM SLUCAE MOJNO UTVERJDAT6 , CTO SLOI POLUCALIS6
KRISTALLICESKIE (/1 , 2 /) *
P* C$SLOI , ODNOVREMENNO SKONDENSIROVANNYE NA PODLOJKI IZ
STEKLA , SLHDY I PLAVLENNOGO KVARQA , IMELI PRAKTICESKI
ODINAKOVOE SOPROTIVLENIE POR4DKA 12 *
C$PRI DLITEL6NOM XRANENII V VOZDUXE SOPROTIVLENIE
VOZRASTAET NEZNACITEL6NO (ZA 40 SUTOK NA 1 , 8 PCT.) *
C$ZAVISIMOST6 SOPROTIVLENI4 OT TEMPERATURY V INTERVALE OT
KOMNATNO1 DO 130 DEG CL$C BLIZKA K 3KSPONENQIAL6NO1 *
C$PRI MNOGOKRATNYX QIKLAX NAGREVANIE - OXLAJDENIE TOCKI NA
GRAFIKE LOG R $\neq$ F (1/T) DOSTATOCNO TOCNO LOJATS4 NA ODNU
I TU JE KRIVUH *
P* C$DL4 VY4SNENI4 VLI4NI4 VOZDUXA BYLI VYPOLNENY
IZMENENI4 ZAVISIMOSTI SOPROTIVLENI4 OT TEMPERATURY
OBRAZQOV TELLURA V VAKUUME *
C$REZUL6TATY IZMERENI1 V OS4X LOG C$R I 1/T MOGUT BYT6
PREDSTAVLENY DVUM4 OTREZKAMI PR4MYX S IZLOMOM PRI
TEMPERATURE OKOLO 90 DEG. LC$C (RIS. 3.) *
RIS. 3, C$ZAVISIMOST6 LOG CL$R $\neq$ F (1/T) DL4 OBRAZQA
TELLURA , KONDENSIROVANNOGO NA GOR4CUH PODLOJKU *
C$RESTNIKOM NA VERXNE1 KRIVO1 OTMECENO NACALO IZMENENI4
ZAVISIMOSTI V VAKUUME (SRAZU JE POSLE IZGOVTOLENI4
OBRAZQA) *
C$JIRNA4 LINI4 OTVECAET XODU ZAVISIMOSTI , SN4TO1 V
VOZDUXE *
C$NIJNIE QIKLY OTVECAHT IZMERENI4M V VOZDUXE SPUST4 DES4T6
DNE1 POSLE IZGOTOVLENI4 OBRAZQA *
P* C$POSLE KAJDOGO QIKLA NAGREVANIE - OXLAJDENIE
SOPROTIVLENIE OBRAZQA PADALO *
C$POSLE POLUCASOVO1 VYDERJKI V VAKUUME PRI TEMPERATURE 130
DEG LC$C SOPROTIVLENIE NESKOL6KO UVELICILOS6 , OSTAVA4S6
VSE JE MEN6WE PERVONACAL6NOGO *
P* C$PRI ZAPOLNENII VAKUUMNO1 SISTEMY VOZDUXOM
SOPROTIVLENIE OBRAZQOV UMEN6WALOS6 *
C$POSLEDNIE NAGREVANI4 OBRAZQA V VOZDUXE IZMEN4LI XARAKTER
ZAVISIMOSTI SOPROTIVLENI4 OT TEMERATURY V STORONU
SPR4MLENI4 KRIVO1 LOG R $\neq$ F (1/T) UMEN6WENI4 EE NAKLONA *

b) The Translation

(0)--(0)--(0)-- PAGE 92 (0)--(0)--(0)--(0) //EXPERIMENTAL
//RESULTS //AND THEIR //DISCUSSION .
    CONDENSED ON COLD SUPPORT THE LAYERS OF TELLURIUM

POSSESSED RESISTANCE , WHICH LIE WITHIN THE LIMITS SEVERAL HUNDREDTH KILOOM .

THE MEASUREMENT OF RESISTANCE IN THE MAJORITY OF CASES WAS CARRIED OUT IN AIR .
THE STRAIGHT AND BACK COURSES OF TEMPERATURE RELATION OF RESISTANCE UPON HEATING AND COOLING DO NOT COINCIDE , YET AFTER EACH RING HEATING - COOLING THE RESISTANCE OF FORM AT THE GIVEN TEMPERATURE INCREASES (CF. FIG. 1) .

PROLONGED OBSERVATION FOR THE BEHAVIOR OF THE FORMS OF TELLURIUM , NOT SUBJECTED TO THERMAL TREATMENT AND BEEING AT ROOM TEMPERATURE , SHOWED IRREVERSIBLE INCREASE OF RESISTANCE WITH TIME .

THE REALTIONS OF RESISTANCE FROM THE TEMPERATURE OF THE FORMS OF TELLURIUM , CONDENSED ON WARMED UP SUPPORT (150 - 160 DEG. //C) , WERE GIVEN ON FIG. 2 .
AND IN THIS CASE OCCURS SHARP INCREASE OF RESISTANCE OF FORM AFTER THE FIRST RING OF HEATING .
REPRODUCTION CURVE LOG R # F (1/T) INSTALLS AFTER 4 - 5 RINGS HEATING - COOLING .
FIG. 1 //RELATION LOG //R # F (1/T) FOR THE FORM OF TELLURIUM , WHICH WAS CONDENSED ON COLD SUPPORT .
THE UPPER STRAIGHT LINE RESPONDS TO INSTALLING REGIME .
FIG. 2 //RELATION LOG //R # F (1/T) FOR THE FORM OF TELLURIUM , WHICH WAS CONDENSED ON HOT SUPPORT .
UPPER CURVE RESPONDS TO INSTALLING REGIME .

THE FORMS OF GERMANIUM , CONDENSED ON COLD SUPPORT , POSSESSED RESISTANCE IN DOZENS MEGOM .
CONDENSED ON SUPPORTS , WHICH WERE HEATED UP TO 500 - 550 DEG. //C , FILMS OF GERMANIUM HAD RESISTANCE , WHICH LIES WITHIN THE LIMITS FROM 7 UP TO 30 KOM, (MAJORITY 10 - 16 KOM,) .
IN THIS CASE IT IS POSSIBLE TO AFFIRM , THAT LAYERS WERE OBTAINED CRYSTALLINE (/1 , 2 /) .

LAYERS , SIMULANEOUSLY WHICH WERE CONDENSED ON SUPPORTS OF GLASS , MICAS AND MELTED QUARTZ , HAD PRACTICALLY THE EQUAL RESISTANCE OF ORDER 12 .
UPON PROLONGED STORAGE IN AIR RESISTANCE INCREASES INSIGNIFICANTLY (FOR 40 DAYS ON 1 , 8 PERCENT) .
THE RELATION OF RESISTANCE FROM TEMPERATURE IN RANGE FROM ROOM UP TO 130 DEG //C IS CLOSE TO EXPONENTIAL .
UPON REPEATED RINGS HEATING - THE COOLING OF THE POINT ON DIAGRAM LOG R # F (1/T) SUFFICIENTLY ACCURATELY ARE PLACED ON THE SAME CURVE .

FOR THE EXPLANATION OF INFLUENCE OF AIR WERE ACCOMPLISHED CHANGES OF RELATION OF RESISTANCE FROM THE TEMPERATURE OF THE FORMS OF TELLURIUM IN VACUUM .
THE RESULTS OF MEASUREMENTS IN AXES LOG //R AND 1/T CAN BE REPRESENTED BY TWO SEGMENTS OF STRAIGHT LINES WITH BREAK AT TEMPERATURE ABOUT 90 DEG. LC$ C (FIG. 3.) .
FIG. 3, //RELATION LOG //R # F (1/T) FOR THE FORM OF TELLURIUM , WHICH WAS CONDENSED ON HOT SUPPORT .

BY THE CROSS ON UPPER CURVE WAS NOTED THE BEGINNING OF CHANGE
OF RELATION IN VACUUM (AT ONCE HOWEVER AFTER THE PRODUCTION
OF FORM) .
THE ALIPHATIC LINE RESPONDS TO THE COURSE OF RELATION , WHICH
WAS RECORDED AIR .
THE LOWER RINGS RESPOND TO MEASUREMENTS IN AIR AFTER TEN DAYS
AFTER THE PRODUCTION OF FORM .
    AFTER EACH RING HEATING - COOLING THE RESISTANCE OF FORM
FELL .
AFTER A HALF HOUR,S EXTRACTION IN VACUUUM AT TEMPERATURE 130
DEG LC$ C RESISTANCE SLIGHTLY WAS INCREASED , REMAINING
HOWEVER LESS INITIAL .
    UPON THE FILLING OF VACUUM SYSTEM BY AIR THE RESISTANCE
OF FORMS WAS DECREASED .
THE LAST HEATINGS OF FORM IN AIR CHANGED THE CHARACTER OF
RELATION OF RESISTANCE FROM THE TEMPERATURE ASIDE OF THE
RECTIFICATION CURVE LOG R $\neq$ F (1/T) THE DECREASES OF ITS
SLOPE .

The RAND Corporation

THE TYPOLOGY OF WRITING SYSTEMS

ARCHIBALD A. HILL

In one of the most authoritative recent books on writing systems, David Diringer classifies them into pictographic scripts, ideographic scripts, analytic transitional scripts, phonetic scripts, and alphabetic scripts.[1] The classification is essentially the same as that which has been in use since Taylor.[2] It has clearly proved its usefulness, yet since views of language, the entity from which writing is derived, have changed very greatly in eighty years, it would seem worth while to re-examine the nature and varieties of writing. Negatively, the current classification invites criticism in at least three ways. First, phonetic scripts (as Diringer is aware) should properly include both syllabaries and alphabets, instead of merely the former. Second, alphabetic scripts can be employed in such different ways that they represent fundamentally different approaches to the representation of speech — as for instance, with English and Finnish, both of which use the same letters. Third, the name ideographic for one of the main divisions, would for most modern linguists, seem unfortunate. That is, many linguists would assert that all writing represents speech, either audible or silent, and can never represent ideas which have not yet been embodied in speech.[3] A modern approach to writing systems would be one which would answer these criticisms, and more importantly, would place every system of writing in relation to that which all systems represent, language. It is such a classification which is proposed here.

Before the discussion proper can begin, it may be well to describe some of the basic assumptions on which it is built. The entities of language which include those I shall use are the discourse, which consists of one or more sentences; the sentence, which consists of one or more phrases; the phrase, which consists of one or more words; the word, which consists of one or more morphemes; the morpheme, which consists

---

[1] David Diringer, *Writing* (London, Thames and Hudson, 1962), pp. 21-25. See also, the same author's *The Alphabet, a Key to the History of Mankind* (New York, The Philosophical Library, 1948)
[2] Isaac Taylor, *The Alphabet, an Account of the Origin and Development of Letters* (London, Kegan, Paul, Trench and Co., 1883), 2 vols. Another important recent work which also follows nearly the same classification is I. J. Gelb, *A Study of Writing, The Foundations of Grammatology* (London, Routledge and Kegan Paul, Ltd., 1952).
[3] On the misleading assumption that a writing system can represent pure ideas, completely divorced from language, see Benjamin Lee Whorf, "Decipherment of the Linguistic Portion of the Maya Hieroglyphs", *Annual Report of the Smithsonian Institution* (1941), pp. 479-502. See also A. A. Hill, review of J. E. S. Thompson, *Maya Hieroglyphic Writing*, *International Journal of American Linguistics*, 18 (1952), pp. 184-186.

of one or more phonemes. The smallest linguistic unit is thus the phoneme; strictly speaking, the largest linguistic unit is often taken to be the sentence, with units larger than sentences thought of as belonging to stylistics. For the purposes of this paper, the dividing line between linguistics and stylistics can be disregarded. Besides the units here mentioned, one other will be relevant. This is the morphophoneme, defined as the class of sounds which fill a given slot within a given morpheme. The distinction between phoneme and morphophoneme is useful for understanding writing systems, and is adopted for that reason. Transformational analysts, on the other hand, deny the utility of the phoneme, and define the smallest unit as what I have called the morphophoneme.

With regard to these entities, writing systems can all be classified in terms of which units are recorded, and how. All systems record, or attempt to record the utterance, but some systems regard the sentence and all smaller units as irrelevant. Some systems record the morphemes, thus recording words, phrases, sentences, and discourses as successions of morphemes. Some systems record phonemes or groups of phonemes, identifying all larger units as successions of phonemes. There are thus three main divisions of writing systems; — discourse systems, morphemic systems, and phonemic systems. It is striking that many linguistic entities fail to appear as the basis of writing systems anywhere in the world. It is perhaps understandable that there are no sentence systems, since as transformational theory now tells us, the number of sentences in every language is infinite. Discourse systems would seem, at first sight, to be open to the same objection — that since the number of discourses is also infinite, an infinite number of symbols would be required to record them. Actually, all discourse systems are partial only. The reason why there are no sentence systems would then seem to be that the partial symbols which would be appropriate for sentence systems are also appropriate for combinations of sentences, so that all partial systems of this type become discourse systems.

It is quite striking, though not by any means always recognized, that there are no systems based on words.[4] The reason seems to be that unless words are identified by their phonetic content, they must be identified in terms of units of meaning. The result is that a non-phonetic system forces analysis of the meaning of words, and results in symbols which are nearly equated with the linguists' concept of the morpheme, which has often enough been defined as the smallest linguistic unit possessed of meaning.

It is often said that the primitive systems consisting of pictures are not properly writing systems at all.[5] A classification such as that proposed here makes it possible to show that these systems are basically the same as more advanced types. The purpose of writing can be said to be unique identification of an utterance. All systems leave some of the linguistic structure out of the record, since not all parts of linguistic structure are required for unique identification. Thus English, for instance, omits

[4] The term *logographic* is often applied to Chinese, or other systems. See below.
[5] Gelb, pages 24-59, puts all such systems in the forerunners of writing.

stress from its writing, and records pitch and juncture only very inaccurately. Morphemic systems leave out the whole phonemic structure, and discourse systems leave out all linguistic units. Since each system is therefore partial, each system relies on the reader's previous knowledge to supply the necessary background for successful identification. All systems rely to some extent on the reader's awareness of what is being talked about for identification, as when the phrase "Watch Repairing", in an English sign is read with the stress of a nominal compound, rather than as an imperative sentence consisting of noun and verb, which would have a different stress. Discourse systems are unique only in that they do not demand that the reader know the language of the recorded utterance, and rely instead to a very heavy extent on knowledge of the non-linguistic background.

Discourse systems can be subdivided into two broad types, though the border between the two may be blurred upon occasion. The first type is the iconic, in which the entities used as symbols are recognizable models of what is represented. This type more or less coincides with Diringer's pictographic systems. An elaborate and well-known example is given by both Diringer and Sturtevant,[6] which consists of a petition for fishing rights sent by a group of Indian tribes to Washington. The tribes were represented by pictures of their animal totems, the lakes in which the fishing was desired, by a map. Lines connected the hearts and eyes of each of the animals with the heart and eye of the crane who led; the crane's heart and eye were connected with the lakes. The meaning was that all were of one mind with their leader, and all wanted the fishing rights.

Systems may still be iconic and possess a considerable degree of convention and sophistication. Diringer gives a simple stick-figure type of drawing of two men and two bows with arrows, which records an Ewe proverb, "two adversaries can not hold the field", or "one must yield".[7]

Conventional systems are those in which there is no immediately discernable model-relationship between the symbols, or symbol arrangement, and the meaning. The best-known system of this type is the Inca system of knotted cords. In so far as these *quipu* represent merely the numbering system, they could be said to be iconic. Yet it seems that they were used to represent the main heads, and even sometimes the kinds of heads or points, of a discourse. It is interesting that conventional writing systems on occasion made use of collections of objects, not representations of them. One such is described by Diringer, from the Lu-tze on the Tibeto-Chinese border. A message consisting of a piece of chicken liver, three bits of chicken fat, a chili, the whole wrapped in red paper, meant "prepare to fight at once".[8]

Far as all these primitive symbolisms are from a modern Chinese or English book, I should like to emphasize once more their kinship to what we are accustomed to

---

[6] Diringer, *The Alphabet*, p. 34, and Edgar L. Sturtevant, *Linguistic Change* (New York, Stechert, 1942), p. 2. The example is ultimately drawn from Schoolcraft.
[7] Diringer, *The Alphabet*, p. 34. The illustration ultimately comes from Meinhof.
[8] Diringer, *The Alphabet*, p. 29.

dignify by the name of writing. No writing system is properly and completely a recording of a discourse. Such a recording could only be something like a color film with sound track. Rather, writing is a partial outline of an utterance, enabling the reader who has the proper background knowledge to identify the utterance uniquely, and to reconstruct a reasonably close parallel to it. In these terms, the mnemonic element in *quipu* or pictorial representations is different only in degree not in kind, from background knowledge demanded of a modern reader. Further, the primitive symbolisms are not so unintelligent in approach to the problem as they have sometimes been thought to be. All writing systems seek to perform their central task as efficiently as possible, leaving out all information beyond that necessary to identification. The primitive systems leave out the most information, it is true, but leaving out information is characteristic of all systems.

The systems which Diringer calls analytic transitional scripts are those which I have called morphemic scripts. Diringer's name is by no means the only one which has been applied to such typical examples of this group as the scripts of Egypt, Mesopotamia, China, and Central America. Gelb, for instance,[9] has a spirited discussion of the names 'ideographic' and 'logographic', of which he much prefers the latter. Even in Diringer's terminology, the dividing line between ideographic scripts and transitional scripts is by no means clear. I shall not describe the great morphemic systems at any length, but will point out that all of them show somewhat similar tendencies. There are often simple iconic signs for meaningful forms, like the sign for Chinese /šan (high level tone)/, 'mountain', which was originally an outline of a peak. There are also composite signs, which attempt to represent the semantic content of a word by symbolism which can often be amusingly ingenious, as the well-known Chinese writing of the character for woman repeated, to indicate 'quarrel'. There are also rebus types, with phonetic transfer. These types of morphemic or lexical symbols are not as interesting as a method which seems to be found in all of these scripts, and which in some of them has developed to the point where it is the basic device in the system. This is the system of giving two components for each sign, one semantic, the other phonetic, thus identifying the morpheme precisely by the intersection of the two. The system could be illustrated in English by a hypothetical word- character made by drawing two strokes for the semantic indicator, and a fruit for the phonetic indicator. The composite symbol would be a sort of puzzle, like saying 'think of something which has to do with the number two, and sounds like a fruit'. The answer, of course, is *pair*. This system can be illustrated from Chinese with the character for /kuŋ (high level tone)/, 'work'. The character can be used as the phonetic indicator in several composite writings, with various other characters as the semantic indicators (or as they are commonly called, determinants). With the character for 'heart', the combination indicates /kuŋ (high level tone)/ 'impatience', with the character for 'water', the combination is read /jaŋ (high level tone)/ 'torrent, flood'. With the character for 'talk, words', the combination becomes /jaŋ (high level tone)/, 'quarrel'. From

[9] Gelb, *op. cit.*, p. 106-107.

Mesopotamian writing, the system can be illustrated by the Sumerian writing for the deity, *Aššur*. The sign is composed of a semantic determinant, that for deity, and a phonetic component to be pronounced *Aššur*, meaning either the city or the God of that name.[10] As for the occurrence of two-part signs in Central America see Thompson's statement that Maya characters consist of main character, and 'affix'.[11] In Egyptian writing, a slightly more complex example is a three-part sign. The first part of the sign is the symbol which spells 'ear', *mester*. This form is, however, used phonetically, to indicate a word of similar sound, *mestem*, 'eye-paint'. The identification is accomplished by adding to the first sign a phonetic indicator, indicating that the termination of the word is -*m*, and a semantic indicator representing 'something under the eye'. The puzzle is a three-part one — 'think of something which sounds like 'ear', ends in -*m*, and comes under the eye'.[12]

The use of indicators, in addition to the basic morphemic signs, is a practice which leads to the system of writing which alone, it seems to me, deserves the name logographic, since as in the Egyptian example given above, the complex sign represents a specific word, which often may be polymorphemic. Aside from such composite signs, no morphemic system seems to be regularly polymorphemic, except for occasional petrified sequences like the English &. The community which has most fully developed this logographic use of a basically morphemic system by the addition of phonetic indicators, is Japan. The common way of writing is use of Chinese characters for the lexical morphemes, plus the purely Japanese kana symbols to indicate the termination. The kana symbols are typical bi-phonemic or syllabic signs, and the habit of writing with Chinese characters thus followed by kana is called *kana-majiri*, or 'mixed kana'. An example is the following sentence

KOno HITO wa YOi

This man subj good

The underlined sequences are written with kana characters, and thus clearly indicate that the word *yoi*, for instance, is intended, rather than some other form such as *konomi*, 'liking', 'fondness', which is written with the same Chinese character, but followed by the kana for -*mi*. The Chinese character which appears in both these words is itself a complex one, consisting of the character for *woman* and *child*, put together to indicate anything particularly good or pleasant. As such, then, it has no pronunciation, or rather, no relation to an individual word until a kana termination-indicator is added. It is worth pointing out that a secondary function which the kana in kana-majiri perform is that of indicating the boundaries of words and constructions.

The remaining great class of writing systems are those which record the phonemes of language. There are several subdivisions within this class, and the first can be called

[10] Gelb, *op. cit.*, p. 101.
[11] See my review of J. E. S. Thompson, *Maya Hieroglyphic Writing*, *IJAL*, 18 (1952), p. 185, and Thompson's reply, *IJAL*, 19 (1953), pp. 153-154.
[12] E. A. Wallis Budge, *Easy Lessons in Egyptian Hieroglyphics* (London, Kegan Paul, Trench, Trubner, 1899), p. 37.

the partial phonemic systems. Strictly speaking the name is not perfectly accurate, since all phonemic systems are to some extent partial, in that all slight or omit the supra-segmental phonemes. The name as used here is limited to a special group, those that limit themselves to a single class of phonemes within the large group of segmentals. The class designated, of course, are the Semitic writing systems, which limit themselves to writing the consonants, leaving the vowels to be supplied in accord with what best fits the context. There is both a structural and a historic reason for this peculiarity of ancient Semitic writing. The structural reason is that there is a high degree of correspondence between Semitic lexical morphemes, and abstractions consisting of three consonants; grammatical and derivational morphemes tend to occur as series of vowels dovetailed into the three-consonant roots to form the pronounceable words. To quote a hackneyed Arabic example, the abstraction /-q-t-l-/ underlies the whole series of words having to do with killing, such as *qatala* 'he killed', *qutila* 'he was killed', *qatl* 'murder', and *qitl* 'one who was killed'. In such a language, there is a plain invitation to record the consonant 'roots' alone, since these are the basic lexical elements, and to disregard the vowel morphemes, since these are often enough plain from the context. The historical reason for this peculiarity is that Egyptian scripts, the ultimate source of Semitic writing, had similar consonant indicators, though in pairs rather than triplets. These consonantal spellings were used as phonetic indicators in Egyptian, and thus constituted a precedent.

The systems which can be called polyphonemic are much more common. These are the types which have usually been called syllabaries, though there is seldom an exact correspondence between the syllables of a language using such a script and the written symbols. The polyphonemic scripts are characteristically two-phoneme symbols, together with symbols for vowels alone. Thus a word like *ability* (V CV CV CV) would be written with a single vowel for the first syllable, and symbols for consonant and vowel for the remaining syllables. Occasionally, as needed, there will be signs for single consonants, or for more than two phonemes. A typical example, and an interesting one, is the syllabary designed for Cherokee by Sequoyah. Cherokee has a rigid phonotactic structure, consisting almost altogether of VCV ... or CVCV ... The only closed syllables end in the single consonant *s*, and the only prevocalic clusters consist of a velar stop and following *w*. Accordingly, Sequoyah created symbols for /s/, and five syllables consisting of /gw-/ and a following vowel. With these, he could record the segmental phonemes of his language perfectly, and it is interesting to note that the only mistake made in analysis was that he provided the script with distinctions between [t] and [d], a distinction not needed in Cherokee phonemics.[13] It is unnecessary to enumerate the many polyphonemic systems which are in use, or have been so. The Japanese kana systems, and the writing of the Cretan Linear B are among the best known. The nature of polyphonemic systems, however, makes them suitable to languages with the phonotactic characteristics found in

---

[13] Diringer, *The Alphabet*, pp. 175-177. For Cherokee phonemics, see Ernest Bender and Zellig S. Harris, "The Phonemes of North Carolina Cherokee", *IJAL*, 12 (1946), pp. 14-21.

Cherokee. For a language like English, which permits heavy consonant clustering both before and after vowels, such systems work particularly badly. As Gelb points out, English *strength* in a typical polyphonemic script, would come out something like *se-te-re-ne-the*. It is also true that there is good reason why these scripts follow a CV pattern. Following this pattern, Japanese kana writing makes use of 65 symbols, five of which are for isolated vowels. To provide only for the two additional sets CVC and VC, would require 15 times as many symbols, or 975. Yet Diringer points out that there is one script, that of Woleai in the Carolines, which may have made systematic provision for CVC, though since information is scanty, the statement is not certain.[14]

When we pass from polyphonemic systems to monophonemic systems, we have reached the familiar alphabetic writing systems, about which we need say little. Yet alphabetic writing systems are possible of being classified in ways other than the familiar genetic. There are two main divisions — phonemic alphabets, and morphophonemic alphabets. Ancient Greek, Old English, and modern Finnish writing is phonemic, or mainly so. That is, there is a near approach to one symbol per phoneme, and this one symbol is employed without variation whenever the phoneme occurs. Modern English (and most other modern systems) are to varying extents morphophonemic. Whenever there are varying spellings for individual phonemes, and these spellings are fixed in accord with the morpheme which is being spelled, the writing system is morphophonemic. Morphophonemic spellings can be like those of modern German, where *Tag* and *Dach*, though ending in the same consonants before pause, are spelled differently since the final consonants are differentiated before case endings. Here the variation is essentially systematic and serves to show a regular kind of morphemic variation — it tells the reader that he must make a variation in the inflected forms of *Tag* which he does not make in *Dach*. A more pervasive type of morphophonemic spelling is that which occurs when a series of different phonemic spellings are merely used to identify differing morphemes. This is the general practice in English, where a given sequence such as /sáyt/ is spelled *sight*, *site*, or *cite*. Morphophonemic spelling, it is a truism to say, has been introduced all over the world by the printing press. It may not be quite so obvious to point out, in connection with modern spelling, that the objects of a good spelling system are two-fold. A speaker of the language should be able to pronounce correctly any sequence of letters that he may meet, even if they were previously unknown, and secondarily, to be able to spell any phonemic sequence, again even if previously unknown. Most modern systems, such as Spanish, French, or Hungarian fulfill the first aim fairly well, and fail primarily in the second. The peculiar badness of the English system lies in the fact that it fails about equally in both. How badly it fails was once illustrated for me by the difficulty an Oriental student encountered in transliterating his name into English. The sequence of English phonemes was /cúw/. He could have chosen *Chew*, *Choo*, or *Chue*, but instead chose *Chough* — about the worst spelling which is possible. Morphophonemic spelling,

[14] Diringer, *The Alphabet*, pp. 446-448.

when it goes as far as it does in English, brings the linguistic systems full circle back to morphemic writing, so that it is just about as true of English that we spell our morphemes by selecting strokes and placing them in the right order according to partially logical rules, as it is of Chinese.

University of Texas

HAUSA PERSONAL PRONOUNS

CARLETON T. HODGE

The presentation of pronominal elements in Indo-Hittite and Afro-Asiatic languages has generally avoided close analysis into morphemes. The work of George L. Trager on Russian, Arabic and French morphology is a noteworthy exception.[1] The possibility of such an analysis is often admitted; its practicality is just as often debated. The present author once considered an analysis of the Persian pronouns as 'somewhat clumsy but possible'.[2] A similar attitude is expressed by M. H. Goshen-Gottstein with regard to Biblical Hebrew. He remarks of the pronouns that "one may similarly agree that these are not free unjoinable morphemes, but rather complexes of mutually bound morphemes". This approach he rejects on several grounds, including the fact that "it would definitely assume a type of continuous bound morphemes which are not 'functionals'".[3] The balance between simplicity of presentation (paradigmatic listing) and rigor of presentation (complete analysis) has usually been tilted toward simplicity. This is understandable, and practical handbooks will necessarily choose the simpler form. Nevertheless, as Trager insists, "Any departures from rigorousness in the direction of pedagogical 'easiness' or the like should be made by starting from the full analysis and with explicit description of what is done and why".[4] It is in this spirit that the following effort is made.

An attempt to depart from the traditional treatment of Hausa pronouns was made by the present writer some years ago.[5] Although labelled 'pronoun alternants' (=allomorphs), the resultant charts were mere rearrangement of paradigmatic features. A much more complete chart of the same nature, given in the Hausa Basic Course, is the basis for the accompanying table.[6]

The occurrence of the forms found on the table is as follows:

---

[1] George L. Trager, "Russian declensional morphemes", *Lg.* 29.326-338 (1953); with Frank A. Rice, "The personal-pronoun system of classical Arabic", *Lg.*, 30.224-229 (1954); "French morphology: verb inflection", *Lg.*, 31.511-529 (1955) — see pp. 511-512 for the theoretical base; "French morphology: personal pronouns and the 'definite article'", *Lg.*, 34.225-231 (1958).
[2] Review of G. Lazard, "Grammaire du persan contemporain", *Lg.*, 34 (1958), p. 114.
[3] M. H. Goshen-Gottstein, "Semitic morphological structures — the basic morphological structure of Biblical Hebrew", *Studies in Egyptology and linguistics in honour of H. J. Polotsky* (Jerusalem, 1964), p. 109.
[4] *Op. cit., Lg.*, 31.512.
[5] Carleton T. Hodge, *An outline of Hausa grammar* (Baltimore, 1947), pp. 28-29.
[6] Carleton T. Hodge and Ibrahim Umaru, *Hausa Basic Course* (Washington, 1963), pp. 238-239.

Table of Hausa Pronouns

	1s	1pl	2sm	2sf	2pl	3sm	3pl	3sf	imp
1	nii	muu	kay	kee	kuu	šii	suu	'itaa	
1a	ni	mu		ke	ku	ši	su	'ita	
2.1	ni	mu	ka	ki	ku	ši	su	ta	
2.1a	nì	mù	kà	kì	kù	šì	sù	tà	
2.2	ni	mu	ka	ki	ku	ši	su	ta	'a
2.2a	nì	mù	kà	kì	kù	šì	sù	tà	'à
3	nì	nà	kà	kì	kù	sà	sù	tà	
3a	ǹ								
4.1	'a	mù	kà	kì	kù	sà	sù	tà	
4.1a	'								
4.2	'wa	mù	kà	kì	kù	sà	sù	tà	
5	nì	mù	kà	kì	kù	yà	sù	tà	'à
5a	ǹ					ỳ			
6						y	su		
7	ǹ	mù	kà	kì	kù	ỳ	sù	tà	'à
7a	n					y			
8	'ìn	mù	kà	kì	kù	yà	sù	tà	'à
9	'i	mu	ka	ki	ku	ya	su	ta	'a
9a	n								
10	na	mu	ka	ki	ku	ya	su	ta	'a
11	na	mukà	ka	kikà	kukà	ya	sukà	ta	'akà
12	naa	mun	kaa	kin	kun	yaa	sun	taa	'an
13	naà	mwaà	kaà	kyaà	kwaà	yaà	swaà	taà	'aà
13a		maà					saà		
14	nàà	mwàà	kàà	kyàà	kwàà	yàà	swàà	tàà	'àà
15						s	saa		

1. Independent pronouns. 1a. Alternate forms of these.

2.1 High tone suffixes to the verb. E.g. /yaamaṅtaaši/ 'he forgot him'. 2.1a Alternate low tone suffixes to the verb. E.g. /yaabaamù/ 'he gave [it] to us', /yaamaṅtaašì/ 'he forgot him'.

2.2 High tone suffixes to /zaà/ 'go' and /baà/ (negative verb). E.g. /zaàni/ 'I'll go', /baàmu dàšii/ 'we don't have it'. 2.2a Alternate low tone forms (less frequent): /zaànì/ 'I'll go'.

3. After /ma/ 'to' (/mi/ before /nì/, alternate /mu/ before /kù/, /sù/). /mù/ rather than /nà/ is used by some speakers. 3a. /ǹ/ occurs as a colloquial alternate to /nì/: /maǹ/ 'to me'.

4.1 and 4.1a After /n/ ~ /na/, /ṛ/ ~ /ta/. E.g. /'ùbaanaa/ ~ /'ùbaana/ 'my father', /'ùbankà/ 'your father', /hùùlaataa/ ~ /hùùlaata/ 'my hat', /hùùlaṛkà/ 'your hat'.

4.2 After /naa/, /taa/ forming 'mine, yours', etc. E.g. /nààwa/ 'mine' (possessed item masculine), /tààwa/ 'mine' (possessed item feminine), /naasà/ resp. /taasà/ 'his'.

5. After /baa/ in negative progressive construction: /baasù taašìì/ 'they're not getting up'. 5a. /ǹ/ and /ỳ/ are alternate forms after /ba/ (short): /baǹ tàfiyàà/ 'I'm not going'. See 14. for other alternate forms.

6. After /mà/, /màà/ to form 'one who has, ones who have': /màygidaa/ 'householder', /mààsugidaa/ 'householders'.

7. After /za/ ~ /zaa/ (future prefix): /zaǹtàfi/ 'I'll go' /zaakàtàfi/ 'you'll go',/zaỳtàfi/ 'he'll go'. 7a.The alternates /n/ and /y/ (without separate tone) occur after low tone negative prefix /bà/: /bàntàfiba/ 'I didn't go'. Otherwise 7 forms follow /bà/.

8. Neutral verb aspect,[7] initially and after /kadà/: /mùtàfi/ 'let's go', /kadàmùtàfi/ 'let's not go'.

9. Before existential /nàà/: /'inàà jiràà/ 'I'm waiting', /yanàà dàšii/ 'he has it'. 9a. /n/ is used by some speakers instead of /'i/.

10. Before /kèè/ (relative) and /kàn/ (habitual): /mèè mukèè jiràà/ 'what are we waiting for?', /mukànjee k'walloo/ 'we usually go play soccer'.

11. Relative perfective prefixes: /'àbindà kikàganii/ 'the thing you (f.) see', /'àbindà naganii/ 'the thing I see'.

12. Perfective prefixes: /naazoo/ 'I came', /munzoo/ 'we came'.

13. Indefinite future prefix: /naàyi k'òòk'arii 'ìnsàyaa/ 'I may try to buy one', lit. 'I may make effort that I buy'. 13a. /maà/ and /saà/ are alternate, more colloquial, forms. /kaà/ also occurs where /kwaà/ would be expected. This is considered a replacement by /kaà/, not a form of /kwaà/.

14. Alternate forms used after /baa/ in negative progressive construction: /baaswàà taašìì/ 'they're not getting up'. They are placed here because of the similarity to those in 13.

15. After /maṛà/ 'one who does not have': /maṛàs gidaa/ 'one who does not have a house', /maṛàsaa gidaa/ 'ones who do not have houses'. /maṛà/ also occurs without a suffix: /maṛà gidaa/ 'one who does not have a house'.

Distributionally the pronouns in 1 may be independent, those of 2-6, 14, 15 are enclitic or post-base, those of 7-13 proclitic or pre-base. It is clear from the table that there is a high degree of formal similarity and even identity among these pronominal elements. The phonemic sequence /ta/ (with no tone implied) occurs in every instance of the third person feminine. The same may be said of /ka/ in the second person masculine singular. On the other hand, the second person singular feminine /ki/ and the second person plural /ku/ show that the /k/ of /ka/ occurs in other combinations. The third person masculine singular offers the greatest complexities. Following is an

---

[7] I am indebted to F. W. Parsons for the concept of a neutral prefix here.

effort to present the morphemes which compose these forms. Each is given an identifying letter, a label, and is then listed as a set of allomorphs.

A First person: /na/ ~ /n/ ~ /m/ ~ /'i/ ~ /'wa/ ~ /'a/ ~ /'/
B Second person: /ka/ ~ /k/
C Third person: /s/ ~ /š/ ~ /sa/ ~ /ya/ ~ /y/
D Third person feminine: /ta/ ~ /t/
E Second person feminine affix: /i/ ~ /y/
F Plural: /u/ ~ /w/ ~ /a/ ~ /aa/ ~ /n/ > /m/[8]
G Singular suffix: /i/
H Independent pronoun affix: /'/ + V ~ /'/ + /y/ ~ /'i/ + /'/ ~ /'/
I Dependent tone: /'/ or /`/
J Impersonal: /'a/ ~ /'/
K Aspectually neutral: /`/ ~ zero before verb bases, /'/ before other bases.
L Perfective: /'a/ ~ /'n/
M Relative perfective: /'/ ~ /'kà/
N Indefinite future: /aà/
O Negative associative: /àà/

A list of other, conditioning, factors must be given. These are not here analyzed into morphemes but are, of course, analyzable. These 'environmental determinants' (with identifying letters) are:

a	/n/ ~ /na/ [4.1]		j	/baa/ [5, 14]
b	/naa/ ~ /na/ [4.2]		k	/za/ ~ /zaa/ [7]
c	/ṛ/ ~ /ta/ [4.1]		l	/kadà/ [8]
d	/taa/ ~ /ta/ [4.2]		m	/bà/ [7, 7a]
e	/ma/ [3]		n	/kàn/ [10]
f	/mà/ ~ /màà/ [6]		o	/kèè/ [10]
g	/maṛà/ [15]		p	/nàà/ [9]
h	/zaà/ [2.2]		q	Verb base taking pronoun
i	/baà/ [2.2]			prefixes [7-13]

(Numbers in parentheses refer to the notes on the pronoun table.)

The above orders (A to O and a to q) have no great significance. A—I will, however, take care of the pronouns which function as nouns, as well as certain other affixes. J—N are associated with the verb but combine with A—F. Of the determinants a—m occur before the pronominal morphemes, n—p after them and q before and after.

Table 2 restates Table 1, giving the morphemes involved and, to the left, relevant conditioning factors, both indicated by letters.

---

[8] See below on A /m/, F /n/ > /m/.

Table 2

		1	AGH	AFH	BH	BEH	BFH	CGH	CFH	DH	
q		2.1	AGI	AFI	BI	BEI	BFI	CGI	CFI	DI	
q		2.1a	AGI	AFI	BI	BEI	BFI	CGI	CFI	DI	
h i		2.2	AGI	AFI	BI	BEI	BFI	CGI	CFI	DI	JI
h i		2.2a	AGI	AFI	BI	BEI	BFI	CGI	CFI	DI	JI
e		3	AGI	AFI	BI	BEI	BFI	CI	CFI	DI	
e		3a	AI								
a c		4.1	A	AFI	BI	BEI	BFI	CI	CFI	DI	
a c		4.1a	A								
b d		4.2	A	AFI	BI	BEI	BFI	CI	CFI	DI	
j		5	AGI	AFI	BI	BEI	BFI	CI	CFI	DI	JI
f		6						C	CFI		
k m		7	AK	AFK	BK	BEK	BFK	CK	CFK	DK	JK
m		7a	AK					CK			
q l		8	AK	AFK	BK	BEK	BFK	CK	CFK	DK	JK
p		9	AK	AFK	BK	BEK	BFK	CK	CFK	DK	JK
p		9a	AK								
n o		10	AK	AFK	BK	BEK	BFK	CK	CFK	DK	JK
q		11	AM	AFM	BM	BEM	BFM	CM	CFM	DM	JM
q		12	AL	AFL	BL	BEL	BFL	CL	CFL	DL	JL
q		13	AN	AFN	BN	BEN	BFN	CN	CFN	DN	JN
q		13a		AFN					CN		
j		14	AO	AFO	BO	BEO	BFO	CO	CFO	DO	JO
g		15						C	CF		

The distribution of the first person allomorphs will serve to show how the tables are related:

/na/ occurs with 1) relative perfective /'/ (10, 11) 2) perfective /'a/ (12)
/n/ occurs with
    1) singular suffix /i/ plus independent pronoun affix /'/ + V (1) or /'/ (1a)
    2) singular suffix /i/ plus dependent tone /'/ varying with /`/ (2.1, 2.1a).
    3) singular suffix /i/ plus dependent tone (basically /'/ but varying with /`/) (2.2, 2.2a).
    4) singular suffix /i/ plus dependent tone (always /`/ after /ma/ and /baa/) (3, 5).
    5) dependent tone /`/ after /ma, /ba/ (3a, 5a), /'/ before base /nàà/ (9a).
    6) neutral verbal aspect /`/ (7), zero (7a).
    7) indefinite future /aà/ (13).
    8) negative associative /àà/ (14).
    9) plural /a/ plus dependent tone /`/ after /ma/ (3).

/'in/ occurs with neutral verbal aspect /'/ (8).
/'i/ occurs with dependent tone /'/ before base /nàà/ (9).
/'wa/ (with low high tone part of this allomorph) after /naa/, /taa/ (4.2).
/'a/ (with high tone on /a/ and the preceding syllable) after /na/, /ta/ (4.1).
/'/ occurs with /na/, /ta/ (4.1a).
/m/ occurs 1) with indefinite future /aà/ (13a), 2) before plural /u/ or /w/ (1-5, 6-14).

/m/ is not simply an allomorph but a portmanteau, being first person (nasal) plus plural (labial component). A similar analytic problem arises with /yaà/ and /saà/ (13, 13a), both being analyzed as third person plus /aà/. Although this was not done above, one could posit a plural allomorph zero, alternating with /w/, for /saà/, /swaà/. A zero allomorph of neutral verbal aspect is posited for /n/ and /y/ in 7a.

Indiana University

CHAMPION OR STAR?

HENRY M. HOENIGSWALD

In Greek *prōtagōnistḗs* means 'chief actor in a play'. It contains *prôtos* 'first' and *agōnistḗs* 'fighter, contestant' (*agōnízomai* 'contend, fight'; *agṓn* 'struggle, contest'). For a technical term like this the mode of formation is fairly normal;[1] in addition there are *deuter-* and *tritagōnistḗs* 'second' and 'third actor', respectively, as well as the more commonplace compounds like *antagōnistḗs* 'opponent, competitor' directly from *antagōnízomai* 'struggle against, prove a match for, vie with, act a part in rivalry with'.

Protagonist seems to have been English since Dryden (1671). It is natural that it should mean (1) "one who takes the leading part in a drama; the chief character in a novel or story around whom the action centers" as Webster's Third has it. But why does it also signify (2) "the spokesman or leader for a cause, the principal mover, CHAMPION" and "the supporter of an idea or action, ADVOCATE"? These latter meanings are perhaps the dominant ones in America. How anciently they are entrenched in British English it is difficult to know. NED lists "a leading personage in any contest; a prominent supporter of any cause" as a second meaning but the proceeds to quote, from 1839-52 (Bailey) "Thou the divine protagonist of time, The everlasting sacrifice" and, from *a* 1859 (De Quincey) "The great talker — the protagonist — of the evening" with perfectly bland metaphorical extensions of the classical meaning. It is perhaps not even with the quotation from Morley (1877) "If social equity is not a chimera, Marie Antoinette was the protagonist of the most execrable of causes" that we see the meaning "champion, advocate for a cause" clearly and centrally established. Its origin is a puzzle which these dictionaries not only fail to solve but which they ignore.

One cannot help thinking that the answer is contained in the synchronic picture. It is hard to maintain descriptively that *protagonist* still falls into its etymological components. *Agony* is too far away in meaning to let the second part of *protagonist* stand out, and words like *agonistic* are technical in a sense that *protagonist* is not. The prefix *proto-* may be somewhat more alive but its antevocalic variant *prot-* is also hopelessly restricted. The only real anchor far and wide is *antagonist*. The word appears in 1599 (Ben Jonson) glossed as "Your antagonist, or player against you" and then, freely, from 1607 (Milton) on. By now it is of course surrounded with a

---

[1] Kretschmer, Glotta 10 (1920), 40.

complete immediate family of its own (*antagonistic antagonize antagonism*, etc.) whether through independent learned borrowing or generated analogically.

NED remarks, under *antagonize*, that "in England, antagonizing forces must be of the same kind, but in the political phraseology of the U.S. a person may antagonize (i.e. oppose) a measure" (the evidence is from 1882). In keeping with this we are given an American entry for *protagonism* from the New York Evening Post (1909), where the phrase is "a protagonism of common sense, candour, and progress".[2]

Apparently the old pair *protagonist* (with *prot(o)*- as its first part): *antagonist* in its relative isolation tended to be reinterpreted, at least in America, as an instance of the then thoroughly familiar opposition *pro*- (from Latin *prō*) : *ant(i)*- 'for : against'.[3] To quote NED once again, *pro*- in this sense began around 1825 and became frequent and productive in the nineties, "usually in antithesis to *anti*-". It is fair to say that this reinterpretation could not have taken place if -*agon*... had remained an active item in the English vocabulary. But it may explain why a protagonist, quite unclassically, is now a champion or advocate as well as a first actor.[4]

University of Pennsylvania

---

[2] NED Supplement.

[3] That this *pro*- tends to have secondary or tertiary stress with open juncture is not a fatal counter-argument, considering the accentual and junctural alternations, both optional and conditioned, with which prefixes in the learned vocabulary are beset. Certainly *protagonist* can have a tertiary stress on the first syllable.

[4] In deference to the setting for which this note is destined it should be pointed out that our problem seems to have a French counterpart, possibly based on a parallel development. The pair *pro*- : *anti*- has of course been part of international European verbiage during the last seven decades or so. [I see now that H. W. Fowler's *Dictionary of Modern English Usage*, s.v. offers the same explanation.]

THE GOTHIC GENITIVE PLURAL -ē:
FOCUS OF EXERCISES IN THEORY

WINFRED P. LEHMANN

Linguistics in the time Professor Dostert has been a central figure in many of its activities has been open to experimentation, to examination of old problems with new approaches. A tribute can best reflect in one area his openness in all of his activities to new procedures: the incorporation of linguistics in language teaching which is now general; the introduction of contemporary linguistics to areas abroad which had scarcely heard of the subject; the similar role of introducing mechanized procedures, such as those available with computers, to a discipline facing masses of data that cannot be managed by a linguist and his card file. In commemorating his receptivity to new ideas, his readiness to expose old problems to new approaches combined with a willingness to admit that a new approach may provide us with insights rather than a final solution, I examine a problem in Germanic linguistics, treating the linguistic system from an abstractly structural point of view.

Alone of the Indo-European languages, as well as of the Germanic dialects, Gothic masculines and neuters and some feminines — the *i*-stems and those inflecting like the masculines, *u*-stems and root nouns — have long -ē as genitive plural marker in contrast with -ō in the other feminine declensions and reflexes of Germanic -ō in the other Germanic dialects. Various explanations, from the latter part of the nineteenth century to recent publications, have met little acceptance. A brief review illustrates the methodology of various periods of linguistic activity.

1. Gothic alone continued an ablaut variant of the normal Indo-European genitive plural, Möller PBB 7.489 (1880).

2. The ē took its vowel quality from the genitive singular of the *a*-stems, van Helten PBB 17.570-73 (1893); 35.273-75 (1909). Though based on analogy, this suggestion is not unlike the one proposed here and might be converted by a sympathetic reader to a structural explanation.

3. Indo-European -ō became -ē under certain circumstances, Mahlow, Die langen Vokale AEO 55, 105-110 (1888).

4. Final -jō of the *a*-stems became -jē and this ending spread, Osthoff, MU 1.240ff. (1878).

5. The ē may be the regular reflex of IE -ẽm < -*e-om*, Loewe, Germanische Sprachwissenschaft 2.9 (1933). Krahe, Germanische Sprachwissenschaft, leaves the question open 2.9 (1957).

The assumption that we must account for the -ē by determining a special development from an earlier item in the phonological system, or by means of a specific sound change of some kind underlies these five early attempts at explanation.

6. Starting from a different approach Brugmann, IF 33.272-84 (1913-14), proposed to explain the ē-forms from neuter nominative/accusative singulars, noting that in *i*-stems the stem vowel is missing before the -ē, e.g. *stadē* as opposed to *þrijē*; Old High German, with final -o, maintains the -*i*-, e.g. *liudio*. The genitive plural *barnē* accordingly developed from the adjective *barnēi̯an* 'childish'; this was made by suffixing -*yo*- to the locative ending -*ē*, and appending the case ending.

In this proposal of Brugmann's we may note on the one hand a dissatisfaction with attempted explanations based on individual phonological items alone, on the other an analysis drawing on morphological patterns. But unless we have some evidence for suffixes added to suffixes, an explanation like Brugmann's seems to us ad hoc.

7. Again seeking a solution in morphology, Sehrt proposed that the -*ē* was an instrumental-ablative which survived in the genitive, Studies in honor of Hermann Collitz 95-100 (1930).

8. The most recent attempt is that of Must, Language 28.218-21 (1952), who suggests that the ending really was an -*ī* (which he considers regular in the *i*-stems), but that the scribes wrote it *ē* to distinguish it from the relative particle. This suggestion assumes for Gothic scribes a sophistication which is not evident in the literary world today, except for the rare instances cited by Must. If however one were to admit that the Gothic scribes were as acute in graphemic analysis as some have assumed for Wulfila in phonology, one would still have to accept Must's explanation for the -*ī* and its spread from *i*-stems to other masculines and neuters.

Possibly our materials are inadequate to solve the problem. Possibly inadequate ingenuity has been applied previously. Have our predecessors dealt with it too narrowly from a fragmented approach with virtually exclusive attention to the development of individual sounds? It may be that an insight can be found through the application of a structural approach.

Such an approach would seek an explanation in the phonological and morphological systems of Gothic. This approach has the appeal of restricting its solution within Gothic; since the -*ē* is found only in Gothic it very likely resulted from characteristics of the language which existed at the beginning of our era to possibly the fourth century.

The most striking of these is the peculiar short vowel system. Disregarding complexities and variations in views, the pertinent peculiarity is its short vowel system of three members — see Twaddell, Language 24.147 (1948) — in contrast with a long vowel system of four:

	front	back	front	back
high	i	u	ī	ū
low		a	ē	ō

Structurally a single low entity in the short vowel system corresponds to two in the long vowel system: *a* corresponds to *ē* and *ō*.

When we examine the noun paradigms we find that the pertinent marker of the genitive singular is a consonant or a consonant cluster following a vowel which in the masculine and neuter is front, in the feminine back. In the *n*-stems, which are similar in the three genders, we find:

		Masculine	Neuter		Feminine
	nom.	guma	hairtō	but	tuggō
Sg.	gen.	gumins	hairtins		tuggōns
		FRONT		VS.	BACK

In the vowel declensions we again find this contrast with the feminine:

	nom.	dags	waurd	but	giba
Sg.					
	gen.	dagis	waurdis		gibōs
		FRONT		VS.	BACK

We may conclude that the essential marker of the genitive in the masculine and neuter was a front vowel.

Equipped with a phonological system in which there was no contrast of low vowels when short, speakers of Gothic may have also treated the long low vowels as non-contrasting morphologically, and they may have selected -*ē* from the morphologically non-contrasting unit {*ē ō*} for the masculine and neuter plurals, e.g.

	nom.	dagōs	waurda	gibōs
Pl.				but
	gen.	dagē	waurdē	gibō
	nom.	gumans	hairtōna	tuggōns
				but
	gen.	gumanē	hairtanē	tuggōnō

This proposal for the origin of the -*ē* presupposes no special phonological development (in older terminology, no special sound law), no aberrant pre-Gothic form, merely a selection occasioned by the phonological and morphological structure of Gothic.

It may gain support when we note that the vowels of masculine and neuter genitive singulars in North Germanic were not front, e.g. Runic *godagas*, and accordingly would not have established a front contrast as marker of the masculine/neuter genitive. Also in Old English and Old Saxon there are reflexes of a back vowel, as in Old Saxon *dagas*. Nor did the pre-stages of these dialects have a three-member, short vowel system. Accordingly they differed from Gothic in their phonological and morphological structures in such a way that there was no situation which might lead to the formation of a genitive plural ending in a front vowel comparable to that of Gothic -*ē*. The differing structure of the other dialects in phonology and morphology therefore aids us in understanding why they did not share the development in Gothic.

This explanation would account for the presence of -ē where it occurs, its absence elsewhere. Since the marker of the genitive was frontness as opposed to the nominative, we expect -ē in those paradigms in which the genitive singular is characterized by a front vowel:

the ɔ-stems	dags	: dagis	:: dagōs	: dagē
	waurd	: waurdis	:: waurda	: waurdē
the i-stems	gasts	: gastis	:: gasteis	: gastē
the u-stems	sunus	: sunaus	:: sunjus	: suniwē
the n-stems	guma	: gumins	:: gumans	: gumanē
	hairtō	: hairtins	:: hairtōna	: hairtanē
the r-stems	brōþar	: brōþrs (<-is)	:: brōþrjus	: brōþrē
the nd-stems	nasjands	: nasjandis	:: nasjands	: nasjandē
consonant stems	baurgs	: baurgs (<-is)	:: baurgs	: baurgē

but not

the ɔ̄-stems	giba	: gibōs	:: gibōs	: gibō
the ɔ̄n-stems	tuggō	: tuggōns	:: tuggōns	: tuggōnō

As noted above, the pattern for some inflections was set by corresponding paradigms, such as the ɔ-stems for the i-stems; the -jɔ-stems, -iɔ-stems and -jɔ̄-stems also follow the pattern of the base paradigm, in which the fronted marker of the genitive was either not employed (feminines) or was characteristic (masculines and neuters).

But can we admit such a high degree of structural awareness among speakers of a language? Is it realistic to assume that morphological categories may be marked by relative points, by contrasts in a phonological system rather than by specific phonemes? May we then ascribe to the morphological structure of a language phonological innovations? A proper evaluation of the role of structure as languages undergo change may be possible when we have data on linguistic modifications from a great variety of languages.

The University of Texas

ON THE ETYMOLOGY OF *SCARF*

KEMP MALONE

The NED recognizes five nouns and three verbs with the form *scarf*. Of these, I will not take up *scarf* sb.³, a variant of *scarp*, nor *scarf* sb.⁴, the name of a bird. I begin with *scarf* sb.², the oldest of the *scarf* words in English, if we may go by dates of occurrence. The earliest quotation given in the NED for this word is dated 1497 and reads, "Certeyn Scarffe Tymbre price — viijˢ vjᵈ". It was taken from *Naval accounts and inventories of the reign of Henry VII* 1485-97 (Navy Records Soc. 1896), p. 312. The NED defines *scarf-timber* as 'timber in short lengths for scarfing'. The process of scarfing is explained thus by Peter Nicholson in his book *The new practical builder and workman's companion* (1823), p. 80:

... the art of connecting two pieces of timber together, in such a manner as to appear like one piece. (NED)

This very broad definition brings to mind an earlier one of *dovetailing* quoted in the NED under *dovetail* sb.:

1565-73 COOPER *Thesaurus*, *Securicla* ... A swallowe tayle or dooue tayle in carpenters workes, which is a fastning of two peeces of timber or bourdes togither that they can not be away.

And obviously scarfing and dovetailing are akin, in their aims at least.

The editors of the NED, in their etymological note under *scarf* sb.², say,

Words of related form and identical meaning (chiefly belonging to the nautical vocabulary) are found in several mod. langs., but recorded much later than in English: ... Sw. *skarf*, Norw. *skarv* piece added to lengthen a board or a garment, also the joint or seam by which this is effected; Sw. *skarfva*, Norw. *skarva*, *skjerva* to lengthen by joining or sewing on an additional piece ... The fact that the Sw. words are not, like those in the other langs., exclusively technical, but have a wider meaning, seems to afford a slight presumption in favour of Scandinavian as the ultimate source. ...

The editors fail to cite ON *skarfr* piece, presumably because it did not come to their notice (it is wanting in the Cleasby-Vigfússon *Icelandic-English Dictionary*). J. Fritzner however duly recorded it in his *Ordbog over det gamle norske Sprog*, with this definition:

Stykke som paa skraa frahugges Enden af en Fjæl eller Stok, saaledes at hele Endefladen medtages deri f. Ex. i Tilfælde af at man vil sammenfælde 2 Bord med deri i saadant Øiemed tildannede Ender ...

Piece that is cut slantwise off the end of a board or beam, in such a way that the whole end surface goes with it, for example in case one wishes to join 2 boards with ends on them shaped for such a purpose (i.e. for joining) ...

If I understand aright Fritzner's example, the *skarfr* is the piece that is cut off (and presumably scrapped) when one shapes a board to be joined, at one end, to another board. Cutting the old ends off slantwise makes the new ends come to a point, that of one board to the right, that of the other to the left, and when the ends are joined their edges, if properly cut, will come together all along the line, making a good fit, easy to fasten securely.

Besides this example Fritzner gives a quotation, taken from verses of ancient date that have come down to us in the *Hervararsaga*. I quote directly from the saga (Fritzner has only the last four words of the passage, thrown into the nominative construction):

> Ek mun þar enskis eyris krefja
> né skjallanda skarfs or golli

'There I will demand no money, nor clinking gold piece.'

We have to do here, it would seem, with a coin, though the speaker (Gizurr) conceivably was represented as thinking simply of a piece of gold, irrespective of its form; if so, it might have been a coin, a ring, or anything else golden that would clink. The word is also entered, in its modern form *skarfur*, in Blöndal's *Islandsk-Dansk Ordbog*, where it is marked obsolete and glossed 'Skærv (en Mønt)' i.e. 'mite (a coin)'.

The NED editors say nothing about Danish *skar(v)* piece either, though this noun is cognate with Norwegian *skarv* and Swedish *skarf*, which they do cite, as it is with Icelandic *skarfr*. Of the corresponding verb, *skarve* or *skarre* in early modern Danish, *skarfue* (i.e. *skarfve*) in Old Danish, they say, "Da. has in this sense *skarre*, the relation of which to the Sw. form is obscure." Obviously they were not aware that in Danish *skarve* as well as *skarre* occurred; it still occurs in written though hardly in spoken Danish.

The big *Ordbog over det danske Sprog* gives as its first meaning for *skar(v)*

stykke, der er øget til ell. sammenfældet med noget andet; især om lap (paa tøj), tømmerstykke olgn.

piece that is added to or joined with something else; especially of patch (on clothes), piece of timber and the like.

The first two meanings given for the corresponding verb are

(tøm.) fælde et stykke tømmer ind i et andet ved udskæring i dette, hvori det første indpasses, ved skraaskæring af de ender, der sammenføjes, ell. paa anden maade, saaledes at der til at fastholde de to stykker kun behøves bolte; ogs.: forlænge (en bjælke olgn.) ved at tilsætte et stykke paa den angivne maade;

(timber) join one piece of timber to another (1) by a cutting out in the one into which the other is fitted, (2) by a cutting slantwise of the ends that are joined, or (3) in some other way, so that only bolts are needed to keep the two pieces joined; also: lengthen (a beam or the like) by adding a piece as set forth above;

(dial.) m.h.t. andre ting, især tøj, reb olgn.: indføje et stykke i et andet for at forstørre, forlænge det ell. som erstatning for et slidt parti, som lap olgn.; ogs.: samle, sammenføje to stykker ell. forlænge et stykke ved tilsætning af et andet.

(dial.) of other things, especially clothes, rope and the like: add one piece to another in order to enlarge, lengthen this or as replacement for a torn or worn part, as patch or the like; also: join two pieces or lengthen one piece by adding another.

According to the *Ordbog*, Danish *skar(v)* piece is the same word as early modern Danish *skarv* little coin, mite and MLG *scharf* shard, mite, and the corresponding verb *skarve* or *skarre* is cognate with OE *scearfian* etc. Here the *Ordbog* echoes an etymology of long standing, an old consensus. The editors of the NED reject the etymology, though offering nothing in its place. They say,

The Sw. *skarf* has commonly been referred to the Teut. root * *skerb-*, *skarb-*, represented by OE *scearfian* (= OHG *scarpôn*, G. *scharben*) to cut into shreds, OE *sceorfan* str. vb., to gnaw, bite, scarify, Du. *scherf* (= OHG *scirbi*, G. *scherbe*) potsherd; but affinity in meaning seems wanting.

In my opinion the affinity that the editors did not find is there and the old consensus is sound. I will begin my discussion of the point with OE *scearfian*.
In some contexts this verb, like its cognate, German *scharben*, clearly means 'chop up, mince' (though hardly 'shred'), witness a sentence quoted (from *Leechdoms*) in the Bosworth-Toller dictionary:

Genim ða ylcan wyrte, scearfa hy ðonne, and gnid swyðe smale to duste
'take that same herb, then cut it up, and rub very small, to powder'.

This sense is technical; it belongs first of all to cook-book speech and so to that of medicinal preparations. But in ordinary speech (*ge*)*scearfian* means 'cut off' or 'cut down' rather than 'cut up'. Thus, the simplex glosses Latin *succidere* 'cut off (from below), cut down' (Vulgate) in the Lindisfarne *Luke* 13.7 and *gescearfian* glosses the same word in *Luke* 13.9. The passage is the parable of the barren fig-tree. Note that the OHG cognate *scarbôn* means simply "cut in two'.

As a denominative verb, *scearfian* is to be derived from an unrecorded proto-English (or pre-English) noun which in classical OE would have had the form **scearf*. This noun and its derivative have the same base, of course, a gradational variant of the base *sceorf* found in OE *sceorfan* bite. And since *sceorfan* means 'bite' the noun **scearf* presumably meant 'bit, piece' (i.e. the portion bitten off). But biting is not the only way to divide a whole into bits or pieces; often cutting with some tool (e.g. knife or saw) will do the work even better. We need not wonder, then, that OE *scearfian* may mean 'cut off'. Whether the noun had come to mean 'part cut off' (alongside or instead of its earlier sense 'part bitten off') before the derivative verb *scearfian* was formed we shall never know, but we do know that the cognate ON *skarfr* might mean 'part cut off.' If a whole is a mass of metal it may be divided into parts by minting, and the parts got in this way, commonly called coins, are also called bits or pieces, as in *threepenny bit* and *gold piece*. Hence the meaning 'mite' for Icel. *skarfur* (obs.), MLG *scharf*, and Danish *skarv*. But in the verses quoted above, *skarfr* means 'piece of money,' not 'mite' (i.e. 'small piece of money').

In 14th-century English and thereafter the noun *piece* may also be used as a verb. I quote the first two definitions of the verb given in the NED:

1. To mend, repair, make whole, or complete by adding a piece or pieces; to patch. 2. To join, unite or put together, so as to form one piece; to mend (something broken) by joining the pieces; ...

Note also the phrase *piece out*, defined in the NED thus: 'to complete, eke out, extend, or enlarge by the addition of a piece'. In like manner (so I think) the Scandinavian noun *skarf* piece gave rise to a verb having meanings identical, or nearly so, with those of English *piece* vb. Hence Swed. *skarva*, Norw. *skarve*, and Dan. *skarve* or *skarre* (see above). This verb in turn had its influence on the noun, which came to mean 'piece added or joined to something else'. Since all the Scandinavian languages already had in ON *stykki*, Dan. and Norw. *stykke*, and Swed. *stycke* (cognate with OE *stycce*) a perfectly good word for 'piece', their *skarf(r)* was excess baggage in the generic sense and could readily develop specialized meanings like the ones given above. What now of English *scarf*? The definition of *scarf* sb.² in the NED reads as follows:

1. *Carpentry* and *Shipbuilding*. A joint by which two timbers are connected longitudinally into a continuous piece, the ends being halved, notched, or cut away so as to fit into each other with mutual overlapping. b. *Shipbuilding*. The overlapping of adjacent timbers in a ship's frame, ... [Sense b, first recorded in the 18th century, is marked obsolete.]

Compare the corresponding definition in the big *Century Dictionary*:

In *carp.*, a joint by which the ends of two pieces of timber are united so as to form a continuous piece; also, the part cut away from each of two pieces of timber to be joined together longitudinally, so that the corresponding ends may fit together in an even joint.

Note that the second part of this definition agrees with Fritzner's definition of ON *skarfr* (see above). *Webster's Third New International Dictionary* gives two definitions relevant at this point:

1: either of the chamfered or cutaway ends that fit together to form a scarf joint 2: SCARF-JOINT

The three dictionaries agree in calling the joint itself a scarf. Only *Webster's* gives 'chamfered or cutaway end' as another meaning of the word, and only the *Century* gives 'part cut away from each of two pieces to be joined ...' as another meaning. One wonders if the editors of the *Century* misunderstood an informant who had in mind ends already shaped for joining but expressed himself badly. But of course the meaning in question may actually have survived to the present. Unluckily the editors give no quotation and I have found none.

Both the NED and the *Century* fail to record yet another sense, defined thus in *Webster's*: 'the beveled face of a stump or log produced by the undercut in tree felling'. Compare the *Dictionary of American English* under *Scarf, n.*³, where the definition reads: 'A V-shaped or diagonal cut through a limb or tree'. The two definitions deal with the same thing but approach it differently: the DAE in terms of the action (a cut), *Webster's* in terms of the state of things after the action. The etymological conjecture in the DAE ("?Variant of *kerf*") is without merit and *Webster's* inclusion of this sense under its ³*scarf* (the NED's *scarf* sb.²) is surely right.

Scarf v.² (NED) is defined briefly enough: 'to join by a scarf-joint'. The verb, since it takes the form *scarf* (not *scarve), must be from the noun and makes no etymological problems. That the noun got into English from some foreign source is evident from the initial /sk/ and that this source was Scandinavian seems reasonably clear, though the NED editors flirt with a hypothetical OF *escarf, itself presumably Scandinavian in origin.

They go more confidently to French for *scarf* sb.¹ H. C. Wyld in his *Universal Dictionary* was much less confident. He writes,

16th cent., not in M.E. The origin & history of the word are difficult. Connexion w. O. Fr. *escarpe*, said to be fr. *escreppe* 'pilgrim's scrip', ... is hard to explain, seeing the final -*f*; cp. also Du. *scherf* 'officer's sash'.

I have not found this Dutch word (Middle Dutch had *scharpe*, replaced in modern Dutch by *sjerp*<German *schärpe*) and suspect it of being English *scarf* in Dutch dress; in earlier modern English *scarf* was pronounced /skærf/ and the Dutch might well have imitated this with *scherf* /sxerf/. (Wyld could hardly have had Dutch *scherf* shard, fragment in mind.)

In the 16th century *scarf* was the English name for a strip or band of cloth (wool or silk) worn round neck or waist or slantwise across the body; a sling for a bad arm and a bandage or blindfold over the eyes might also be so called. A piece cut off the end of, say, a bolt of cloth would make a perfectly suitable scarf and I conceive that *scarf* sb.¹ is in origin the same word as *scarf* sb.²

The sense 'piece cut from the end (of something)' is recorded for ON *skarfr* only with reference to timber, but since we have plenty of later evidence from Denmark, Norway, and Sweden that both noun and verb were said of cloth too, we may reasonably think that Scandinavian *skarf* was taken into English in two senses: (1) 'piece of timber or cloth cut from one end of a larger piece' and (2) 'piece of timber for lengthening a board or beam'. The second sense is recorded in 15th-century English; see the quotation given at the beginning of this paper. The first sense is implied in our earliest quotation, that of 1555, for *scarf* sb.¹ (where Lady Vane calls a scarf "my handy worke") and could perfectly well have given rise to the senses of that word found in English documents of the 16th century. In sum, the etymology here proposed for *scarf* sb.¹ makes no real difficulties whether phonological or semantic.

Scarf sb.⁵ and its verb remain. They are whaling terms, entered as Americanisms in the *Dictionary of American English* (DAE) and the *Dictionary of Americanisms* (DA), though not so marked in the NED. I quote the NED entries:

A longitudinal cut made in a whale's body. 1851 H. MELVILLE *Whale* II.xxv.181. As the blubber in one strip uniformly peels off along the line called the 'scarf'. 1874 C. M. SCAMMON *Marine Mammals* 63 (Cent.) A scarf is cut along the body and through the blubber, to which one end of a tackle is hooked.

trans. To make a 'scarf' or incision in the blubber of (a whale). Also *absol.* 1851 H. MELVILLE *Whale* II.xxv.182 The heavers singing, the blubber-room gentlemen coiling, the mates scarfing, the ship straining, and all hands swearing occasionally. 1887 GOODE, etc. *Fisheries U.S.* v.II.278/1 The second mate 'scarfs', or cuts the body blubber.

Here NED and DAE rightly derive the verb from the noun; the DA has "Origin obscure. Cf. *scarf*, n." The NED gives no etymological note for the noun; DAE and DA have "Origin obscure", to which DA adds "?f. *kerf*", with no explanation of the phonological difficulties. *Century* and *Webster's* agree in entering a sense 'groove' under their *scarf*[1] and [3]*scarf* (answering to NED *scarf* sb.[2]) respectively, with particular reference to the whaling term, and in my opinion they were right in doing so. Scarfing in carpentry involves cutting grooves and it would be natural enough for a sense 'groove' to arise. The word *scarf* and the kind of work it denotes were of course especially familiar in nautical circles and the crews of whaling ships, many of whom were trained carpenters and shipbuilders, might be expected to transfer such terms as *scarf* to their work in cutting up whales. Certainly the evidence indicates that they did so; it is not easy to find another source whence they could have got the word.

The Johns Hopkins University

LEXICAL REDISTRIBUTION IN MODERN ENGLISH *SAY* AND *TELL*

ALBERT H. MARCKWARDT

One of the problems which almost every teacher of English as a foreign language encounters is that of teaching his students the proper use of the verbs *say* and *tell*. In many languages there is just a single verb which performs most of the functions which speakers of English assign to these two: thus German *sagen*, French *dire*, Spanish *decir*. Consequently, for native speakers of these and many other languages, acquiring even a near-native command of these verbs becomes a matter of bifurcating a lexeme and learning a couple of syntactic constraints: *say* may not be followed by the indirect object without a preposition; *tell* may not introduce a direct quotation or an indirect quotation unless it is preceded by the indirect object. In reality, the situation is somewhat more complex than this, but these are its broad outlines.

It is interesting to note that with many features of English, a learning problem of some difficulty for non-native speakers often calls attention to an interesting historical development. This is true, for example, of the current status of *much* and *many*, of *some* and *any*, of the various devices for indicating future time. The current distribution of *say* and *tell* offers striking support to this general observation.

Like Modern English, Old English also had two verbs with the general meaning of 'say' or 'speak'. These were *cweðan*, a strong verb of the fifth conjugation, and *secgan*, one of the four verbs of the third class which clearly preserved the features of that conjugation. Both of these occurred with several prefixes, among them *be-*, *on-*, and *wið-*. In addition, the verb *tellan* was also a part of the Old English lexicon, but it was used chiefly in the sense of 'reckon' or 'count', and somewhat less often with the meaning 'relate, recount'. What has happened, then, in the millenium separating the language of King Alfred from our own is that *cweðan* became obsolete although the preterit *quoth* continued in use long after the other forms of the verb had disappeared, *tellan* shifted in meaning, and syntactical factors came to govern the distribution of *say* and *tell*. It is the purpose here to determine, insofar as possible, the chronology of these changes in the hope that some light may be thrown upon the language processes which were involved.

It will probably be most convenient to deal first with *cweðan*, since this verb does not survive in Modern English. In Old English it appears to have had the highest incidence of use of the three verbs which are involved in this complex relationship.

A Grouped Frequency Word-List of Anglo-Saxon Poetry[1] shows it to have occurred 430 times in the entire poetic corpus of this period as compared to 380 for *secgan*. Both of them are within the first one hundred words occurring most frequently. *Tellan* appears only about one-fourth as often as the others.

There seems to be little doubt that *cweðan* was used more frequently in Old English to introduce a direct or an indirect quotation than for any other purpose. The two earliest citations listed in the *Oxford English Dictionary*, both from the Vespasian Psalter, introduce direct quotations: "Dryhten cwæð to mē, 'Sunu mīn ðū earð'", (ii. 7) and, "Ðonne bið cweden tō mē ... 'Hwēr is God ðīn?'" (xli. 4) *Beowulf* 199 illustrates the use of the verb to introduce an indirect quotation: "Cwæð, hē gūðcyning ofer swanrāde sēcean wolde ..." With indirect quotations, however, the use of the connective *þæt(te* is probably more frequent, as in 857, "Monig oft gecwæð, þætte sūð nē norð be sæm twēonum ofer eormengrund ōþer nænig under swegles begong sēlra nære, rondhæbbendra, rīces wyrðra." Of eighteen occurrences of *cweðan*, *ācweðan*, and *gecweðan* in *Beowulf*, all but two introduce a quotation.

It is of particular interest to note that when the person addressed is mentioned, *tō* is invariably employed as an introductory word in Old English. It is not until the fifteenth century that an indirect pronominal object appears immediately after the verb, as in the alliterative romance of Alexander (line 4325): "I sall quethe þe forqui & quat is þe cause." Occasionally *cweðan* and *secgan* occur in juxtaposition in what on the surface, at least, seems to have been virtually synonymous usage. *Beowulf* 93 has, "Sægde sē þe cūþe frumsceaft fīra feorran reccan, cwæð þæt se Ælmihtiga eorðan worhte, wlitebeorhtne wang, swā wæter bebūgeð ..." But even here it is *cweðan* which introduces the indirect quotation, and *secgan* might be more accurately translated as 'told' or 'related'.

To all intents and purposes, *cweðan* was finished as a verb with the general meaning of 'say' or 'tell' by the beginning of the fifteenth century, and was probably infrequent in use well before that time. It continued in two special functions. That form of the verb which had the prefix *be-* became specialized in meaning, indicating formal assignment of property by will. The earliest use of *bequeath* in this sense is to be found in a charter of Eadweard written in 1066:[2] "Swa ful fre and swa forð swa he it sainte Petre bequað." Here it is interesting to note that the indirect object does appear without an introductory *to*, as it also does in Chaucer's *Gentilesse* (lines 17-18): "But ther may no man, as men may wel see, Bequethe his heir his vertuous noblesse." The preposition did not begin to appear in constructions of this kind until the fourteenth century. For a brief period, chiefly during the fourteenth and fifteenth centuries, the verb *quethe* without the prefix acquired this same meaning.

The other relic of *cweðan* is to be found in the continuation of the historically irregular preterit form *quoth* to introduce a direct quotation. In its separate treatment

---

[1] John F. Madden and Francis P. Magoun, Jr., *A Grouped Frequency Word-List of Anglo-Saxon Poetry* (Harvard University, 1961).

[2] John M. Kemble, ed., *Codex Diplomaticus Aevi Saxonici*, 1839-48, IV, 191.

of the past tense form, the *Oxford English Dictionary* comments: "The verb is always placed before the subject, and the clause is commonly inserted parenthetically toward the beginning of the words quoted, but may also precede or follow the whole sentence or speech." The inversion of subject and verb dates from 1200. *Quoth* continued in dialect, chiefly Scots, and literary use until very late in the nineteenth century, but it is obsolete today. Just when it began to acquire an archaic flavor is difficult to say.

The earliest recorded meaning of *tellan* in Old English was 'to recount', 'to enumerate', or 'to relate'. When so used, it referred to an extended narrative or to a series of associated facts. The now obsolete meaning of 'to reckon' or 'to estimate' appears just about as early, but it did not survive much beyond the beginning of the fifteenth century. *Tell*, in the sense of communicating information, facts, and ideas, in contexts where the verb *say* might have been equally appropriate, first appears in the twelfth century. There are two noteworthy features about the early use of the verb in this sense. The indirect object was often present, as in: "Gode tiðinge ... us telleð ... seinte Lucas on þe holie godspelle",[3] and, "He ... tolde hire al is þouȝt".[4] This was simply a continuation of the earlier use of the indirect object in contexts where the verb had the meaning of 'relate' or 'recount'. It is still a feature of the use of the verb today, and one not currently shared by *say*.

Indirect quotations were quite regularly introduced by *tellan* with *that* serving as a connective. Sometimes the indirect object preceded the object clause; on other occasions it was omitted. The *Anglo-Saxon Chronicle* furnishes an instance of the latter in the entry for 1046: " Þa ... Sweȝen ... tealde þæt his sciperes woldon wændon fram him buton he þe raðor come." In *Jacob's Well* (203) the indirect object precedes the indirect quotation: "I teld ȝou þat a schouyl hath iij. partys: a scho, an heued & an handyll."

It would seem, therefore, that once the verb *tell* had become firmly established with the meaning 'to make known, to communicate', it had virtually attained its Modern English status. Its current distinctive feature of including the indirect object in the structure was already there. Thus, by the early Middle English period, *tell* had moved in and *cweðan* was on its way out. To complete the account, we need only to trace the changes in the use of *say*.

There are three developments in connection with this verb which appear to be noteworthy. First of all, there is its gradual emergence as the principal device for introducing a direct quotation. The early examples of the use of the verb for this purpose seem either to be part of a somewhat more complex structure or are employed to introduce a speech decidedly more formal than the *he said* and *I said* of ordinary conversational interchange. The following, for example, serves as the introduction to the formal announcement of Beowulf's death: "Lȳt swīgode nīwra spella sē ðe næs

---

[3] R. Morris, *Old English Homilies*, Series II, *EETS*, Vol. 43 (London, 1873), p. 31.
[4] Carl Horstmann, *Early South-English Legendary*, *EETS*, Vol. 87 (London, 1887). Life of Beket, 1188.

gerād, ac hē sōðlice sægde ofer ealle."⁵ Likewise, Wiglaf's speech of reproach to his companions, prior to Beowulf's final battle with the dragon, for their failure to support their leader, is introduced by *sægde*, but the formal nature of discourse is again suggested by a parallel construction with *maðelode*: "Wīglāf maðelode, wordrihta fela sægde gesīðum — him wæs sefa geomor —"⁶.

Typical of the somewhat complex structures in which *secgan* appears in connection with a directly quoted statement is the following from Mark xiv. 38 of the Old English translation of the Gospels: "Wē ӡehyrdon hine secgan ic towurþe þis hand-worhte tempel." In the twelfth-century Lambeth Homilies a parenthetical clause intrudes between the verb and the quotation it introduces: "Soðlice he walde seggen ӡif he mihte speken, wa is me þet ic efre dude swa muchele sunne."⁷ It is not until the thirteenth century that introductory *say* appears with any great frequency in such simple constructions as, "I-her me, dohter,' he seið".⁸ and "At ilka mattyng þei seide 'chek'."⁹

Of all the uses of *secgan* in Old English, that of introducing an indirect quotation was by far the most frequent. The following example from the Blickling Homilies is typical: "Sē engel hire sæӡde þæt hēo sceolde modor bēon hire Scyppendes."¹⁰ The verb *cweðan* also appeared in this construction more frequently than in any other. The difference between the two, however, was that in the case of *secgan*, this construction though common was but one of many in which the verb is to be found. It had a far greater range of meaning and use than did *cweðan*.

Two syntactic developments occurred to give *secgan* the structural range that it has today. First, the use of the inflected dative from of the noun or pronoun for the person addressed was replaced by the prepositional construction. That is to say, constructions such as, "Sey him on ðin stede to gon",¹¹ were replaced by, "Says to mi folk on þiskin wis, þat þey me mak a sacrifice".¹² The *to* began to appear in the early fourteenth century. Instances of the dative construction, particularly with pronouns, can be found well into the fifteenth century and suggest that the *to* can scarcely have been considered obligatory until the beginning of the sixteenth.

Moreover, during the fifteenth century the connective *þæt* began to be eliminated as an introductory element; the object clause containing the indirect quotation followed directly after the introductory *say*. The *Towneley Mysteries* have, "Say him I com",¹³ and a century later we find, "Thou saist thou art as much my friend as any man can be".¹⁴ By this time, as we have seen, *cweðan* had fallen into almost total disuse except for the preterit *quoth*; *say* had taken over its functions.

[5] Lines 2897-2899.
[6] Lines 2631-2632.
[7] R. Morris, *Old English Homilies*, Series I, EETS, Vols. 29, 34 (London, 1868), p. 35.
[8] F. Furnivall, *Hali Meidenhad*, EETS, Vol. 18 (1866), p. 6.
[9] Robert Manning of Brunne, *The Story of England*, ed. F. Furnivall, Rolls Series, Vol. 87 (London, 1887), p. 378, line 11399.
[10] R. Morris, *The Blickling Homilies*, EETS, Vol. 83 (London 1880), p. 9.
[11] R. Morris, *The Story of Genesis and Exodus*, EETS, Vol. 7 (London, 1865), line 4114.
[12] R. Morris, *Cursor Mundi*, EETS, Vol. 57(London, 1874), line 6063.
[13] G. England and A. W. Pollard, *The Towneley Plays*, EETS, Vol. 71 (1897), ix. 137.
[14] Timothy Kendall, *Flowers of Epigrammes* (London 1577), p. 18.

While *say* was assuming certain areas of meaning formerly expressed by *cweðan*, it was also losing certain of its functions to *tell*. Definition 7 in the *Oxford English Dictionary* ascribes the following range of meaning to *say*: "To deliver (a speech a discourse); to relate (a story); to express, give (thanks); to tell, speak (truth, lies); to express (one's opinion)." To all of this, the label *obsolete* is attached. The use of *say* in the sense of 'relate' occurs quite frequently in *Beowulf*. "Hwæt, þū worn fela, wine mīn Unferð, bēore druncene, ymb Brecan spræce, sægdest from his sīðe", (*ll*. 530-532), and again, "þa wæs ēaðfynde þē him elles hwær gerūmlicor ræste sōhte ... ðā him gebēacnod wæs, gesægd sōðlīce swēotolan tācne, healðegnes hete". (*ll*. 139-142). Other instances are to be found in lines 90, 273, 582, 875, 1049.

To sum up, what the developments of the last one thousand years amount to are in effect the obsolescence of *cweðan*, the assumption of most of the functions of *cweðan* by *say* (OE *secgan*), a shift in the meaning of *tell*, away from the notion of reckoning or estimating toward that of recounting, and in so doing, taking on certain earlier uses of *say*. Syntactically, *tellan* required no change to reach its present state, but in the case of *secgan* the use of *to* to signal the person addressed became obligatory.

Since all of these changes appear to overlap in time, it is difficult to maintain that any one of them triggered the process. It is worth noting, however, that the fifth class of Old English strong verbs, of which *cweðan* was a member, underwent a high incidence of loss in the transition from Old English. Moreover, such fifth-class strong verbs as did survive, *tread, see, speak*, all give evidence of marked changes in their pattern of vowel alternation, as did *quoth* of course. This is in striking contrast to such strong verb conjugations as the first and parts of the third, which show a strong tendency not only to survive but also to retain the essential qualities of their patterns of internal vowel change: *e.g., drive, drove, driven; sing, sang, sung*. One might conjecture, therefore, that the unsatisfactory and somewhat confusing phonetic makeup of the fifth-class verbs makes the obsolescence of *cweðan* an understandable phenomenon, and as the range of its use became more and more restricted, the way was prepared for the changes in the meaning and structure of *secgan* and *tellan*.

Princeton University

LANGUAGE, LINGUISTICS AND THE THREE CULTURES*

RAVEN I. McDAVID, JR.

Even if I had illusions of expertise, a half-dozen years of intimate association with Mencken's *The American Language* would make it impossible for me to assume the role of expert[1] in the face of the practical experience of the composition teacher. However active I may have been in linguistics, I have never had a voice in organizing a composition program, and it has been more than nine years since I last graded a batch of freshmen themes. Yet conceding my small right to tell the composition teacher what his objectives and methods should be, I can assert from my own freshman experience, a generation ago, that the course in composition can be one of the most stimulating in the curriculum for the student, that it can powerfully shape all one's later attitudes toward language, and that — as in my own experience — it can even determine the direction of one's career.[2] One may even generalize this experience into a lesson for English departments who are worried about recruitment to the profession: the composition instructor works more closely with the student than does any other faculty member during the critical years when students are settling upon their vocations. Consequently, when any English department, however lustrous its reputation, relegates the teacher of composition to second-class citizenship and when appointments are made, turns its back to those who have achieved distinction in this field, it is not only exhibiting a pitiful myopia and dishonoring its own profession, but helping to cut its own throat.[3]

---

* This is a slight revision of a paper delivered at the meeting of the Conference on College Composition and Communication, Chicago, Illinois, April 5, 1962.

[1] See *Euphamism*, Ch. VI, sec. 7. esp. pp. 348-349, in the one-volume abridgement edited by Raven I. McDavid, Jr., with the assistance of David W. Maurer (New York, Alfred H. Knopf, Inc., 1963). In South Carolina, in my boyhood, the folk definition of an *expert* was "a damned fool a thousand miles from home".

[2] Of all the English courses, undergraduate or graduate, the composition course taught by A. T. O'Dell of Furman University in the winter and spring of 1929 is sharpest in my memory, and the course which incited me to choose English as my undergraduate major. Had I accepted the kindly dean's suggestion of a less exacting composition instructor, I would never have made this choice. As with other irreversible decisions, it is amusing to speculate: I might well have gone on to greater wealth and prestige, say, as a physicist; I could never have become a linguist, and subsequently an anthropologist. What is even more important is that, even in those moments when I most bitterly cursed the fate that had nudged me into the teaching of English, I never regretted choosing O'Dell's section.

[3] Few English departments have senior appointments in the teaching of composition; of those who have the title, must manage to evade the intent by appointing some practitioner of critical mumbo jumbo.

It is out of this experience and from this perspective that I speak to the text that the practical composition teacher, like the theoretical linguist, must have a wide range of interests in the academic community. Neither can work effectively by tying himself to a single division of learning, but for his own purposes must learn to communicate with all. If, as Clemenceau said, war is too serious a business to be left to the generasl, the teaching of composition is too important in our society to be entrusted to departments of English alone — at least so long as they are dominated by those whose intellectual concerns are restricted to the history and criticism of literature.[4] If the linguist is more actively and overtly concerned with the problem of interdisciplinary communication than most composition teachers have been, it is because through necessity his discipline has reached the point of sophistication where he cannot understand language by humanism alone but must work with the physical and biological and social sciences as well — to their mutual benefit.

The fact that such an obvious statement must be made — indeed, the fact that it can be made — is an unfortunate commentary on the exponentially growing body of facts in all disciplines, and on the disgraceful lack of communication that muddies much of our intellectual and academic life. Francis Bacon could take all knowledge to be his province, and succeed to the point where some people still claim him as the real author of certain popular dramatic productions registered under the name of a Warwickshire petit-bourgeois. Milton could seriously propose that a proper education should fit its recipients for performing all the offices public and private, of peace and war — and fill the gaps between poetic composition and government service by teaching, along with other subjects, the elements of geography and astronomy. Jefferson and Franklin, even, could achieve distinction in a variety of fields, theoretical and practical. But too often today the pack-instinct is to rend asunder those who transgress conventional departmental boundaries, even if their teaching and scholarship require it. The member of an English department who feels a need to work closely with anthropologists or psychiatrists is characterized at best as an anomaly, at worst in terms still unprintable after court decisions permitting the publication of *Lady Chatterly's Lover* and *Tropic of Cancer*. This pedestrian, even paranoid, provincialism is our century's version of the Miltonic fable of dismembered truth, itself frankly analogized from the sad legend of Osiris.

The reason for this lack of communication is not merely the amount of new data and for some disciplines an increasing dependence on intricate machinery. The blandest humanist could profitably relegate to mechanized retrieval systems much of the sterile boon-doggling of compiling bibliographies.[5] Nor is this barrier attributable

---

[4] This argument has been made, of late, by a number of distinguished scholars, notably Warner G. Rice of the University of Michigan. To my knowledge, no successful counter-argument has been made — only prescription and vested interest. In cold fact, assigning composition (like army K.P.) to all staff members, regardless of vocation, is a sure way to make composition courses drudgery to teachers and students and to thwart creative scholarship on all levels.

[5] Many kinds of apparatus, designed for other purposes, are readily adaptable to humanistic scholarship — if the scholars would make use of them. Such information retrieval centers as that at

merely to the tendency of our age toward specialization, for specialists existed in Pharaonic Egypt — notably in the embalmer's craft. It is not that the principles of the new knowledge are excessively recondite, for there have been sound popularizations of most of the new disciplines, except perhaps of the thaumaturgy by which the professional humanists, such as the literary critics, arrive at their conclusions. It is not, I hope, simple anti-intellectualism, though the closed minds which so many students of literature bring to interdisciplinary programs and take away, *virgines intactas*, would be presumptive evidence in any well-ordered court of law. Perhaps it is primarily the swift march of events — the fact that older boundaries, intellectual as well as political and economic and social ones, are breaking down, and the essential indivisibility of knowledge, as well as the essential indivisibility of mankind, must be understood and established — or there will soon be no mankind, much less any opportunity to expand the frontiers of human knowledge. And as these older boundaries break down, those who have enjoyed a comfortable respectability within their segregated compartments[6] — whether academic or social — are bewildered and afraid, and seek to evade the responsibility of adjusting to the rush of events by pretending that it isn't happening, and that it can't happen if they deny long and loudly enough the possibility that it will happen.[7] More objective thinkers, less imprisoned by sterile departmental creeds and more concerned with developing the potential talents of all mankind, see that these barriers must go, so that each investigator, of whatever department, may feel free to work with those who are concerned with the problems he wishes to solve. True, no person can be chemist, poet, statesman and historian at once; but equally true, any person in any discipline who excludes in advance any other discipline from his potential interest is lobotomizing himself. To take a crude example, a little knowledge of statistics could inform the teacher of English literature whether over a period of time his set examinations were effectively separating the good students from the poor ones, or were simple meaningless ceremonial.[8]

The crippling effects of a limited perspective have naturally worried many of our best minds. For a long time the engineer and the student of agriculture were the stock butts of humanistic wit; but it is noteworthy that in recent years the better schools of science and technology have responded to this criticism by insisting on enough

---

Western Reserve University have vainly attempted to encourage their English departments to use their facilities.

[6] A number of grim morals may be drawn from the fact that in the Southern states a traditional humanistic education is still prized as a social ornament, and social science denigrated as busy-bodyish meddling — and violence is most hallowed as a way of dealing with embarrassing questions. One wonders if there is only chance parallelism between the attitudes toward the outside world of professional humanists and professional Southerners.

[7] And when the march of events pushes them to recognize, titularly, a new discipline, the traditional humanists often act to evade their responsibilities; for example, many of them still apply the label of *linguist* to anyone whose dissertation lay in Old or Middle English literature — as if every hookworm-ridden Mississippian were *ipso facto* a parasitologist.

[8] I shall not ask literary moghuls to reveal the extent to which they have had the validity of their tests examined by outsiders, but shall leave this as a matter of conscience between them and their confessors. My own experience in administering such tests is that the questions screen rather poorly.

general education to enable their graduates to fulfill their obligations as literate citizens. In recent years, in fact, the shoe has been on the other foot, so that a distinguished teacher of English could remark wryly, "No one is so narrowly technological in his viewpoint as the professional defender of the humanities." Indeed, it is probable that many introductory courses in physics today are more genuinely humanistic in their implications that many of the courses in Shakespeare taught in our graduate schools.[9]

In the great educational debate of the Age of Sputniks the differences between these disciplinary attitudes have become dramatically apparent. The scientists, by and large, do not merely want more massive injections of science into the curriculum; they want an evolving program of scientific education, responsive to the changes in knowledge, and they wish to see a more general understanding of the larger implications of science for the world in which we have to live, as ominously epitomized in $E = MC^2$. But the humanists too often call merely for larger doses of what they have hitherto given. The new programs that they propose are, if anything, more provincial, more isolated from the physical and social sciences than what they have heretofore been peddling.

To those who object that science deals with cumulative knowledge, the humanities with unchanging verities, I can only reply that when I took my doctorate in English literature, Henry James was considered a very dull dog, and any critic who then might have ranked Donne ahead of Milton as a poet would have been referred to a psychiatrist.[10]

Whatever other merits Sir Charles Snow may have, he deserves the evangelical Protestant's traditional showers of blessing for bringing this problem into the open. "The Two Cultures and the Scientific Revolution" noted the lack of communication between the physical scientists and the humanists, and suggested that the greater responsibility fell on the latter, since they were the more articulate group, less aware of the limitations of their disciplines, and less receptive to new ideas from outside their immediate traditions. As a member of an English department I regret that the validity of Sir Charles's argument has been empirically demonstrated by the reactions of the two groups. Whatever the motive, the physical scientists seem relatively humble toward the great values of the humanistic tradition, even though they may not comprehend them, while the humanists seem not only satisfied with their scientific ignorance

---

[9] By an interesting coincidence, this point was also made by H. A. Gleason, Jr., of the Hartford Seminary Foundation, at another session of the CCCC Convention of 1962. See his "What Is English?", *College Composition and Communication*, Vol. XIII, No. 3 (Oct. 1962), pp. 1-10.

[10] And to those who glibly proclaim that they know so much more about literature and literary values than did the graduate professors of the 1930's, I recommend the punch-line of Mark Twain's Birthday Dinner Address. As a matter of fact, under Allan Gilbert, whom (parroting a phrase) along with A. T. O'Dell I revere as much as any man may this side of idolatry, the graduate students at Duke underwent a rigorous exploration of the texts of Donne and Sidney and others of that age. To such students, much of the fashionable intellectual prestidigitation by which reputations in criticism are currently being attained seems both trivial and hackneyed. Moreover, point-integrating in his teaching, Gilbert always insisted that a work of art be viewed in its total cultural context, and considered any discipline relevant if it enriched the interpretation.

but resentful of efforts to dispel it, whether the effort originates with a physicist or with one of their own colleagues.

Whether by accident or by deliberate intent to polarize his argument, Sir Charles did not include in his discussion the social and behavioral sciences. To complete the picture, my anthropological colleague Lloyd Fallers has recently presented an alternative view — "Two Cultures Are Not Enough"[11] — showing that for many problems of our age neither the traditional humanities nor the new physical sciences, nor both together, can supply the answers, but must call in the disciplines concerned with society, culture and personality. It is inevitable that the newly developing nations utilize the devices of Western technology; but it is imperative for the peace of the world that this technological development not result in the same shattering of cultural values that it brought to the American Indian, to the Negro brought as a slave to work the rice and cotton plantations and then turned loose to fend for himself, and to the displaced rural inhabitants of the one-time agrarian South. The whole United States is still paying heavily, and will always have to pay, for ignoring the lessons of the social and behavioral sciences in these instances;[12] whenever these lessons are ignored today in Asia or Africa or Latin America, only Moscow and Peking can profit.

Because the social and behavioral sciences are closer than the physical sciences to the matter and methods of the humanities — one might call them the human sciences — it should be hoped that through them a rapprochement among the disciplines could be made. Edward Sapir was a poet and perceptive literary critic, as well as a psychologist and a master of several branches of anthropology. Ruth Benedict was also a poet; her presidential address to the American Anthropological Association urged a closer understanding between anthropology and literature. At the Darwin Centennial, Alfred Kroeber — the last of the universal anthropologists — insisted that anthropology must keep its affiliations with the humanities. And other anthropologists have insisted that imaginative literature — and they specifically exclude the literature of explicit social documentation, the tracts in novel-guise of Upton Sinclair and Erskine Caldwell — often provides deeper and more accurate insights into the human condition than the best formal ethnography.[13] Yet on the other side the response has been less enthusiastic; not only are the social scientists favorite straw men for verbal clobbering when style is an issue[14] (though I defy any objective observer to find a socio-

[11] Originally published in the October 1961 *Bulletin of the Atomic Scientists*; reprinted in *Context: A University of Chicago Magazine*, Vol. I, No. 2 (Fall 1961), pp. 19-23. In the London *Times Literary Supplement* (Oct. 25, 1963), pp. 839-844, Sir Charles speaks favorably of an emerging culture of the social and behavioral sciences, which must be considered in future evaluations of academic attitudes.
[12] The century of neglect of the American Negro, following Emancipation, with the almost universal unspoken assumption that the problem would cure itself if nobody talked about it, is currently yielding a whirlwind in the deterioration of our major cities. Its educational implications (with which even the professional humanists might be concerned) are set forth in grim particularity in James B. Conant, *Slums and Suburbs* (New York, McGraw-Hill, 1961).
[13] This observation is frequently made by my colleague Julian Pitt-Rivers, and is the basis on which our seminar "Novelists as Ethnographers" is organized.
[14] Naturally enough, the professional humanists with the greatest vested interest in maintaining academic *Apartheid* are most eloquent in assuming this as a datum; having read a spate of documents

logical term more obfuscatory than Mr. Faber's Mr. Eliot's "objective correlative"), but any student of literature who seeks insights from the perspective of social history, psychology or anthropology is immediately déclassé in the eyes of high-church humanists (unless, like Mencken, he is dead and therefore metaphorically embalmed for veneration). It is even reported that in some institutions, departments on the humanistic side have opted for continuing poverty in *Apartheid*, — the poverty about which they are perpetually griping — rather than accept funds that would have brought some students and faculty members into closer collaboration with the social sciences.[15]

Yet at this time, when any major policy decision may determine whether mankind is to continue as a species, we cannot morally accept the forcible segregation of academic disciplines, any more than we can accept the forcible segregation of ethnic groups. Like other kinds of segregation, it has to be overcome, and it will be. And the instrumentality through which it will be overcome is the discipline of linguistics, the serious systematic study of language phenomena, not because it sometimes promises quick or painless solutions to long-standing practical problems, but because it impinges on all kinds of academic disciplines. In fact, the broad spectrum of linguistics as an ordered body of knowledge is what, in essence, made me become a linguist. Wavering between mathematics and history as primary interests, but taking a doctorate in English literature with a dissertation involving political philosophy, I was drawn into the study of American dialects, with particular emphasis on their relationships to sociocultural differences, because this study seemed to provide a more systematic interpretation of the complicated sociocultural matrix in which I had grown up than had been provided by any of the conventional academic disciplines to which I had previously been exposed. Having committed myself to language in its social and cultural relationships, it was but a small — though inevitable — step to acquire prefessional status as an anthropologist. And in the last few years I have joined McQuown, Hockett and Austin in examining the implications of linguistic phenomena for the investigation of psychiatric problems. Each new facet of linguistics seems to make all the rest more meaningful, and to provide deeper understanding of all the related disciplines, not the least of these being the teaching of literature. Thanks to this experience, I can now give a much better course in Milton than I have ever given in the past.[16]

---

composed at various levels on both sides of the barbed wire, I can only agree with George Ade, "It All Depends", and deplore the lack of controlled studies. See my forthcoming essay, "If Lions Were Sculptors".

[15] The number of foreign students at American universities is approaching 100,000; at some institutions renowned for graduate programs they already constitute 20% of the student body, with a large proportion unable to profit from their opportunities because they have an inadequate command of English. Yet in many of these institutions English departments have resisted requests from other departments and schools that some provision be made to assure these students an adequate command of the language in which their instruction will be conducted.

[16] A decent respect for the dignity of the individual would not prescribe this particular succession of experiences for all of our professional colleagues, even if we were sure they could survive it. Yet if

If one thinks seriously about the implications of linguistics, as expounded by recent scholars in the field and those who have made a serious effort to comprehend them, one may see that these implications derive from two basic propositions.

First, to quote the definition given by Herskovits as developed from those of Sapir and Sturtevant,[17] "A language is a system of arbitrary vocal signals, by means of which social groups cooperate and interact and by means of which the learning process is effectuated and a given way of life achieves both continuity and change."[18]

Second, language is that characteristic that taxonomically most clearly differentiates mankind from all other forms of life.[19]

If we prepare an exegesis of these propositions, we are inevitably led into all divisions of knowledge. It is for this reason that such bodies as the Linguistic Society of America arose, to provide a common meeting place where the phenomena of language and their implications could be discussed without the restraint of departmental boundaries. It may be interesting, if old hat, to examine a few of these implications.

1. Like the physical sciences, linguistics studies systems, each system made up of ordered concurrences and patterns of constituents, and therefore susceptible to formulaic statements, of varying degrees of complexity according to the scale of the description.[20] Such formulaic statements, for two languages juxtaposed, may determine where the critical problems of second-language teaching will lie, or where the greatest areas of complexity in any given language are. From acoustics we have learned, thanks to Joos and others, that in a given language each phoneme has its own characteristic profile, regardless of the individual voice-set of the speaker; and in turn, the knowledge of the acoustic manifestations of linguistic signals is reflected in better designs of communication equipment. And from quantum mechanics we draw inferences as to the nature of phonemic systems and the problems of phonemic change.

2. Phonetics of the older sort has been long referred to the anatomy of the vocal organs, and — whatever we may say about particular theories[21] — there has been a profitable discussion of the relationships between these two interests. We are just now beginning to see something of the relationships between linguistic signals and neural circuitry. The relationship between language learning in childhood and language loss in the complex of communicative disorders called aphasia has been explored, and

---

it can so enrich one member of the profession, it would seem a phase of the greater stupidity to close its opportunities to others.

[17] See Edgar H. Sturtevant, *An Introduction to Linguistic Science* (New Haven, Yale University Press), 1947, p. 2.

[18] Melville J. Herskovits, *Man and His Works*, 2nd ed. (New York, Alfred A. Knopf, 1960). The chapter in which this definition occurs is appropriately entitled "Language, the Vehicle of Culture".

[19] This definition originated with John Kepke of Brooklyn, one of the most influential American linguists of the mid-century, though known far less widely than he should be.

[20] This emphasis on the systematic nature of linguistic phenomena constitutes the essential identification of linguistics with the sciences and the greatest area of disagreement between linguists and professional humanists.

[21] See, for example, Kenneth L. Pike, *Phonetics* (Ann Arbor, University of Michigan Press, 1944).

continues to provide rich opportunities for research.[22] We have had suggestions by physical anthropologists that the development of language has been accompanied by certain changes in the structure of the mouth in response to the development of speech-muscles, so that there may be touchstones for determining whether certain skulls are hominid or non-hominid.[23] Through psychology we approach the relationships of linguistic phenomena to tabu; from tapes of psychiatric interviews we have noticed the unconscious alteration of nasality-intensity or basic speech-pitch tempo, as related to the revelation of a driving social insecurity. And on humbler levels we are all familiar with the "Freudian slip", now raised to an art form as the "sick joke" — of which everyone has his favorite examples.

3. With the social sciences, the affiliations of linguistics are well established. The relationship between speech-communities or cultures may be determined by seeing who borrows what words from whom and on what occasions. If there is any such thing as a "cultural psychology", perhaps it has some relationship to the techniques by which borrowing is accomplished. English since 1100, like Japanese throughout recorded history, has been prone to take in new words and adapt them phonologically; German before 1945, Chinese and Old English have apparently preferred loan translations. It would be interesting if we knew — or even plausibly guessed — the reasons why. Placenames and loanwords in dialects, like drumlins and terminal moraines, mark the extent of past cultural inroads. And dialect differences alone reveal a host of historical and socio-cultural features, about which many scholars have spoken at length.[24] The affiliations of geographical dialects with folklore, folk architecture, folk culture, folksongs and folk anecdotes are just beginning to be explored. Only a handful of brave souls have ventured to examine what are the precise dialect touchstones by which persons are accepted or rejected in social groups within an ostensibly open society.[25] But we do know enough, from specific speech patterns in smaller Northern communities, to be sure that so-called school integration by transportation across neighborhood lines is not going to work — is not going to erase the dialect touchstones by which minority groups are identified — so long as playtime and daily living are segregated, and can serve only the sinister ends of those who wish to create a pretorian guard of rootless bully-boys to turn loose upon all objects of their resent-

---

[22] A profitable workshop, under the auspices of the Rehabilitation Codes, brought linguists and specialists in aphasia together at Carmel, California, January 28-30, 1964.
[23] But see Charles F. Hockett and Robert Ascher, "The Human Revolution", *Current Antropology* Vol. V (June 1964). pp. 135-168.
[24] For an early summary of achievements and promises, see R. I. McDavid, Jr., "Dialect Geography and Social Science Problems", *Social Forces*, Vol. XXV (Dec. 1946), pp. 68-72.
[25] Two fruitful lines of investigation have been followed, of late, by Lee Pederson at the University of Minnesota and William Labov, of Columbia University; see Pederson, *The Pronunciation of English in Metropolitan Chicago: Consonants and Vowels*, Dis (MS) (University of Chicago, 1964), and Labov, "The Social Motivation of a Sound Change", *Word*, Vol. XIX (Dec. 1963), pp. 273-309. Labov is currently involved in the study of significant social differences in pronunciation in Metropolitan New York, Pederson in the study of lower class Negro speech in Chicago, both in the application of linguistics to the communication problems of the culturally disadvantaged.

ment.[26] As the one-class suburb has developed, we are anxious to find out what are the linguistic traits that characterize the upward route of the Chicago organization man from Park Forest to Oak Park to Winnetka to Kenilworth. We have already become aware of the use of slang and argot to identify a particular in-group, whether of New Critics, ad-writers, narcotic addicts or confidence men. And learning this, we have learned how to make better dictionaries, more accurately keyed to the multivalent society in which standard English is spoken — though the children of those who could never abandon the notion of the literal inspiration of Scripture, as presented in Elizabethan English, seem to have as hard a time abandoning the notion of the literal inspiration and infallibility of a large-scale dictionary published in NewEngland.[27]

Where the humanities are concerned, I am more diffident, because these affiliations are well rehearsed of old. So well rehearsed they have been that Carroll[28] did not feel necessary to include the study of literature as one of the disciplines allied to linguistics. We ought to take it for granted that no one is competent to discuss a literature until he is thoroughly immersed in the structure and history of the language in which that literature is written, for ignorance can result in poor texts and wronghead judgments, like Dryden's notorious evaluation of Chaucer's versification. The editor and the printer who produced the text Dryden used had made no effort to preserve the orthography of the Chaucerian manuscript, for in the Seventeenth Century the *e* could come and go in writing or print according to the need to justify a line and present a neat page; furthermore, it is not likely that Dryden would have known the significance of the *e*'s even if they had been faithfully preserved. So the most delicately fluid verse in English is adjudged as having a quaint, rude charm. But if every schoolboy knows this, too few of us are aware that a language system exists as of a particular time and place, and by its nature permits and prohibits certain kinds of manipulations for literary effect. Where inflections signal grammatical relationships, as in Latin or Ojibwa, word order can be manipulated rather freely; where word order carries the signal-burden, as in English or Chinese or Malay, we can make few shifts without altering the message. Quantitative verse is good for classical Latin, because vowel

---

[26] This statement may antagonize soft-headed do-gooders who had rather move people around than face the problem of fundamental attitudes. But children normally do *not* acquire their speech patterns in school, but from those among whom they live and play. Warren, Ohio, is too small to have segregated high schools, but during my stay at Western Reserve University (1952-57) every Negro freshman native to Warren showed such characteristic "Negro" grammatical features as the omission of inflectional endings, both in speech and in writing. My colleague Sol Tax also points out that in housing — until the public becomes better educated — there is a fundamental distinction between *integration* and so-called *non-discrimination*. It is gratifying to learn that the basic sociolinguistic conclusions of this paper are supported by Conant's *Slums and Suburbs*.

[27] Most of the breast beaters who deplore the so-called "permissiveness" of *Webster's Third New International Dictionary* (1961) do not know the tradition of lexicography in England and America, as surveyed by Joseph Friend, James Hulbert, Mitford M. Mathews, James Sledd and DeWitt Starnes and Gertrude Noyes. But Leonard Bloomfield long ago showed that it is impossible to discuss such problems rationally with those to whom the preconception is more important than the fact. "Secondary and Tertiary Responses to Language", *Language*, vol. XX (April 1944), pp. 45-55.

[28] John B. Carroll, *The Study of Language* (Cambridge, Mass., Harvard University Press, 1954).

quantity was high on the scale of structural features; syllable-counting verse is good for French, where stress is not phonemic but rhetorical; stressed verse fits English. The syllabic structure of Italian encourages double and triple rime, and permits *terza rima* with ease. The syllabic structure of English consigns double and triple rime, today, largely to such humble verse-forms as the limerick, and gives to attempts in *terza rima* a patent flavor of artificiality, as translators of Dante know to their sorrow.[29] And the critic who pays attention to the superfixes in a language cannot only distinguish good readings from bad, but can specify his judgment. Here one could talk indefinitely; but I leave the discussion to those who have labored longer than I in this vineyard.[30]

In recent years England has seen the rise of a group called the linguistic philosophers. Whatever their ultimate promise, they do not yet seem to have made contact with the descriptivists. Being heavily data-oriented myself, I find it all I can do to operate in the Bloomfield tradition — working with actual corpora of utterances, sorting out things that are the same from things that are different, and determining what combinations are possible and in what order. But however mechanistically we must approach our data, we must be intrigued by the implications of the Whorf hypothesis[31] that a linguistic system imposes its categories on the analysis of the universe by its speakers. Yet as LaBarre has pointed out, a slavish mechanical attempt to approach culture by literal analogies from the categories of language is a disservice to ourselves and to Whorf's memory alike.[32] Perhaps some day the linguists and anthropologists and psychologists and philosophers will devise a technique for evaluating the ways in which the structure of a language inescapably influences the structure of the patterns

---

[29] In our multivalent world, it is a pitiable ethnocentrism that talks about "general poetics" or "general prosody" while restricting itself to conventions set up from classical Hellas west. To take a simple problem, Pike suggests that metaphoric expression is alien to the conventions of many cultures. Probably no man since Sapir has been conversant with a wide enough variety of languages and cultures to generalize about prosody; and Sapir was both too humble and too intelligent to make such generalizations.

[30] Dissatisfied aesthetes should ask themselves how often they have invited linguists to participate in these dialogues *as linguists*, or how willing they have been to put aside what they assume about rhetorical tradition until they become acquainted with the organization of the linguistic system on which they must build their teaching of rhetoric.

[31] This hypothesis was enunciated in "The Relationship of Habitual Thought and Behavior to Language", originally published in *Language, Culture and Personality* (*Essays in Memory of Edward Sapir*, Kenosha, Wisconsin, 1939; reprinted by the University of Utah Press, 1960), pp. 75-93. It is included in *Language, Thought and Reality*, Selected Writings of Benjamin Lee Whorf, edited and with an Introduction by John B. Carroll, Foreword by Stuart Chase, (Cambridge, Mass., The Technology Press of Massachusetts Institute of Technology and New York, John Wiley and Sons, Inc., 1956) pp. 134-159. It has been frequently discussed at length, notably in *Language in Culture*, a symposium directed by Harry Hoijer, *What Linguists Tell Anthropolists*, in William M. Austin (ed.), *Georgetown University Monograph Series on Languages and Linguistics*, No. 11 (Washington, D.C., Edmund A. Walsh School of Foreign Service, Institute of Languages and Linguistics, 1958), pp. 73-78. Memoir No. 79, *The American Anthropologist* (Chicago, 1954) (*Comparative Studies of Cultures and Civilizations*, No. 3).

[32] Weston LaBarre, *What Linguists Tell Anthropolists, op. cit.*

of thought and behavior of those who speak the language — if that influence exists, as I believe it does.

In the meantime, having begun with dissatisfaction toward any academic discipline that constricts one's intellectual explorations, this paper may, more hopefully, end on a global scale, with the observation that peace may be nearer a reality when everyone learns that grammatical categories and syntactic arrangements are arbitrary, like departmental membership or even nationality. When we are sophisticated enough to take in stride the existence, as structural features, of clicks and lateral affricates, of four-person verbs and voiceless vowels, of nouns with tense and verbs with gender and all the other kinds of linguistic phenomena that we encounter if we range wide enough, we may also become sophisticated enough to accept as good for those to whom they come naturally a wider range of economic and social and cultural and political institutions than our middle-class representative democracy and mixed economy now utilize. And we will hope that each American organization of scholars and teachers, and its opposite numbers in all cultures, will continue to help students to use their languages more effectively, so that we may all make clearly known our legitimate aspirations and understand the aspirations of other in the one kind of world we must have if we are to have any world at all.

University of Chicago

COMPUTATIONAL MORPHOLOGY*

MILOS PACAK

The purpose of automatic morphological retrieval is the identification of word forms which can be segmented into their basic productive components (morphemes). By 'productive' components are meant those components which convey grammatical or semantic information which is, or could be, relevant in automatic language data processing.

The establishment of the distributional classes and subclasses of productive morphemes will constitute a reasonable basis for automatic morphological retrieval.

It is clear that the very possibility of any kind of language data processing depends, in the main, upon the construction of an adequate rapid-access storage device and of a well-organized dictionary. The recent development of computers with large disc memories will make it possible to store and retrieve the great amounts of linguistic data which it is necessary to have in the dictionary for the automatized analysis of natural languages.

The old discussions of the organization of dictionaries in terms of segmented versus unsegmented word forms are no longer of crucial importance. However, the prevailing opinion is that the segmentation of word forms into stem morphemes and inflectional morphemes in highly inflected languages is still to be preferred over nonsegmentation for such practical reasons as the decrease in the size of the dictionary, the faster look-up, and so on.

Since the Georgetown University Machine Translation Project has always focused mainly on translation from Russian into English, it was necessary to design a system of morphological analysis which would be as complete as possible for Russian and which would be applicable to other inflected languages as well.

It is not the purpose of this article to describe this system of morphological analysis in detail; this description can be found elsewhere. The purpose is rather to point out some interesting features of the research.

Description of A Morphological System

The word-form in inflected languages can be defined as a grammatically characterized

* The author expresses his grateful appreciation to Dr. R. R. Macdonald for commenting on this paper and especially to Dr. L. E. Dostert, whose accomplishments as director of the Georgetown Machine Translation Research Project provided the opportunity to write this paper.

unit. The order of morphemes within the word-form is rigid, but the order of word-forms relative to each other is usually variable.

It is assumed by some linguists that this fact justifies a contrast between morphology and syntax. On the other hand, it can be argued that the inflectional morphemes in Slavic languages are markers not simply of morphological relationships, but of morphosyntactic relationships, and, for this reason, it does not seem useful to draw a sharp distinction between morphology and syntax.

Any analysis of an inflected language must discuss the inflections in terms of their morphosyntactic functions. As has already been pointed out, inflectional morphemes serve as markers of syntactic relationships and so help to indicate the boundaries of syntactic connections.

The system of morphological analysis which was developed at Georgetown University was focused on the identification of inflectional suffix-forms, on their admissible correlations with classes of stem morphemes, and on their morphosyntactic functions. The stem morpheme is defined here as a segment of an inflected word-form which can be correlated with the maximum set of inflectional morphemes; it is considered to be a constant segment. The inflectional suffix-form is here defined as all those inflections which have one particular form, whether they represent one particular morpheme or several; it is considered to be a variable segment.

The relationship between the major classes of stem morphemes and inflectional suffix-forms may be represented as the functional dependence of the dependent variables upon the independent constant,

$$f(x, y),$$

where x is the distributional class of the stem morpheme (which is the constant), and y is the class of the inflectional suffix-form (which is the variable).

The morphosyntactic value of an inflected form is the logical sum of the class or subclass of the stem morpheme and the class or subclass value of the inflectional suffix-form

$$(x_m, y_n),$$

where x is the class of stem morpheme and subscript m denotes a subclass of x, and where y is the class of the inflectional suffix-form and subscript n denotes a subclass of y.

The morphosyntactic value of a given inflected form is shown in:

a. the category of case and number if the stem morpheme belongs to the class of nominals or pronominals, excluding the personal pronouns,

b. the category of case and number, gender, animateness, form (long or short) and degree of comparison is the stem morpheme belongs to the class of adjectivals, including participle forms,

c. the category of gender, number, voice, tense and person if the stem morpheme belongs to the class of verbals,

d. the category of case and number if the stem morpheme belongs to the class of personal pronouns.

Classes of Stem Morphemes

The First Approach:

In one approach to the research, the classes of the stem morphemes were established only on the basis of the distribution of inflectional suffix-forms.

The resultant number of stem classes in the various form classes in Russian is as follows:

a.	Nominals	91
b.	Adjectivals functioning as modifiers	29
c.	Pronominals, including numerals	32
d.	Verbals	39

The stem classes were set up by treating every different suffix-form separately (-A is distinct form -JA, U from JU, and so on through the following list: A/JA; U/JU; I/Y; IM/YM; AM/JAM; AX/JAX; IX/YX; YJ/IJ; OM/EM; YE/IE; AJA/JAJA; UJU/JUJU; AMI/JAMI; YMI/IMI; EMU/OMU; OGO/EGO).

This type of distribution corresponds to a certain extent to the traditional distintion between 'soft' and 'hard' types of declension.

This approach has the advantage that it can be used if Russian is either the source or target language.

The Second Approach:

The second approach used the complementary distribution and mutual exclusiveness of classes of inflectional suffix-forms in relation to classes of stem morphemes (if A, then $\bar{B} + \bar{C}$; if B, then $\bar{A} + \bar{C}$; if C, then $\bar{A} + \bar{B}$). Examples are given below.

By this procedure it was possible to combine the soft and hard types of declension into a smaller number of classes and to eliminate, to a certain extent, the traditional distinction between them.

For example, the following fifteen different declension types of the first approach were combined into one class, or into two classes if the distinction of animateness as against inanimateness is observed: STOL, FLAG, KORABL6, MUZEJ, PALEC KARANDAŠ (inanimate types); SLON, BRAT, KRESTJANIN, KNJAZ6, SOSED, AKADEMIK, KON6, GEROJ, TOVARIŠČ (animate types).

The distribulion of inflectional suffix-forms within this class (class M-I/A, where M indicates masculine, I indicates inanimateness, and A animateness) is as follows

a. If Ø, then $\bar{6}$ + $\bar{J}$;
if 6, then $\bar{\emptyset}$ + $\bar{J}$;
if J, then $\bar{\emptyset}$ + $\bar{6}$.

The morphosyntactic value of -Ø/-6/-J is nominative and accusative singular if the subclass is M-I, or nominative singular only if the subclass is M-A.

b. If -OV, then -ĒV + -ĒJ;
if -EV, then -ŌV + -ĒJ;
if -EJ, then -ŌV + -ĒV.

The morphosyntactic value of -OV/-EV/-EJ is genitive plural if the subclass is M-I, or genitive and accusative plural if the subclass is M-A.

c. If -Y, then -Ī;
if -I, then -Ȳ.

The morphosyntactic value of -Y/-I is nominative and accusative plural if thesubclass is M-I, or nominative plural only if the subclass is M-A.

d. If -U, then -JŪ;
if -JU, then -Ū.

The morphosyntactic value of -U/-JU is dative singular.

e. If -OM, then -ĒM̄;
if -EM, then -ŌM̄.

The morphosyntactic value of -OM/-EM is instrumental singular.

f. If -E, the morphosyntactic value is prepositional singular.

g. If -AM, then -JĒM̄;
if -JAM, then -ĒM̄.

The morphosyntactic value of -AM/-JAM is dative plural.

h. If -AMI, then -JĀM̄Ī;
if -JAMI, then -ĀM̄Ī.

The morphosyntactic value of -AMI/-JAMI is instrumental plural.

i. If -AX, then -JĀX̄;
if -JAX, then -ĀX̄.

The morphosyntactic value of -AX/-JAX is prepositional plural.

The pairs of allomorphs -I/-Y, -U/-JU, etc., can be classified as replacive inflectional suffix-forms because their morphosyntactic function and value is identical, and their occurrence is conditioned by the phonological determination of their distribution.

An identical procedure was used for determining the distribution of replacive inflectional suffix-forms with regard to other major classes of stem morphemes.

The effect of this second procedure was to reduce the number of stem classes of nominals from 91 to 59, and to reduce the number of stem classes of pronominals and adjectivals from 61 to 17.

However, this second procedure is one-directional and can be used only if Russian is the source language. But it does have the advantages that the number of classes of stem morphemes is substantially smaller than in the first approach, and that there are more mechanisms for ensuring correct matching of stems and inflectional morphemes. Moreover, accurate encoding by human coders is much simpler and faster, and the number of human errors is consequently smaller.

Distribution of Inflectional Morphemes

The distribution of inflectional morphemes is described in terms of their
    (a) co-occurrence with stem morphemes;
    (b) morphosyntactic function.

a) *Co-occurrence with Stem Morphemes*

The identical inflectional suffix-form can occur with stems of any number of major word-classes, for example:

1) One word-class:
-AX/-JAX occurs only with nominals;
-AJA/-JAJA occurs only with adjectivals;
-ETE/-ITE occurs only with verbals.

2) Two word-classes:
-AM/-JAM occurs with nominal and pronominal stems.

3) Three word-classes:
-E occurs with nominal, pronominal and adjectival stems.

4) Four word-classes:
-$\emptyset$ occurs with nominals, pronominals, adjectivals and verbal stems.

b) *Morphosyntactic function*

Case homonymy is extremely widespread in Russian as well as in other Slavic languages. There is no type of declension in which all six cases have different forms. Consequently, it is appropriate to classify the inflectional suffix-forms according to their morphosyntactic function. This can be done in the following way:

1) The inflectional suffix-form is monovalent if it has a single morphosyntactic value (i.e., if it refers to one case and one number only).

2) The inflectional suffix-form is polyvalent if it has more than one morphosyntactic value (i.e., if it refers to more than one case in the same number of in different numbers[1]).

The monovalent inflectional suffix-forms are:

-EMI/-IMI/-YMI	instrumental plural
-OMU/-EMU	dative singular
-6JU	instrumental singular
-AMI/-JAMI	instrumental plural
-AM/-JAM	dative plural
-AX/-JAX	prepositional plural
-UJU/-JUJU	accusative singular (adjectival)
-AJA/-JAJA	nominative plural (adjectival)

All other inflectional suffix-forms are polyvalent.

One of the most productive and, at the same time, most ambiguous inflectional suffix-forms is -I and its allomorph -Y.

The total morphosyntactic value of -I/-Y within the major class of nominals is genitive singular (s2), dative singular (s3), prepositional singular (s6), nominative plural (pl) and accusative plural (p4).

In theory, there are 3125 (5^5) potential morphosyntactic combinations possible for -I/-Y within the class of nominals. However, only 9 combinations of morphosyntactic values actually exist.

The admissible combinations are:

1. REAKQI-I	s236 pl4
2. MYŠ-I	s236 pl
3. SANATORI-I	s6 pl4
4. ZELEN-I (singulare tantum)	s236
5. STEN-Y	s2 pl4
6. P4T-I (cardinal numeral)	p 236
7. ŽEN-Y	s2 pl
8. STOL-Y	pl2
9. PROLETARI-I	s6 pl

The inflectional suffix-form -I/-Y is monovalent if it occurs with the following subclasses of nominals:

10. AKADEMIK-I	pl
11. ZNANI-I	s6
12. VOZN-I (singulare tantum)	s2

---

[1] The class of verb inflections is not treated in this paper. See Pacak, M., "Morphological Abstraction of Russian Verbs"; *Machine Translation*; M.I.T., Vol. VI (November 1961).

Altogether, then, the inflectional suffix-form -I/-Y exhibits 12 different morphosyntactic values.

The range of the morphosyntactic values of -I/-Y within the class of modifiers is more restricted. If -I/-Y occurs with the adjectival subclass of the type OTCOV-, it is the marker of the nominative plural if the noun modified by OTCOVY is animate, or the marker of the nominative and accusative plural if the noun is inanimate.

Otherwise -I/-Y is the marker of the short form of the plural in adjectivals, including the participles. The categories of case and gender are unmarked in the plural of the short forms.

Patterns of Morphosyntactic Polyvalencies

The patterns of morphosyntactic polyvalencies in nominal, pronominal and adjectival forms can theoretically be divided into three major classes:

  I. Case and number are both ambiguous;
 II. Case is ambiguous but number is unambiguous;
III. Number is ambiguous but case is unambiguous.

Practically, in Russian, only Class I and Class II are to be found. The type of polyvalency of Class III is not found.

Class I

There are 15 subclasses in which both case and number are ambiguous.

1.	PROLETARI-I	(prepositional singular; nominative plural)
2.	ZEN-Y	(genitive singular; nominative plural)
3.	DOL-EJ	(instrumental singular; genitive plural)
4.	IVANOV-YM	(instrumental singular; dative plural)
5.	VS-EM	(instrumental & prepositional singular; dative plural)
6.	DOKTOR-A	(genitive & accusative singular; nominative plural)
7.	OSTROV-A	(genitive singular; nominative & accusative plural)
8.	SANATORI-I	(prepositional singular; nominative & accusative plural)
9.	QAPL-E	(instrumental singular; genitive & accusative plural)
10.	SOLDAT-Ø	(nominative singular; genitive & accusative plural)
11.	GLAZ-Ø	(nominative & accusative singular; genitive plural)
12.	VS-E	(nominative & accusative singular; nominative & accusative plural)
13.	MYŠ-I	(genitive, dative & prepositional singular; nominative plural)
14.	REAKQI-I	(genitive, dative & prepositional singular; nominative & accusative plural)
15.	TAKSI	(all cases both singular and plural).

Class II

There are 14 subclasses in which case is ambiguous, but number is not.

1. SAXAR-U   (genitive & dative singular)
2. STOL-Ø   (nominative & accusative singular)
3. SLON-A   (genitive & accusative singular)
4. LES-U   (dative & prepositional singular)
5. STOL-Y   (nominative & accusative plural)
6. ŽEN-Ø   (genitive & accusative plural)
7. Č-EM   (instrumental & prepositional singular)
8. IVANOV-U   (dative & accusative singular)
9. BEDNOST-I   (genitive dative & prepositional singular)
10. POL-E   (nominative, accusative & prepositional singular)
11. IVANOV-A   (feminie nominative singular; masculine genitive & accusative singular)
12. IVANOV-YX   (genitive, accusative & prepositional plural)
13. ST-A   (genitive, dative, instrumental & prepositional)
14. PORTN-OJ   (masculine nominative & accusative (inanimate) singular; feminine genitive, dative, instrumental & prepositional singular).

Distributional Table of Morphosyntactic Polyvalencies

Class I: Case and number ambiguity

Number of values	Number of subclasses having that number of values
2	4
3	7
4	2
5	1
12	1
Total	15

Class II: Case ambiguity only

Number of values	Number of subclasses having that number of values
2	8
3	4
4	1
6	1
Total	14

This table shows the distribution of morphosyntactic polyvalencies within Classes I and II. For example, within Class I there are four different dyadic subclasses; reference to the preceding list will show that these are:

1. locative singular and nominative plural.
2. genitive singular and nominative plural.
3. instrumental singular and genitive plural.
4. instrumental singular and dative plural.

Representation of Data

There are several ways of representing the results of a morphological or of any other linguistic analysis in a computable form.

Algorithmic Tree Representation

The algorithmic tree representation is demonstrated by means of the inflectional suffix-form -J and its morphosyntactic distribution within the major class of nominals.

The symbolic notation s14 p24 is a coverall for the widest range of morphosyntactic values of -J under all circumstances; these values are nominative singular (s1), accusative singular (s4), genitive plural (p2) and accusative plural (p4). The actual ranges of morphosyntactic values are s14 (nominative, accusative singular), p24 (genitive, accusative plural), s1 (nominative singular) and p2 (genitive plural), depending on the subclass of the nominal stem (the symbols MA, MD, MH, MP, MI, M$, FA, FB, F1, ND, are here used to represent different subclasses of nominal stems).

MA	MUZEJ	M$	PROLETARIJ
MD	KRAJ	FA	LINIJA
MH	SANATORIJ	FB	STAJA
MP	CAJ	F1	MARIJA
M1	GEROJ	ND	ZNANIE

Logical Formulae

The same type of morphological analysis for the suffix-form -J can be written as four logical formulae.

Formula 1: [(MA v MD v MH v MP)] ⊃ *AD*
Formula 2: [(F1)] ⊃ *HJ*]
Formula 3: [(M1) v (M$)] ⊃ *A*
Formula 4: [(FA) v (FB) v (ND)] ⊃ *H*

COMPUTATIONAL MORPHOLOGY

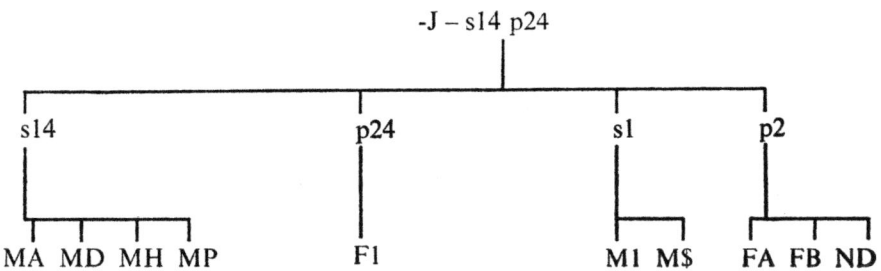

Matrix Representation

The distribution of inflectional morphemes can be represented by a set of matrices which are constructed separately for every inflectional suffix-form with its allomorphs.

The matrix for the inflectional suffix-form -J is given as an example.

Matrix for -J

	MA	MD	MH	MP	M1	M$	FA	FB	F1	ND
s1	+	+	+	+	+	+	−	−	−	−
2	−	−	−	−	−	−	−	−	−	−
3	−	−	−	−	−	−	−	−	−	−
4	+	+	+	+	−	−	−	−	−	−
5	−	−	−	−	−	−	−	−	−	−
6	−	−	−	−	−	−	−	−	−	−
p1	−	−	−	−	−	−	−	−	−	−
2	−	−	−	−	−	−	+	+	+	+
3	−	−	−	−	−	−	−	−	−	−
4	−	−	−	−	−	−	−	−	+	−
5	−	−	−	−	−	−	−	−	−	−
6	−	−	−	−	−	−	−	−	−	−

The subclass of the stem morphemes of nominals are listed across the matrix, and the separate morphosyntactic values are listed down the matrix.

A plus sign at the intersection of column and row indicates that -J has the morphosyntactic value to the left of that row, provided that it is matched with the subclass of nominal stems at the top of that column.

Three-dimensional Table

The construction of a three-dimensional table could also prove useful in morphosyntactic analysis.

The subclasses of the stem morphemes are listed parallel to the x-axis and the particular inflectional suffix-forms are listed parallel to the y-axis. The intersection of the horizontal row and vertical column defines a line parallel to the z-axis which can be considered as containing the morphosyntactic values which are the logical sum of the values of the stem and of the inflectional morpheme.

Three-dimensional Table

	MA	MD	MH	MP	Ml	M$	FA	FB	Fl	ND
-J	s14	s14	s14	s14	s1	s1	p2	p2	p24	p2
-Ø	—	—	—	—	—	—	—	—	—	—
-A	—	—	—	—	—	—	—	—	—	—
-JA	—	s2p14		—	s24	s24	s1	s1	s1	—
-E	s6	s6	s6	s6	s6	s6	s36	s36	s36	s14
-O										
etc.										

The three-dimensional table has the advantage that all admissible combinations can be represented on one table instead of in a series of matrices. In some cases, however, it may be more advantageous to use matrices because they can be more easily replaced and controlled. The preference for using either one large three-dimensional table or a set of smaller matrices will depend on the type of computer which is available.

Both the table and the matrices are flexible; additional subclasses of stem morphemes and additional inflectional morphemes can easily be incorporated into the table without changing the logical basis.

REFERENCES

Dostert, L. E., "Automatic Translation and Language Data Processing", *Vistas in Information Handling*, Vol. 1, Chapter 5 (Spartan Books, Washington, D. C., 1963).
Garvin, P. L., "A Study of Induction Method in Syntax", *Word*, Vol. 18 (August, 1962).
Harris, Z. S., *Structural Linguistics* (The University of Chicago Press, 1961).
Hayes, D. G., "Research Procedures in Machine Translation, *Natural Language and the Computer*, Chapter 4 (McGraw-Hill Book Company, 1963).
Lamb, S. M., *Outline of Stratificational Grammar* (University of California, 1962).
King, G. W., "The Requirements of Lexical Storage", *Georgetown University Monograph Series on Languages and Linguistics*, No. 10 (1959).
Macdonald, R. R., "General Report 1952-63"; *Georgetown University Machine Translation Research Project*, Paper No. 30 (June 1963).
Mel'chuk, I. A., "Morphological Analysis in Machine Translation", *Problemy Kibernetiki*, No. 6 (1961).
Nikolajeva, T. M., "Opyt Algoritmiceskoj Morfologii Russkogo Jazyka", *Strukturno-Tipologiceskie Issledovanija* (Akademija Nauk, USSR, Moskva, 1962).
Nida, E. A., *Morphology* (The University of Michigan Press; Ann Arbor, 1963).
Lehmann, W. P. & Pendergraft, E., "Structural Models for Linguistic Automation", *Vistas in Information Handling*, Chapter 4; (Spartan Books, Washington, D. C., 1963).
Oettinger, A. G., *Automatic Language Translation* (Harvard University Press, Cambridge, Massachusetts, 1960).
Pacak, M., "Morphology in Terms of MT", *Advances in Documentation and Library Science*, Vol. 3, Part 2, Chapter 36 (Interscience Publishers; New York, 1961).
Pacak, M., "Syntagmatic Limits of Morphological Sets", *Methodos* No. 49-50, Vol. XIII (Milano, Italy, 1961).
Henisz-Retman, B., "Morphological Analysis of Polish Nouns", *Georgetown University Machine Translation Research Project* (June 1962).

Georgetown University

THE PHONEMIC INTERPRETATION OF EARLY GERMANIC NAMES

HERBERT PENZL

Germanic names in Greek and Latin sources have provided welcome material for a period in which Germanic texts are not yet available. They have been used for historical phonology, e.g., to establish details of the relative and absolute chronology of Germanic vowel changes. It is the purpose of this paper to examine briefly the methods used in this interpretation and their validity. Two general assumptions have been made: firstly, that names reveal phonemic change like other linguistic material, and secondly, that the Germanic sounds are reflected by the Greek and Latin graphemes used. The first assumption can be shown to be correct by the reflexes in names of such sound changes as, e.g., the High German consonant shift or Old High German or Old English umlaut. Occasionally, to be sure, a more conservative, traditional representation is found in names than in common nouns: e.g., the 6th, 7th century $ē$ in *Suebi Suevi*.[1] Otherwise, the frequently closer connection of names with place and time in history would seem an advantage in establishing the absolute chronology and the localization of sound-changes reflected by them.

The Latin and Greek reflexes of the Germanic vowels have been taken to be of two types synchronically, either matching, that is phonetically identical with their source, or indicating sound substitutions ("Lautsubstitution", "Lautersatz"). This is the point where our reexamination has to start: we must assume that, unless the foreign phoneme is actually borrowed, any rendering of sound values of another language in names, or in loanwords in general, is a phonetic 'sound substitution', no matter how close reflex and source can be phonetically: e.g., *Dagalaifus* with Germanic *a and *ai, *Saxones* with *a* for Gmc. *a but Latin *ks* for Gmc. *hs, etc.[2]

But there are other types beside the strictly phonetic substitution that can be observed. A morphophonemic or phonotactic substitution shows in the reflex its regular phonotactic structure rather than the phonetic value of the source or necessarily any later phonemic change in the borrowing language: OHG *zins, minta*, OE *minta* OHG *Chobilinza* 'Koblenz' from Latin *census, ment(h)a, Co(n)fluentia* indicate the Germanic nonoccurrence of /e/ before nasal clusters rather than the value of the

---

[1] M. Schönfeld, *Wörterbuch der altgermanischen Personen- und Völkernamen* (1911), pp. 212-215; A. Bach, *Deutsche Namenkunde* (1953), II, 1, §30.
[2] Schönfeld, pp. XXIf., 68f., 199f.; Siegfried Gutenbrunner, *Die germanischen Götternamen der antiken Inschriften* (1936), p. 14ff.

underlying Latin vowel or a later Gmc. sound-change $e > i$.[3] The 6th century spelling *Buccelinus* (beside Greek *Boutilīnos*) may reflect the late Latin palatalized stop before palatal vowels rather than a Germanic value different from [t].[4] A third substitution type that we can call morphemic substitution shows in the reflex the influence of existing morphemes, sometimes against the values of the source; this has often been called "folk etymology". An example is the Latin form *Longobardi*, beside *Langobardi*, influenced by the Latin morpheme *long-*.[5] A fourth substitution type is analogical substitution, as, e.g., in the High German place-name form *Eichholz* for Low German *Ekholt* (1373)[6] or in the Latinized 8th century form *Stratburg* besides *Strazburg*[7] where the substitutions seem to be based on many parallel High German-Low German and Latin-Old High German consonant correspondences. For these phonetic, phonotactic, morphemic, analogical substitutions mentioned we assume oral Germanic sources and analyzable written indications of their oral Latin or Greek reflexes. Written sources and various resulting transliteration or transcription reflexes or orthographic transfers in the spelling of names, not to mention purely scribal errors, can further complicate the phonemic interpretation. But the recognition of all four types of substitution is essential even for only synchronic analysis. Germanic names in classical texts have to be analyzed like minimal texts by themselves.

In the diachronic analysis of Germanic names, however, still a much greater variety of possible interpretations has to be recognized; invariably a comparison of two or more Latin or Greek reflexes is involved. Bremer[8] published in 1886 a list of Germanic names with IE *$\bar{e}$ in classical texts: the various Latin and Greek *e* and *a* spellings, e.g., *Suevi*, Cheruscan *Chariomerus* (third century), Alemannic *Vadomarius* (4th century) appear to show the gradual spread of the $\bar{a}$ type in the various German dialects. Differing forms within the same dialect can reflect a lowering of original [ɛː] or [æː] to [aː] or a phonemic coalescence with the formerly nasalized $\bar{a}$ before Germanic *h*, which may, as Lüdtke and Moulton suggest, well have been brought about by the origin of a new $\bar{e}$, the so-called $\bar{e}_2$.[9]

But the graphemic differences between Latin reflexes do not necessarily reflect a phonemic change in the Germanic sources. The Latin reflexes with *o* and *a* in medial and stem syllables, respectively, for IE *o in words like Ceasar's *Marcomanni*, *Ariovistus*, Tacitus' *Langobardi*, *Chariovalda* were interpreted as indicating two stages in the merger of Pre-Germanic *o and *a into one phoneme usually written *a: it

---

[3] O. Bremer, *Idg. Forschungen* 26 (1909), 148ff.
[4] Th. Steche, *ZfdPh* 62 (1937), 3f. assumes a Germanic affricate.
[5] Schönfeld, p. 150-152 calls it "lateinische Volksetymologie". Analogical remodeling is also frequent among inflexional and derivational affixes.
[6] Bach, II, 2, §528.
[7] Bach, II, 1, §68, J. Schatz, *Althochdeutsche Grammatik* (1927), §138, W. Braune-W. Mitzka, *Althochdeutsche Grammatik* (1953[8]) §83, Anm. 3.
[8] *PBB* 11 (1886), 1ff.
[9] H. Lüdtke, *Phonetica* 1 (1957), 157ff. W. G. Moulton, *PBB* 83 (1961), p. 35, fn. 1. The new /ā/ followed coalescence of Pre-Germanic */ā/ and */ō/ into /ō/. Caesar's *Bacenis* with *a* for IE *$\bar{a}$, PGmc. *$\bar{o}$ may reflect a Celtic source or conceivably point to Gmc. [ɔː].

allegedly occurred first in stressed, then in unstressed position.[10] In 1962 W. P. Lehmann suggests also the possibility of interpreting the spellings as Latin and Greek reflexes of allophonic variations in the Germanic sources, the unstressed allophone being more velar and rounded and therefore rendered by Latin *o* not *a*.[11] This analysis points out the important fact that phonetic substitution in borrowed forms, whether they are names or other loans, provides phonetic, that is allophonic information that cannot be obtained from graphemic or orthographic or naive spelling evidence.[12] Only the phonemic principle makes it possible, by the way, to place beside the old diachronic interpretation of the two stages of the merger of **a* and **o* a synchronic analysis of [o] and [a] as coexistent allophones. But the continued existence of forms with medial *o* in words like 6th century *Ostrogothae* suggests morphemic or phonotactic substitution in the medial syllable beside the phonetic substitution in the stem syllable; the early medial *o* in *Marcomanni* may reflect a genitive plural ending.[13] In other forms Celtic beside Germanic sources may be reflected (e.g., in *Ariovistus*).[14]

Name forms have been quoted in pursuing the prehistory of Germanic **u* and **o*, **e* and **i*. Collitz convincingly showed that *o* in Latin *Gotones*, *Gothi* beside *u* in *Gutones* was not proof for an earlier Gothic [o] but either derived from a Greek phonetic substitution for Germanic *u* or the reflex of West Germanic usage.[15] The relative dates of the occurrence of *i* and *e* in such forms as Caesar's *Tulingi*, *Tencteri*, then Tacitus' *Inguiomerus*, Tacitus' *Fenni* versus Ptolemy's *Finni*, Tacitus' *Segimerus* versus Velleius Paterculus' *Sigimerus* have been used to postulate a relative and absolute chronology of Gmc. [e] > Gmc. [i] in different positions; first before velar nasal plus consonant, particularly outside of the main stress; then before other nasal clusters; then before *i* in the next syllable.[16] Not only the scarcity of the material but also the contradictory chronology does not permit this diachronic interpretation. Does this name material throw any light then on the controversial question of the phonemic status of *[e] and *[i] in Proto-Germanic or Common Germanic, that is, whether in the overall pattern they should be reconstructed as two phonemes or as one with two main allophones in a distribution parallel to that of *[u] and *[o]?[17] The answer must be negative too. But such forms as those quoted above, also *Semnones* with *mn* from **bn*, and *Segestes*, indicate two phonemes /i/ and /e/ for the first century A.D. in Germanic dialects. The Germanic name forms cannot be expected to show after the phonemization reflexes of the original allophonic distribution in all

---

[10] O. Bremer, *Idg. Forschungen* 14 (1903), 363 ff., Schönfeld XVII f.
[11] W. P. Lehmann, *Exercises to Accompany Historical Linguistics* (1962), p. 82 f.
[12] "Methoden der Lautbestimmung in der historischen Sprachwissenschaft", *Proceedings of the Fourth International Congress of Phonetic Sciences*, Helsinki 1961 (1962), pp. 719-722.
[13] Schönfeld, 161 f., Rudolf Much, *Die Germania des Tacitus* (1959²), p. 368, quotes ON *markamenn* 'Bewohner der *Markir*'.
[14] Fn. 10 above; E. Prokosch, *A Comparative Germanic Grammar* (1939), p. 103.
[15] H. Collitz, *JEGPh* 1 (1897), 220-238.
[16] Schönfeld, p. XVIII ff., O. Bremer, *ZfdPh* (1896), p. 250 f., O. Höfler, *PBB* 77 (Tübingen 1955), 428-448, H. Fromm, *ZfdA* 88 (1957), 94 ff.
[17] W. G. Moulton, *PBB* 83 (1961), 9-12.

instances. The evidence, moreover, suggests that the Latin reflexes do not show phonetic substitution, which alone could prove specific Germanic sound values, but rather, if not Celtic sources are also involved,[18] a type of analogical substitution that could have resulted from the contrast between classical Latin and certain varieties of Spoken Latin where apparently a partial coalescence between Latin *e* and *i*, always a very wide, open vowel, had taken place. In analogy to classical *i* versus rural *e* correspondences, not the phonetic *i* but the hyperdialectical, analogical *e* may have sometimes been used for Germanic [i].[19] Germanic dialectal differences may also account for Latin *e* and *i* before *nn*.[20]

To summarize: Four types of sound substitution have to be recognized in the synchronic phonological analysis of early Germanic names. This makes the specific phonetic identification of Germanic sound values through their Latin or Greek reflexes very difficult. Only phonetic substitution, none of the other three types can reveal Germanic allophones. In the diachronic interpretation of differing reflexes of an assumed identical Germanic source-phoneme, we have to consider the following possibilities: the differences may be essentially just orthographic; they may be based on different types of synchronic sound substitution (e.g., in *Langobardi*); they may be reflecting contemporary but different Germanic dialects (*Gotones*, *Gutones*) or Germanic forms and forms with third language sound substitutions, e.g., Celtic or Greek ones in the Latin reflex. The differences may also reflect regional or social varieties and their interaction within the borrowing language (*Fenni* and *Finni*; *Sigimerus* of 30 A.D. and *Segimerus* of 100 A.D.); they may show a sound-change within the borrowing language (Latin *Buccelinus* and *Butilinus*). Only rarely are contrasting Latin forms numerous and clear enough to allow an unequivocal interpretation as due to changes in the respective Germanic sources (*Chariomerus*, *Vadiomarus*). The constant recognition of the entire range of possible relations between source and reflex in early Germanic names should result in great caution in synchronic and diachronic interpretation, especially in their use for the internal phonological history of Germanic phonemes.

University of California (Berkeley)

---

[18] H. Collitz, "Segimer oder germanische Namen in keltischem Gewande", *JEGP* 6 (1906), 253 ff.
[19] F. Sommer, *Handbuch der lateinischen Laut- und Formenlehre* (1948) §55, E. Sturtevant, *The Pronunciation of Greek and Latin* (1940²) §116 e. M. Schönfeld, *GRM* 4 (1912), p. 254, assumed a Germanic vowel intermediate between [i] and [e].
[20] The Old Norse development in *drekka* (Gothic *drinkan*), *vetr* (Gothic *wintrus*), and the Germanic loan *rengas* in Finnish show the existence of Germanic dialects where high vowels had lower variants before nasals.

SEMOLOGY, METALINGUISTICS, AND TRANSLATION

GEORGE L. TRAGER

The subject matter covered by the words of the title of this article has always been of great interest to Léon Dostert, to whom the present volume is offered. As a small contribution to the study of these very important but still very much neglected parts of linguistics in the widest sense (macrolinguistics, I have called it), I present this examination of a Taos verb base and some of its ramifications.

This is the first of what it is hoped will be a series of intensive Taos vocabulary studies. The specific data for these studies were brought together during the academic year 1962-63, when I was on sabbatical leave from the University of Buffalo, held a National Science Foundation research grant, and was a Fellow of the Center for Advanced Study in the Behavioral Sciences at Stanford. Field work was done at Taos for several months, and analysis of the materials was begun at the Center. For the opportunity to continue and expand my studies of Taos (begun in 1935) in this way, I express may deeply felt gratitude to the institutions named. I must also thank my friend and principal informant of many years standing, who, in accordance with long established practise at Taos, must remain anonymous; his unfailing patience and deep understanding of the aims of anthropological study in general and of my work specifically, alone have made possible such insights into the culture of the Taos as I have discovered.

A complete bibliography of my previous publications on the Taos is not needed here. The last such publication, "Taos IV: morphemics, syntax, semology in nouns and in pronominal reference", *IJAL* 27.211-22, 1961, contains the references to the three previously numbered papers, and between them they list all previous pertinent publications. For the general analytical theory in terms of which semology is distinguished as an area of linguistic analysis, see now my *Linguistics is linguistics* (*Studies in Linguistics, Occasional Paper* no. 10, 1963).

Taos Pueblo is located in northern New Mexico. The language of its over 1000 inhabitants is a Tanoan language — Northern Tiwa language group of the Tiwa subfamily of the Tanoan family of the Kiowa-Tanoan superfamily. Some conclusions about the history of these languages in the upper Rio Grande valley in the last 1500 years are presented in my forthcoming paper, "The Tanoan settlement of the Rio Grande area: a possible chronology", to be published in *Studies in Southwestern ethnolinguistics* (Festschrift for Harry Hoijer).

The speakers of Taos are now nearly all bilingual — many in Taos and Spanish, and the younger and better educated in Taos and English. They are, in varying degrees, participants in the general culture of New Mexico and thus of the United States and of the Western world. They have had contact with American culture for over 100 years, and with Spanish culture for over 350 years. Yet, as will be seen, the structure of their 'thinking', in Taos, is wholly different from their 'thinking' in Spanish or English.

The Taos phonemes that occur in the material that will be presented here are: /p, t, k/ voiceless fortis unaspirated stops before a vowel, more lenis in the 'glottalized stop' clusters; /'/ glottal stop, lenis, released smoothly into the following vowel, whether initial in its syllable or forming a 'glottalized stop' with a preceding stop; /m, n, w, y/; /i, u/ high, relatively tense vowels; /a/ low front, /o/ low back slightly rounded; /uo/ glide from /u/ to /o/ in one syllable; /ą/ low central vowel, nasalized; /´/ primary stress, middle tone; /˝/ primary stress, high tone; /^/ primary stress, low tone; /`/ medial stress, middle tone; /˘/ medial stress, high tone; /"/ medial stress, low tone; weak-stressed (middle tone) unmarked; /+/ internal open transition. (See Taos I, *IJAL* 14.155-60, 1948.)

Taos has inflected nouns and verbs. Noun inflection involves suffixes of noun class, and multimorphemic prefixes indicating the person and number of the possessor and the class of the possessed noun. Verb inflection involves various aspectual, temporal, and relating suffixes, and prefixes — very similar to those of nouns — indicating person and number of the subject and the class of the object. Most Taos bases appear with both noun and verb inflection, and seem to be most easily interpreted as basically verbal; there are some noun bases that are not verbal, and there are the bases of some particles (uninflected) which are not verbal. (See Taos II, *IJAL* 20.173-80, 1954, and Taos IV, for the prefixes and the noun classes.) The symbols ´ and ` over a vowel mean high-tone base and low-tone base respectively; ¯ over a vowel means middle-tone base; bases and other morphemes are shown with hyphens.

The corpus of forms that will be analyzed was all taken from texts of various kinds: narrative, answers to questions of the form 'How do you say...?', spontaneous comment by the informant. All recur numerous times throughout my extensive material, and the ten forms considered here were brought together and discussed with the informant in July 1963, a tape recording being made of the discussion. The discussion confirmed the analyses that had been reached by me previously.

The forms, with usual translations, are (numbered for reference below):

1. 'owǎ *I was there, I was born*;
2. tiwǎ *I called him*;
3. 'owǎmą *I am*;
4. 'ąnwǎmą *I have*;
5. tąwǎpǎ *I claimed*;
6. wǎpŭo'i *former(ly)*;

7. 'ąn'ù+wǎ *I had a child* and 'ąnnö'ù+wǎpŭo *I didn't have a child*;
8. kinąwǎ'i *our customs* and kinąt'óywǎ'i *our Indian way*;
9. wǎna *penis*;
10. 'ąnmok'ûwǎmą *I'm glad, I like it*.

They all contain the base wǎ- *to be, to exist*, which is the topic of our analysis.

Morphemic analysis of the forms shows the following:

1. 'owǎ: 'o- '*it* as subject, *me* as object'; wǎ-. The verb, like all Taos verbs, is "transitive"; the literal meaning, then, is, perhaps, something like 'it [impersonal] made or caused me to be' = *I was, I existed*. The locational connotation, *I was there*, or the reporting of the event, *I was born*, result metalinguistically from the context and situation.

2. tiwǎ: ti- '*I* as subject, entity of class A as object'; wǎ-. The meaning is approximately 'I made him be, exist' = *I called him*. Nouns of class A (see 9 below) always indicate a discrete, isolable, countable entity; when paired with a class B form from the same stem, the A form is "singular", the B form is "plural", and the reference is to an animate entity. It is the combination of context and the semological content that indicates the metalinguistic reference to a person.

3. 'owǎmą: 'o-, wǎ-; -mą stative suffix. The literal meaning is 'it has been made to be in reference to me' = *I am*. An example with incorporated complement is: 'otòbu+wǎmą *I am governor* — tòbúna *governor* (tōbu-, -na class A suffix).

4. 'ąnwǎmą: 'ąn- '*I* as possessor, entity of class A as thing possessed'; wǎ-, -mą as in 3. Here the literal meaning must be something like 'it has been made to be in reference to something of mine' = *I have*. With incorporated complement (=object), we have: 'ąnkwò+wǎmą *I have an ax* (kwóna: kwō-, -na).

5. tąwǎpǎ: tą- '*I* acting on *myself*', reflexive; wǎ-; pǎ- *to make, to cause*. Literally, we have 'I made, caused being for myself' = *I claimed*. The two bases wǎpǎ are in normal transition, with primary stress on the first, indicating that the second functions as a quasi-suffix, the whole being a unit, *to claim* ('make to be for oneself').

6. wǎpŭo'i: wǎ-; pŭo- *to happen*; -'i *that which, he who*. Literally the form is 'that which, he who made [it] be as having happened' = *former(ly)*.

7. 'ąn'ù+wǎ: 'ąn- *my* (possessed of class A); 'ù- *child, son, young* (of animal) — 'ù'úna (-'u- stem-vowel reduplication, -na class A). Referring back to 1 and 4, we get a literal meaning like 'it was made to be in reference to my child' = *I had a child*. The form that corresponds to the negative of this sentence has an extra verbal element: 'ąnnö'ù+wǎpŭo; 'ąn- *my*, -nö- after /n/ for -wò- verb negater, 'ù-, wǎ-, pŭo-, literally, 'it made it be as having happened negatively in reference to my child' = *I didn't have a child*.

8. kinąwǎ'i: ki- 'of us (more than 2)' = *our*; -ną- object of class L (place, locality); wǎ-, -'i. This gives literally something like 'that which made to be something of ours [as it is] locally' = *(that which is) our way, custom*. To get the explicit idea of *Indian*, we have kinąt'óywǎ'i, where t'óyna *Indian, person* (class A) is the incorporated comple-

ment, something like 'that which made to be something Indian of ours [as it is] locally' = *our Indian way*. Note that t'óyna means *human being*, and is rarely, if ever, applied to non-Indians; there is even some hesitation in applying it to Navahos!

9. wăna: wá-, -na class A, literally 'a discrete entity that makes to be' = *penis*. This noun has "plural" wăne, where -ne is the class C suffix; paired nouns A, C are inanimate, the A being a "singular" entity, the C an aggregate or haphazard assemblage of such entities. I have not tried it on informants, but I assume that wăna could be used "figuratively" in the meaning *progenitor*, and its "plural" would then be wănemą class B; paired nouns A, B are animate in reference, and when "plural" are "thought of" (i.e., spoken of) as a systematic set of entities (*set* in the sense of patterned social group or the like).

10. 'ąnmok'ûwămą: 'ąn- *my*, -mo- reflexive = *my own*; k'û- 'good' (a verb base); wá-, -mą. Literally this must be approximately 'it has been made to exist as being good in reference to something of my own' = *I'm glad, I like it*.

From the attempted cumbersome literal meanings, and the structural analyses, it can be concluded that the linguistic, or semological, meaning of the verb base wá- is 'to focus (or bring into focus) existence on (or in relation to) [something or someone]'. Replacing the expressions used above by this phrasing, condensed into 'to focus existence on', we get:

1. 'it focussed existence on me'. The extension of meaning to *I was there*, and further to *I was born* is, as noted, metalinguistic, and identifiable only in the appropriate context.

2. 'I focussed existence on an A'. If the context implies an animate object, the translation is *I called him*, as if to say 'I called him into being [by naming him]'. Interestingly enough explication is needed here: this means *I called him* in the sense of 'I called out to him', 'I called his name'. To say 'I called him [on the telephone]' we say tit'óy'ąmą: ti *I...him*, t'ōy- *person*, — 'ąmą causative (actually a verb base 'ąmą- appearing uncompounded only in the stative, kąmmą *made, caused*): 'I caused him to be a person', as if 'I called him into being as a person [in the machine]'.

3. 'existence has been focussed on me [as someone]'.

4. 'existence has been focussed on my [something]'.

5. 'I focussed existence-making on or for myself [on something]'. It is easy enough to "figure out" that this translates into *I claimed*, when the informant tells us so.

6. 'that which focussed existence as having happened'. This points up very well how a "verb-oriented" semology differs from the kind we have in English: being *former* is stated actively in Taos, as the result of happenings.

7. 'it focussed existence on my child'. Note that in Taos, being born (see 1) and bearing a child are not spoken of physiologically; they are in terms of coming into existence. The negative, 'it focussed existence as having happened negatively on my child', requires the actual linguistic expression of something having happened.

8. 'that which focussed existence on our [way, place]'. Class L reference, always

shown by -na̜- added to class A prefixes, is found not only in such nouns as thə́na *house* (/ə/ is a lower high retracted central vowel), but also as the reference for various kinds of seeming abstract and deverbal nouns; L-nouns in -na, which look like A-nouns, never have a "plural" in C; the deverbal nouns that have L-reference look like C-nouns (-ne), but never have an accompanying A or B. The semology and metalinguistics of L-reference has still to be worked out in detail.

9. 'existence focusser'. That this should come to mean, "in the real world", *penis*, is a metalinguistic accident.

10. 'being good [=goodness] has been focussed on my own [something]'. Here perhaps the something is *self*; when the self is good, one likes something, or is glad.

The discussion presented here may serve to set the stage for further analysis of the semology and metalinguistics of Taos.

Semologically, it appears that the verbs corresponding to English intransitives have a meaning expressible as 'to focus [a state of ...] on'. Without bringing in the data themselves at this point, we may indicate that active or "transitive" verbs can be expressed as "to do [an action]' or 'to perform [a doing of ...]'. We may also put the meaning of the noun classes (cf. Taos IV) into this frame in the following manner: A-nouns, in -na, as animate, 'one who [does ...]' or 'one who [focusses ...] on'; B-nouns, in -nema̜ or -na̜, as "plurals" of animate A's, 'a set or patterned social group which [does ...]' or '... which [focusses ...] on'. Inanimate A-nouns are never subjects, but as objects have the meaning 'an entity on which someone focusses ...'; their "plurals" are C-nouns. Inanimate B-nouns are never subjects; their metalinguistic reference is "singular", and as objects they mean 'a set on which someone focusses ...'; their "plurals" are also C. The C-nouns are never subjects, but as objects they are 'something focussed on or done to, as an aggregate or unpatterned assemblage'; or, when they have L-reference, and this is also true for the L-nouns in -na, they are, as objects, 'something focussed on or done to in a place, or as a locale'. The relative forms in -'i, "plural" -'ina̜ (-na̜ from class B?), mean 'he who' or 'they who' [do or focus ...].

What kind of generalizations, in terms of our title, can be made from this presentation?

The semology comes out of the linguistic structure. Unless a language is structurally analyzed, in its own terms, no satisfactory semology can ever be constructed. "Your old school-teacher's" rhetoric, Latin-based, can perhaps give you kernels of meaning in your own language and set you off on a chain of transformations, but it can never get at the semology — the structure-derived linguistic 'meaning' of a language. Only analysis of structure as structure, at separate levels as needed, passing systematically from one to another, can bring this about.

The metalinguistics comes out of the application of the linguistic material, the semology, structurally and systematically to the non-linguistic culture. This means, of course, that ways must be found to analyze the culture structurally. Anthropologists are far from having worked out such analytical procedures. Reductionistic evolutionism, and pseudo-psychologizing, will never give us the needed analytical tools. Working from linguistic structures might help, however,

For Taos the semology is begun, and since the studies of the language have to be done in a field situation, something of the metalinguistics comes through also, despite the lack of sufficient analytical tools.

What about the translation? This is easy, as long as one has human translators. The Taos informant knows his semology, as a speaker of the language; to the extent that he knows English (and my informant speaks it well, and is highly literate), he knows English semology also. He is actively engaged in metalinguistic application of the semologies to the various aspects of his idioculture. When translation is asked for, in the field-eliciting situation, or in real life, the informant can put together the corresponding semologies in the presence of a metalinguistic situation that he is familiar with, and come up with what we call a 'translation'. Suppose we had to program a machine to translate Taos into English? It could be done, of course, but only after the bulk of the linguistic and non-linguistic cultures of the Taos AND of English speakers had been systematically analyzed, level by level. The human brain of the bilingual informant does this easily. It would be nice to know how.

The University of Buffalo

LINGUISTICS AND THE DESIGN OF PSYCHOLINGUISTIC EXPERIMENTS

EDITH CROWELL TRAGER

In his presidential address in 1963 Charles Osgood said to the members of the American Psychological Association, "What with linguists like Roman Jakobson, Joseph Greenberg, and Noam Chomsky to the left of me, and with psychologists like Fred Skinner, Jack Carrol, Jim Jenkins, and Roger Brown to the right of me — not to mention George Miller, who is usually ahead of me — I feel that I have been rather in the thick of psycholinguistics."[1]

It is certainly significant to both linguists and psychologists that the title of his address was "On Understanding and Creating Sentences". Everyone in linguistics has been aware of the ever-increasing rate of activity in the field of psycholinguistics in the past decade, and, incidentally, of the expanded semantic area of the term "psycholinguistics".

In the broadest sense, psycholinguistic research is obviously anything amenable to the techniques of and relevant to the theory of linguistics, psychology, and psychiatry. Perhaps the term will come to be applied only to those matters that require the joint efforts of experimental psychologists and linguists, both descriptive and theoretical.

Psychiatric linguistics, still in embryonic form, has as one of its chief milestones *The First Five Minutes*[2] by the linguist Charles Hockett and two psychiatrists who worked for two years on the joint analysis of the language, paralanguage, and kinesics of the patient and therapist during the initial five minutes of a psychiatric interview. Another book, to be called *The Natural History of an Interview*, begun when Frieda Fromm-Reichmann was still alive, is under preparation by Norman McQuown, working with the linguists William M. Austin, Raven I. McDavid, Jr., and A. L. Davis, at the University of Chicago. It will be a linguistic, cultural and psychiatric analysis of a movie of Gregory Bateson working with a schizophrenic family. The original hope has dwindled that this psycholinguistic activity, more aptly called psychiatric linguistics, would lead to diagnostic techniques that could be specifically taught to psychiatrists in training. The present, more reasonable, concern is with making psychiatric workers aware of the number and complexity of the messages in

---

[1] Charles E. Osgood, "On Understanding and Creating Sentences" *American Psychologist*, Vol. 18 (1963), pp. 735-751.
[2] R. E. Pittenger, C. F. Hockett, and J. J. Danehy, *The First Five Minutes: A Sample of Microscopic Interview Analysis* (Ithaca, New York, 1960).

the acoustic signal that they and the patient exchange during every second of interaction. The hope is, of course, that increased awareness will lead to increased understanding of the therapeutic problems. The work of Yale's George Mahl is a solid body of data and theory in this and related areas.[3]

There was a psycholinguistic project in 1960-61 at the Walter Reed Army Institute of Research where there were such outstanding people as David McK. Rioch, Robert Galambos, and Joseph Brady. This project, however, involved only a psychiatrist, Edwin A. Weinstein, this linguist, and the people on and in the neurosurgery ward of Walter Reed Hospital. The psychiatrist's aim was to prove the relevance of the Sapir-Whorf hypothesis to the language of brain-damaged patients, whose trauma might be due variously to gunshot wounds, accidents, aneurysms, and tumors. He felt that he could determine in a general way their pre-operative Weltanschauung by learning what he could about their language, i.e. what they talked about and their attitudes toward their chief topics of discussion, such as money, food, kin, and sex. It was hoped that we could analyze their language after surgery, and that thereby we would have martialed evidence to support the Sapir-Whorf hypothesis. There is in preparation my empirical study of the phonology, morphology, syntax, and paralanguage of ten successive interviews with a patient whose physical condition was likely to improve rapidly. His condition and his linguistic pathology did exhibit striking correlations. Perhaps, however, psychiatric research, even when linguistics is involved, is of such a different order from the kind of work discussed below that the term "psycholinguistics" should not be applied to it. It also became clear during that year at Walter Reed that neurolinguistics is a field that ought to be developed, especially since there exists an enormous amount of information on the neuro-anatomy and neuro-physiology relevant to both normal language and to its pathologies, including aphasia.

The term "neurolinguistics" seems to be the logical one for this area,[4] since "psycholinguistics" already refers to an extremely diverse set of studies, speculations and, occasionally, genuine theories. Saporta's useful psycholinguistics reader[5] attests to some of this diversity. Diebold's superb review[6] of that book is at the same time a comprehensive survey of the field, and further enforces the need for the two separate areas of neurolinguistics and psycholinguistics.

Psycholinguistics, however, is the concern of Osgood's paper, in the course of which, incidentally, he makes an interesting reference to an agreement by Gibson and Hebb that perception belongs with meaning rather than with sensation. At any rate,

---

[3] George F. Mahl, "Sensory Factors in the Control of Expressive Behavior", paper presented at the 16th International Congress of Psychology, Bonn, Germany, 1960, which the author states is a fragment of the paper "People Talking When They Can't Hear Their Voices" written while he was at the Center for Advanced Study in the Behavioral Sciences, 1963-64. It has a bibliography of some of his own work and related publications by others.
[4] Edith C. Trager, "The Field of Neurolinguistics", *Studies in Linguistics* 15.70, 71 (1961)
[5] *Psycholinguistics: A Book of Readings*, edited by Sol Saporta, with the assistance of Jarvis R. Bastian. (New York, Holt, Rinehart, and Winston, 1961).
[6] A. Richard Diebold, Jr., Review of *Psycholinguistics* (ed. by Saporta), *Language* 40. 197-260 (1964).

Osgood takes as his point of departure the ground-breaking article by Katz and Fodor[7] wherein they put the sentence *The man hits the colorful ball* through their semantics machine. In a subsequent publication,[8] by the way, Fodor approves of the suggestion that the meaning of a word is a function of the rules for operating with it, but disapproves of the requirement that those rules be denotation rules.

Be that as it may, Osgood discusses three models for a sentence generator, which he calls respectively the kiddie-car model, the horse and buggy model, and the Model T-Ford model — which we must all concede to be marvelously mnemonic nomenclature. The kiddie-car model is typified by Skinner's single-stage behaviorism as expounded in his *Verbal Behavior*,[9] so illuminatingly reviewed by Chomsky.[10] This simple S→R model, applied to language, gives us a finite state grammar, such that a Markov-type generator could produce sentences, since each word is probabilistically dependent on the preceding words. Chomsky and others in his wake have argued that such a sentence generator could not produce a potentially infinite set of grammatical sentences, as linguists certainly suspected all along. Osgood points out that Chomsky never said that the Markov model was erroneous; he merely said that it was insufficient, and I think we should remember that probability doubtless plays a great part in the decoding of sentences, if not the encoding. Also, some terrain not navigable by the kiddie car model is that of self-imbedding sentences. "Self-imbedding" is the term used when the same nested construction occurs more than once. An example of an imbedding sentence follows: "The man who lives in that trailer standing over there that belongs to my mother who only let him have it on suffrance used to go whenever he liked to visit that house on the corner of Third and Magnolia where the Markovs were living when they were married to their respective first spouses who, as you know ... One could continue imbeddingconstructions, it is clear.

It would be more in point, however, to go on to the horse-and-buggy model which really dates back to Hull (1930). He talked in different terms, about two-stage mediation, in which the pure stimulus act produces self-stimulation, rather than being instrumental in itself. This concept, applied to language, gives what we know as phrase-structure grammar. It involves rewrite rules and dictionary rules, and, in the case of English, the rule that S → NP + VP. With this, we can show very neatly by binary tree diagrams the basic sentences that contributed to the final linear sentence. To use the words used by Chomsky in a series of lectures in Berkeley in February, 1964, phrase-structure grammar can show how the deep structure of the sentence is mapped into the surface structure. This model can generate an infinite set of grammatical sentences and transformation rules. It cannot, however, resolve ambiguities or "disambiguate" phrases like "the shooting of the hunters" or the now-classic "visiting relatives can be fun". Are the hunters doing the shooting? or getting shot?

---

[7] J. J. Katz and J. A. Fodor, "The structure of a semantic theory", *Language* 39. 170-210 (1963).
[8] Jerry A. Fodor, Review of *Questions of Meaning* by László Antal, *Language* 39. 468-473 (1963).
[9] B. F. Skinner, *Verbal Behavior* (New York, Appleton-Century-Crofts, 1957).
[10] Noam Chomsky, Review of *Verbal Behavior* by B. F. Skinner, *Language* 35.26-58 (1959).

Are we visiting the relatives? or are they visiting us? This two-stage model doesn't tell us. Osgood puts his horse-and-buggy model in more general terms. Whenever some neutral stimulus is repeatedly contiguous with another stimulus which regularly and reliably elicits a particular pattern of the total behavior, the neutral stimulus will become associated with some portion of this total behavior as a representational mediational process. This is certainly a refinement of Mowrer's statement made ten years ago in *his* presidential address to the APA, where he said that the sentence is a conditioning device. To linguists, this seems like a vast oversimplification, of course. Osgood himself says that this model does not account either for perceptual organization or motor skill organization.

Osgood then moves on to the Model-T Ford theory, or the three-stage mediation-integration model, which takes into account Hebb's Integration Principle. Hebb has a presentation of his theories about the organization of behavior that is of interest to linguists,[11] but the particular statement cited by Osgood is this: "The greater the frequency of paired $S \rightarrow R$, the greater is the tendency for the central correlates to activate each other (redundancy, frequency, temporal contiguity). Motivation and reinforcement have nothing to do with the formation of integrations." Osgood's model does not assume that the units of encoding and decoding must be the same. He takes the word, for instance, as the characteristic unit of the perceived forms of language, but uses the syllable as a unit of the encoding system. He suggests there are three components in the decoding machinery and calls them (1) the Word Form Pool, (2) the Semantic Key Sort, and (3) the Cognitive Mixer. He then takes us through the sentence "The clever young thief was severely sentenced by the rather grim-faced judge", suggesting that when we hear *the*, for instance, we store everything until the noun appears, then decide that it is the subject of the sentence if a verb follows immediately. He suggests that meaning is a bundle of simultaneous semantic features, and that therefore we can disambiguate even a sentence like "Light lights lightly light light lights".

Finally, he points out that Miller has demonstrated that we can measure the increased time needed for sentence-understanding as the number of transformations increases. He says that there is an unpublished account by Neal Johnson, at the University of Ohio, of an experiment in which the subjects had to learn sentences of two different grammatical types (The tall boy/ saved the dying woman. The house/ across the street/ is burning.). He predicted that the probability of transitional error in recall would be greater across phrase boundaries than within them. This proved to be the case. The cupboard is bare, however, when it comes to controlled experiments based on linguistic analysis of sentences — not surprising, since the latter is truly in its infancy.

There are three papers which Osgood could not have seen by Chomsky and Miller

---

[11] D. O. Hebb, *Organization of Behavior* (New York, John Wiley & Sons, 1949). Reprinted by Science Editions (New York, 1961).

in the *Handbook of Mathematical Psychology*,[12] one of which is called "Introduction to the Formal Analysis of Natural Languages". There the authors say "we explicitly reject the common opinion that a language is nothing but a set of verbal responses" and "Our hope is that by clearing away some syntactic problems we shall have helped to clarify the semantic issue if only by indicating some of the things that meaning is not". The (finite) set of rules specifying a particular language constitutes the grammar of that language, says Chomsky, and this means that "a grammar must have the status of a theory about those recurrent regularities that we call the syntactic structure of a language". He says, as Osgood pointed out, that "the syntactic component of a grammar contains rewriting rules and transformational rules". He is more explicit than he has hitherto been when he says that "the phonological component of a grammar ... [is] an input-output device that accepts a terminal string with a labeled bracketing and codes it as a phonetic representation". When the latter statement first hit the linguistic grapevine, where it was stated rather more baldly — like "Who needs phonemes?" — the shot was heard round the linguistic world.

There is a distinct possibility that the techniques that seem so impressively applicable to the semology and syntax of language are much less useful on the levels of morphology and phonology. At any rate, the resulting statements about the phonological component of a grammar seem not very new, or when they *are* new, naive. Certainly, the empirical evidence for the reality of the phoneme has been around for at least 5500 years (in the form of alphabets) and deserves the serious attention of psycholinguistics.

Let me take a moment to make an aside. A situation seems to be emerging in linguistics that already obtains, for instance, in nuclear physics. There, as we know, a research project will involve theoretical physicists, experimental physicists, and nuclear engineers, and the most successful projects, I am told, are those in which there is constant exchange of information among all three of the groups concerned.[13] Obviously, the theoretical physicists' prime concern is the mathematical aspects of the experiments, while the experimental physicists do the actual running of the experiment in the reactor and make the decisions which the nuclear engineers help them implement. It would be productive if more of the theoretical linguists talked to more of the descriptive linguists. Chomsky is certainly willing, and so is Lees, although this is less clear in other cases. The descriptive linguists certainly have a great deal to tell the

---

[12] a. Noam Chomsky and G. A. Miller, "Introduction to the Formal Analysis of Natural Languages", 269-322. b. Noam Chomsky, "Formal Properties of Grammars", 323-418. c. G. A. Miller and Noam Chomsky, "Finitary Models of Language Users", pp. 419-492, *Handbook of Mathematical Psychology*, Vol. II, ed. by R. D. Luce, R. B. Bush, and Eugene Galanter, (New York, John Wiley & Sons, 1963).
[13] The foregoing statement was written months before Hockett gave his "Four Lectures on Theoretical Linguistics", given on July 23-28, 1964 at the Linguistic Institute, Indiana. It is interesting that in his handout for the first lecture, he says, "By theoretical linguistics I mean a field that bears the same relationship to our concrete observational work with individual languages that theoretical physics bears to experimental physics. Theoretical linguistics is mathematical, whenever that is useful, but it is not mathematics. The distinction is crucial. The fancy of the mathematician is bound by no constraints save those of logic. The theoretical linguist is bound by observations..."

theoretical linguists, and only the most rock-ribbed descriptivist can say he has learned nothing from the theoreticians. Those who are in applied linguistics are analogous to the nuclear engineers. Although hardly a separate group yet, they have already furnished insights which a descriptive or theoretical linguist would simply not be able to, because he has no access to the situation which afforded the insight. Such a situation might be the teaching of a foreign language. Certainly the work done by Evan Keislar and Paul Pimsleur is evidence of that.[14]

So Chomsky, who does not pretend to be in touch with field work, makes a statement like this: "Each symbol of the universal phonetic alphabet is an abbreviation of a certain set of physical features." Well, of course, there is no universal phonetic alphabet nor can there be. Chomsky bases this on *The Preliminaries to Speech Analysis* by Jakobson, Fant, and Halle. Some acoustic phoneticians find that in the very grossness of that analysis lies much of its utility. Each distinctive feature covers a probably infinite set of demonstrably differing acoustic signals within each language, and certainly signals that differ widely among different languages. Linguists concerned primarily with phonology have long since learned that there is no goodness of fit between phonemes (regarded as perceptual units and, more trivially, as analytical units) and the continuum we see on a spectrogram. We know that there is no one-to-one correspondence. We are familiar from first-hand experience with the fact that one cannot expect either the linearity condition or the invariance condition to be met.[15]

Chomsky defines the linearity condition thus: each phoneme must have associated with it a particular stretch of sound in the represented utterance. Dr. Henry Truby of IBM has demonstrated by thousands of measurements that in an utterance like /pet/ there is a minimum of fifty percent overlap of the /p/ sound into the short /e/ sound; that there is no steady-state /e/, but rather a /p/-ish /e/ segment followed by a /t/-ish /e/ segment, and that the /t/ is influenced by the /e/ for a good half of its duration.[16] In thinking theoretically about the implications of this disparity between (a) what people believe they are saying and hearing and (b) what they are actually doing, in terms of the physical characteristics of the speech sounds, one has to decide that the linearity condition is nonsensical. While phonemes and classes of allophones are highly relevant to descriptive and applied linguistics, it is pointless to consider allophones in a theoretical discussion since the fact of the matter is that there are as many allophones as there are possible environments. Take /i/ as typical of any syllable nucleus; it may occur before and after all twenty-four of the English consonant

[14] Paul Pimsleur, Larry Mace, and Evan Keislar, "Preliminary Discrimination Training in the Teaching of French Pronunciation", Research report (University of California, Los Angeles, 1961).
[15] It is noteworthy that even Hockett said the following, in his handout accompanying the second lecture of "Four Lectures on Theoretical Linguistics", given on July 23-28, 1964 at the Linguistic Institute, Indiana: "If there is a core of empirical truth in the phonemic theory, it is that a speaker's articulatory motions map a discrete array of all-or-none elements into a continuous signal, and that, to understand what is said, a hearer must requantize the incoming continuous signal, thus recovering or reconstituting the discrete array."
[16] H. M. Truby, "Acoustico-cineradiographic analysis considerations", *Acta Radiologica*, Supplement 182 (Stockholm, 1959).

phonemes when they are in medial and final position, and this means that /i/ already has a minimum of 576 "allophones". And this does not begin to cover the effects of noncontiguous sounds, stress, pitch, paralanguage, and the like. Certainly there is no phonetic alphabet in existence, or likely to be, that can note all the allophones of a phoneme.

The descriptive and applied linguists, however, will continue to work with phonemes and classes of allophones because the nature of language forces them to. The single rather offbeat transcription in the Chomsky-Miller article /t^{h}è.d + sɔw + ðəwz + buks/ casts further doubt on the strength of the phonological theory. Why does Ted have a broad phonetic rendering of its initial /t/? Why is the automatic lengthening before /d/ indicated since this is a "phonemic" transcription? Why the Texan pronunciation of *saw*, followed by a British pronunciation of *those*? Does the pitch mark 3 mean that Trager-Smith would show primary stress on *those*? Why the grave accent? There seems to be a confusion between a psychological reality, the phoneme, and a physical reality, the continuum that is speech.

The statement about the invariance condition suffers similarly. The invariance condition is defined, thus: "To each phoneme A [is] ... associated a certain defining set Σ (A) of physical phonetic features such that each [allophone] of A has all the features of Σ (A), and no phonetic segment which is not a variant of A has all the features of Σ (A)." The example of *writer* vs. *rider* is adduced, since in some dialects these words fall together. True enough, but hardly enough to base a whole theory on. Perhaps we have to say that there is high probability than when a /d/ sound is perceived in an utterance, there will be present on a spectrogram corresponding to it a stop-gap, possibly a voicebar, followed by a spike, then vowel formants with frequencies appropriate to that vowel when it follows an alveolar sound. Similar statements of probable correspondences can be made for each of the analytical units we call phonemes. We also must allow for an indeterminacy principle. That is, there will be cases (possibly more the exception than the rule) when the analytical unit, the phoneme /t/, does not have any of its usual acoustic correlates except shorter duration of the preceding vowel. A much less stringent statement of the invariance condition is required and, in fact, it might be better called a variance condition.

This leads me, at long last, to say that I hope that we shall very soon be able to see carried out a series of experiments designed to test our hypotheses about the phonological and morphological structures of English.

Fruitful experiments involving sentences must be less rigorous at this time because we know so little about sentences. We know a little more about morphology, although the first in the series of contrastive studies, prepared under the aegis of the Center for Applied Linguistics of the Modern Language Association, is rather disappointing on that score in its treatment of German. Let me indicate what kind of analysis of English morphology could be used. See Tables I and II of English verb states below, for an indication of what constitutes a verb phrase.

It is much easier to imagine, however, how a descriptive phonological statement could be used in the design of experiments. See Tables III and IV for such a statement. A series of experiments of very simple design would be possible. We have many monolingual Spanish speakers in this country — enough to furnish a multitude of subjects in different age groups. Since many of us find it counter-intuitive to abandon

TABLE I

Conjugation of verb-states of Modern English in affirmative statements

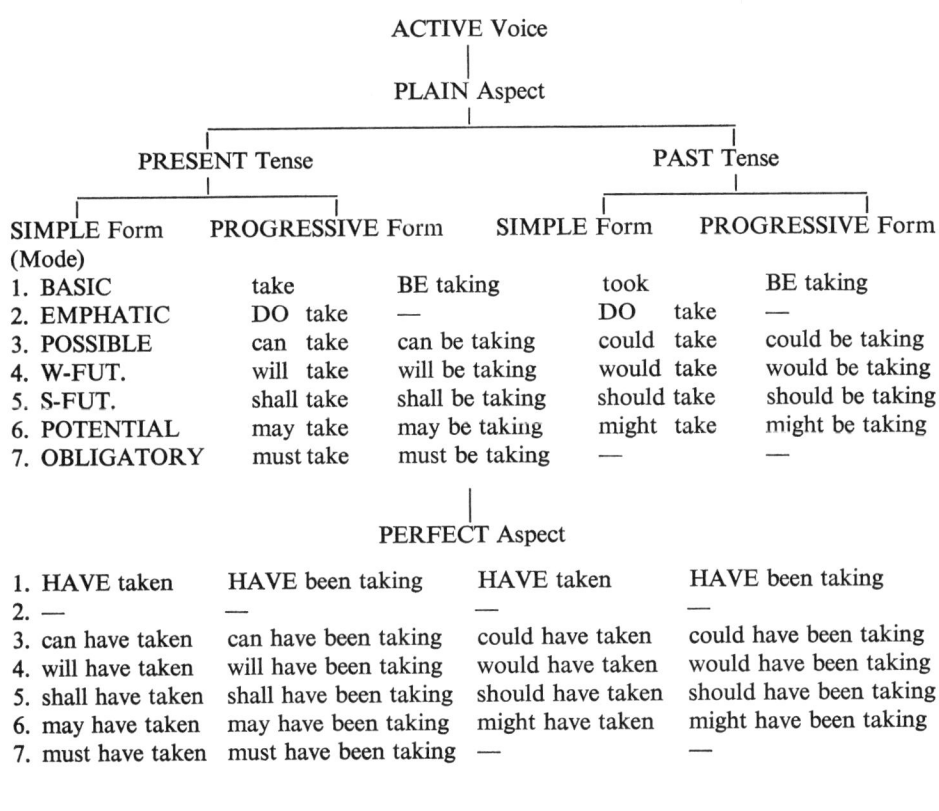

ACTIVE Voice

PLAIN Aspect

	PRESENT Tense		PAST Tense	
SIMPLE Form (Mode)		PROGRESSIVE Form	SIMPLE Form	PROGRESSIVE Form
1. BASIC	take	BE taking	took	BE taking
2. EMPHATIC	DO take	—	DO take	—
3. POSSIBLE	can take	can be taking	could take	could be taking
4. W-FUT.	will take	will be taking	would take	would be taking
5. S-FUT.	shall take	shall be taking	should take	should be taking
6. POTENTIAL	may take	may be taking	might take	might be taking
7. OBLIGATORY	must take	must be taking	—	—

PERFECT Aspect

1. HAVE taken	HAVE been taking	HAVE taken	HAVE been taking
2. —	—	—	—
3. can have taken	can have been taking	could have taken	could have been taking
4. will have taken	will have been taking	would have taken	would have been taking
5. shall have taken	shall have been taking	should have taken	should have been taking
6. may have taken	may have been taking	might have taken	might have been taking
7. must have taken	must have been taking	—	—

Rules

1. Is it active or passive? If passive, look at next table.
2. Is it plain or perfect? If perfect, look at bottom of this page.
3. Is it present or past? If past, look at right-hand side of this page.
4. Is it simple or progressive? If progressive, look at second column of each side.
5. Is it basic or special? If special, look at lines 2-7 of each half of this page.
6. Is it in caps or not? If Have, choose *had* or *have/has*; DO, *did* or *do/does*; if BE, *was/were* or *am/is/are*, according to tense and subject.

TABLE II

Conjugation of verb-states of Modern English in affirmative statements

PASSIVE Voice
PLAIN Aspect

	PRESENT Tense		PAST Tense	
(Mode)	SIMPLE Form	PROGRESSIVE Form	SIMPLE Form	PROGRESSIVE Form
1.	BE taken	BE being taken	BE taken	BE being taken
2.	—	—	—	—
3.	can be taken	can be being taken*	could be taken	could be being taken*
4.	will be taken	will be being taken*	would be taken	would be being taken*
5.	shall be taken	shall be being taken*	should be taken	should be being taken*
6.	may be taken	may be being taken*	might be taken	might be being taken*
7.	must be taken	must be being taken*	—	—

PERFECT Aspect

1.	HAVE been taken	HAVE been being taken*	HAVE been taken	HAVE been being taken*
2.	—	—	—	—
3.	can have been taken	can have been being t'n*	could have b.t.	could have b.b.t.*
4.	will have been taken	will have b.b.t.*	would have b.t.	would have b.b.t.*
5.	shall have been taken	shall have b.b.t.*	should have b.t.	should have b.b.t.*
6.	may have been taken	may have b.b.t.*	might have b.t.	might have b.b.t.*
7.	must have been taken	must have b.b.t.*	must have b.t.	must have b.b.t.*

* rare

SUMMARY OF ENGLISH VERB-STATES

Voice→	Aspect→	Tense→	Form→	Mode
ACTIVE−	PLAIN−	PRESENT−	SIMPLE−	BASIC−
PASSIVE+	PERFECT+	PAST+	PROGRESSIVE+	SPECIAL+
(BE+V−EN)	(HAVE+V−EN)	(V−ED)	(BE+V−ING)	(M+V)

TABLE III

*Spanish and English
Guide to Contrastive Phonology*

A. CONSONANTS

   1. *Phonemic differences*
      a. +Spanish, −English: /ñ/, /x/, /rr/
      b. −Spanish, +English: /v, θ, š, ž, ǰ, ŋ, ð, w, h/
      c. Distributional: −Sp., final /p, b, t, k, g, f, z, m/ and final C-clusters /C+t, d/ /C+s, z/, /r+C/, /l+C/ and combinations.
        +Sp., +Eng.: initial /C+l, r/
        +Eng.: initial /s+C (±l, r)/
        +Sp.: initial /e/ + /s+C (±l, r)/

2. *Phonetic differences*
   a. /p, t, k/ Sp. unaspirated, Eng. asp. before stressed V except after /s/.
   b. /t, d, s, n,/ Sp. dental, Eng. alveolar
   c. /b, d, g/ Sp. [β, δ, γ,] fricatives intervocalically, [b d g] stops elsewhere.
   d. /s/ Sp. [s, z] voiced before voiced C
   e. /r/ Sp. tap, Eng. retroflex, etc.; /rr/ Sp. trill

Contrastive array of phonemic and gross phonetic differences between California Spanish and English

	p b [β]	t d [δ]	č —	k g [γ]
Stops + Fricatives	f	s [z]	—	x
Nasals	m	n	ñ	—
Others	—	l, r rr	γ	—

	p [pʰ/p] b	t [tʰ/t] d	č ǰ	k [kʰ/k] g
Stops				
Fricatives	f v	θ, s ð, z	š ž	—
Nasals	m	n	—	ŋ
Others	w	l, r	γ	h

TABLE IV

Spanish and English
Guide to Contrastive Phonology

B. Vowels
  1. *Phonemic differences*
     a. +Sp.: /i e a u o/, /ai, ei, oi/, /au/
     b. +Eng.: /i e æ ə a u/, /iy, ey, ay, oy/, /uw, ow, aw/, /V+r/
     c. Sp. Vs occur in all positions; Eng. short stressed Vs never final

  2. *Phonetic differences*
     Sp. Vs are short tense and 'pure'; stress does not affect quality.
     Eng. Vs are short and lax, or diphthongal; quality varies with stress.

		Spanish				
		High i	u			
		Mid e	o			
		Low	a			
		English				

Simple Vowels				English	Spanish	Key
	Front	Central	Back	/i/	no equivalent	pit
H	/i/		/u/	/e/	no equivalent	pet
M	/e/	/ə/		/æ/	no equivalent	pat
L	/æ/	/a/		/ə/	no equivalent	putt
				/a/	no equivalent	pot
				/u/	no equivalent	put

Complex Vowels with /y/-glide					
/i/			/iy/	<i> +	see
/e/		/o/	/ey/	<ei, ey>	say
	/a/		/ay/	<ai, ay>	sigh
			/oy/	<oi, oy>	soy
with /w/-glide					
		/u/	/uw/	<u> +	boot
		/o/	/ow/	<ou>	boat
	/a/		/aw/	<au>	bout

the phoneme, why not test the perceptions of English-speaking subjects exposed to a variety of languages and of Spanish-speaking subjects, in the hope of determining just what is the conceptual framework in terms of which they perceive the sounds of another language. The experiments at Stanford did just that for Americans listening to Russian. Since the results are readily available elsewhere[17] I will not discuss them here. They may be of more interest for those concerned with perception than with learning theory.

But our main concern must be more basic. The whole question of the value of the concept of the phoneme has been raised. For theoretical linguistics, it may not be necessary, though I would question even that. But every alphabet in existence, every dictionary, every bit of field work, and every example of language-learning testifies to the existence of the phoneme as a concept. It is a concept shared by all native speakers and hearers of a given language, and also the writers and readers of that language, if they are not congenitally deaf. Certainly it is worth testing experimentally. Subjects should be children of different age groups: most vitally, pre-school children since they are not

[17] These are three technical reports printed in the Psychology Series of The Institute for Mathematical Studies in the Social Sciences, Applied Mathematics and Statistics Laboratories, Stanford University, Stanford, California.
a. P. Suppes, E. Crothers, R. Weir, and E. Trager, "Some Quantitative Studies of Russian Consonant Phoneme Discrimination", *TR* No. 49 (1962).
b. P. Suppes, E. Crothers, R. Weir, "Application of Mathematical Learning Theory and Linguistic Analysis to Vowel Phoneme Matching in Russian Words", *TR* No. 51 (1962).
c. E. Crothers, R. Weir, and P. Palmer, "The Role of Transcription in the Learning of the Orthographic Representations of Russian Sounds", *TR* No. 56 (1963).

yet literate; then, elementary school children, before the age of puberty, which Penfield, in *Speech and Brain Mechanisms*,[18] claims is the cut-off point before physiological changes in the central nervous system make language-learning difficult; young adults, older adults, illiterates, and blind people should also be subjects.

The hypothesis for a whole series of experiments would be this: native speakers of English assign all consonant sounds in an acoustic signal to one of the following 24 categories: /ptck, bdjg, fθsš, vðzž, mnŋ, rlwyh/.

The task in one experiment could be this, using pre-school students: to have them identify the phonemes /k d s v m l/ to a statistically significant level.

The directions might be this. "The word *pig* begins with the same sound as *pin*. Do you hear the same sound in *pill*? Say 'pill' if it starts with the same sound as *pig* and *pin*. Say 'Peggy'. Now I'll say another word. If it begins with the same sound as *pig* and *pin*, say it after me. If it doesn't, keep still. *Rat*. Shh. Don't say anything. Good — *rat* did not begin with the same sound as *pig* and *pin*, so you kept still. Now, every time I say a word that starts with the same sound as *pig* and *pin*, you say it after me. If I say a word that starts with another sound, keep still."

It would take longer to test the pre-schoolers, but it could be done in a language-lab set-up, in short sessions, for all of the 24C in two weeks. The stimuli would be so organized that all possible V's followed each of the C so that we would have data on the classes of allophones.

For a high-school class, the technique would be different although the hypothesis, of course, and the task would be the same. The instructions, however, would be quite different. "You have an answer sheet in front of you for 100 questions. Circle 1, 2, 3, or 4 depending on whether the first, second, third, or fourth word begins with the same sound as you will hear spoken on the tape. You will hear a key word; it will be a regular English word, pronounced twice. Then you will hear four other words; some of them are English nonsense syllables. Indicate which word or syllable begins with the same sound as the key word." Ex: "pat, pat.① rat,② cack,③ bav,④ pal". "You should have circled number 4 because *pal* begins with the same sound as *pat*." Here you could cover the ground more quickly and learn more about the effect of allophone-class on phoneme recognition, by having the V in the beginning word paired in the correct answer with each of the other V's.

It is not at all certain that the results would agree with our common-sense or our traditional linguistic expectations. But certainly, such a series of experiments is basic to any contrastive study in psycholinguistics.[19]

---

[18] W. Penfield and L. Roberts, *Speech and Brain Mechanisms* (Princeton University Press, Princeton, New Jersey, 1959). Reviewed by Eric H. Lenneberg, *Language* 36. 97-112 (1960).

[19] It is not within the scope of this paper to treat the vast literature on speech recognition based on work in experimental phonetics and carried out in such places as the Haskins Laboratories. We will eventually need a careful integration of the acoustic and physiological work done by people like Peter Ladefoged at UCLA, Ilse Lehiste at the University of Michigan, and later at Ohio State University, and William Newcomb at General Dynamics, Rochester, New York. A correlation of the data obtained from controlled psychological experiments, of the sort outlined in this paper, with the results of experimental phonetics will eventually have to be made. Two of many relevant publications

In any case, it is good that basic assumptions about phonology have been questioned; it is good that the windows have been opened and that the stifling air which was rapidly becoming toxic, has been freshened by a renewed concern with syntax and semology. Meaning, after all, is what language is all about. Nobody knows exactly what we mean by "lexical content" but we do know that there are words which refer to perceptual realities (the physical, psychological, sociological and cultural phenomena which individuals are trained to perceive). We know that there are other recurrent partials and grammatical patterns that make it possible to comment on those topics in any given language. All items in a language have significance.

Linguists who were trained in the Bloomfieldian tradition certainly eschew meaning in their presentation of the structure of a language, but just as certainly, we make use of meaning while we are making our analysis of that structure. An analysis of phonology can certainly be done with recourse only to differential meaning. A great deal can even be done with the morphology of words, without recourse to meaning, though this shortly becomes an exercise in futility. With syntax, very little indeed can be done without meaning, and indeed very little was done It is still true that we want descriptions on every level of linguistic structure that have not been determined by or based on meaning. But nobody can deny that we have never stopped using meaning to help us make our analyses.

Generative-transformational grammar merely makes explicit the use of meaning, which is absolutely essential for a complete syntactic description But a theory of grammar in general, or of English grammar in particular, is certainly a different concern from that of many linguists and is perhaps a philosophically more profound one. To specialize in formal linguistics, the theory of grammar, one must know the terminology of computer programming, Boolean algebra, set theory, and symbolic logic, at least.

It should be a source of comfort to some linguists, and of a certain amount of loss of complacency on the part of others, to remember what John Von Neumann said in his brief and beautiful book, posthumously published.[20] Von Neumann was, and is, regarded as a peerless mathematician. He talks on pages 71 ff. about how Turing in 1927 showed that "it is possible to develop code instruction systems for a computing machine which cause it to behave as if it were another, specified, computing machine. Such systems ... are known as *short codes*". There is relevance to the way in which the human central nervous system [CNS] works with natural language, but Von Neumann first goes on to show how the CNS "must definitely have an arithmetical as well as a logical part" although it "manages to do its exceedingly complicated work on a rather low level of precision ... but also to a rather high level of reliability". He says,

---

are these: Morris Halle and K. Stevens, "Speech Recognition: A Model and a Program for Research", *IRE Transactions on Information Theory*, IT-8 (1962), pp. 155-159, Paul L. Garvin and Edith C. Trager, "The Conversion of Phonetic into Orthographic English: A Machine-Translation Approach to the Problem", *Phonetica* Vol. 11: 1-18 (1964).

[20] John von Neumann, *The Computer and the Brain* (New Haven, Yale University Press, 1958).

"We have seen how this leads to a lower level of arithmetical precision but to a higher level of logical reliability: a deterioration in arithmetics has been traded for an improvement in logics." There is an extremely important message for linguists, both in formal and pragmatic linguistics, in what Von Neumann says about language and the workings of the human mind.

He says on the final page of his Silliman Lectures, which he would have delivered at Yale, had he lived, "Thus logics and mathematics in the central nervous system, when viewed as languages, must structurally be essentially different from those languages to which our common experience refers."

He goes on to note that "the language here involved may well correspond to a short code in the sense described earlier, rather than to a complete code: when we talk mathematics, we may be discussing a *secondary* language, built on the *primary* language truly used by our central nervous system".

Von Neumann's penultimate statement is perhaps the most relevant of all to the work that will be done on language in the rest of the twentieth century. "Thus the outward forms of *our* mathematics are not absolutely relevant from the point of view of evaluating what the mathematical or logical language *truly* used by the central nervous system is."

His last statement corroborates what Sapir and Bloomfield and their intellectual descendants have long inferred from their observations of language. He says that his remarks "about reliability and logical and arithmetical depth prove that whatever the system *is*, it cannot fail to differ considerably from what we consciously and explicitly consider as mathematics."

San Jose State College

SOME THOUGHTS ON SPELLING

RUTH H. WEIR

> It is with sadness that I report, as this little volume goes to press, of the untimely death of Ruth Hirsch Weir in California, late in 1965. At the age of thirty-nine so much promise was left unfulfilled. Her books *Audio-visual Aids in Language Teaching* and *Language in the Crib* are well-known and widely respected. Her work on an ideal writing system is stimulating and suggestive. Her teaching opened many doors to students at Georgetown and Stanford Universities.
>
> To her husband and children, on behalf of many friends, colleagues and students, the editor and the scholar for whom she wrote this article, extend their heartfelt sympathy
>
> WILLIAM M. AUSTIN
LÉON DOSTERT

"Unless we adopt a system of Chinese ideographs, and learn by heart a separate arbitrary symbol of every word in the dictionary we must spell phonetically. We may corrupt and confuse our phonetic spelling by etymologic fads, spelling det with a b and foren with an ig, just as we might spell man mapn or mkyan to show that we are descended from apes or monkeys; but we shall not spell man ape nor shall we ever spell cat dog. If we did the only result would be that we should presently spell dogma catma. We cannot get away from phonetic spelling because spelling is as necessarily and inevitably phonetic as moisture is damp."[1] Thus wrote George Bernard Shaw to the Editor of the Times on September 25, 1906. This summarizes as well as anywhere, or better, the frequent argument for English spelling reform and for a phonetic orthography. Much has been said, written, and even done recently to establish auxiliary alphabets of various types to help Johnny read. This attempt to introduce 'phonetic' spelling is by no means confined to English, but also extends to languages like Russian, as Klein has pointed out.[2] However, it is not the subject of this paper to evaluate the advantages or disadvantages of various attempts at respellings; nor is it

---

[1] Abraham Tauber, ed., *George Bernard Shaw on Language* 32 (N.Y., 1963).
[2] Kurt Klein, "Recent Soviet Discussion on Reform of Russian Orthography", *Slavic and East European Journal* 54-61 (1964).

our task, as set here, to discuss a number of problems connected with orthographecs like the nature of the reading process, or what should in fact be learned by children in order to enable them to read, or should a child learn by context with a few letter clues, etc. What does concern us here is the relationship between the spoken and written systems of some languages including English.

It is not surprising that linguists have not paid too much attention to writing for some time. It was a difficult enough task to free ourselves from looking at language only through its written representation, and to accept the vocal-auditory processes as a self-contained, independent system. The victory of accepting the primacy of spoken language has in fact been won so hard that any concession to writing savored of retreat.[3] However, there have been some attempts in the past to view the vocal-auditory processes on the one hand, and the written representation on the other as independent expressions of the same underlying system. Uldall[4] states it in the following manner: "When we say that orthography and pronunciation are expressions of the same language, we mean simply that the orthographic units and the units of pronunciation correspond to, or, better, are functions of the same units of content: the fact that both *kat* and 'cat' are functions of the idea *felis domestica*, as that idea is defined in relation to other English ideas, proves that they are expressions of the same language. It is this mutual function between two planes that constitutes a language: the units of content are defined as such by having an expression, and the units of expression are defined as such by having a content ... The system of speech and the system of writing are thus only two realizations out of an infinite number of possible systems, of which no one can be said to be more fundamental than any other." A similar statement is made by Vachek,[5] looking at the same problem from a different theoretical construct: "Die Orthographie ist eine Brücke zwischen zwei Sprachsystemen, der geschriebenen und der gesprochenen Sprache, eine Summe von Entsprechungen einzelner Bestandteile beider Sprachsysteme ... Der Übergang von einer Norm zur anderen wird Rechtschreibung bzw. Aussprache genannt, je nachdem ob man von der Sprechnorm oder umgekehrt vorgeht."

With some languages, the transition from the spoken system to the written one or vice versa is simpler than with others, but it seems to us that we have to consider the orthographic representation as an independent system, and not merely as a reflex of the sound system of the spoken language. Frequently, the assumption has been made that a 'phonetic' spelling, or in more sophisticated terms, a one-to-one phoneme-grapheme relationship is the ideal orthography for a given language. Joos has conveniently summarized the basic principles as applied to English 'phonetic' spelling reforms in his review of Wijk's book: "For each sound of English, choose one (preferably the commonest) traditional spelling to be used exclusively for that sound, until the spellings are used up, then by analogy create spellings for the remaining

---

[3] Dwight L. Bolinger, "Visual Morphemes" *Language*, 22.333-334 (1946).
[4] H. J. Uldall, "Speech and Writing" *Acta Linguistica* 4.11-16 (1944).
[5] Josef Vachek, "Zum Problem der geschriebenen Sprache", *TCLP*, 8.94-104 (1939).

sounds. For each traditional spelling unit (th, ai, igh, aught, etc.) select one "sound" which is to be exclusive reading for that spelling, until the spellings get too odd, then respell the residue by convenient analogies."[6]

In other words, when dealing with alphabetic writing systems, the only regularity which is desirable is that each written symbol correspond to one and only one phoneme, and that each phoneme be represented by the same written symbol at all times. Thus, in a recent Soviet proposal for spelling reform it was suggested, in addition to proposals to eliminate functionless spellings like double consonants, that the vowel letters *E* and *я* be spelled only under stress, and *u* be written in unstressed position in order to conform to pronunciation.[7] That this would also entail the writing of the same grammatical ending in two forms, depending on the stress position, is ignored. For example, the prepositional case would have to be written *E* in ВВОДЕ (in the water) and *u* in ВКОМНАТИ (in the room) because the former ending is stressed, the latter is not. Obviously, we must ask ourselves if such a rigorous conformity to sound at the expense of grammar would be advantageous, and the answer, in our opinion should be clearly no.

'Perfect alphabetic systems', that is, one-to-one phoneme-grapheme correspondences, have been frequently ascribed to languages like Czech.[8] True, the transition from writing to speech and vice versa is more apparent in Czech than it is in English, but the Czechoslovak Academy states explicitly[9] that "Czech orthography is basically a phonemic one. Some deviation from this principle is mostly conditioned by grammatical or semantic considerations." This statement clearly points to a morphophonemic spelling principle. For example, the voiced: voiceless opposition is neutralized word finally, but the orthography writes *bod* 'point' and *bot* 'shoes, gen pl.' to correspond to the identical phonemic sequence /bot/. Some orthographies, like the Serbo-Croatian one,[10] does show an even closer correspondence between sound and spelling than the Czech writing system permits. In Serbo-Croatian speech, consonant clusters are homorganic as to voice; the orthography recognizes this within word boundaries and spells *vrabac* and *vrɒpca*, 'sparrow' but the very same phenomenon is ignored across word boundaries, e.g. *pod petom* "under the heel". Not even here then can we speak of a perfect phonetic spelling. As a matter of fact, to our knowledge, there is no orthography in existence which would have a one-to-one phoneme-grapheme correlation, indicating in spelling all segmentals as well as phonemes of stress and intonation. And even if this were possible, it certainly remains questionable that it would be desirable. Czech orthography is roughly morphophonemic. Some aspects of the above mentioned Russian spelling reform are undesirable because, in

---

[6] Axel Wijk, *Regularized English. An Investigation into the English Spelling Reform Problem with a New, Detailed Plan for a Possible Solution* (Stockholm, 1959). Rev. Martin Joos *Language* 36.250-262 (1960).
[7] Klein, *op. cit.*
[8] Leonard Bloomfield, "Written Records", *Language* 281-296 (N.Y., 1933).
[9] Československá akademie věd, *Pravidla českého pravopisu*, 9 (Praha, 1958).
[10] Matica Hrvatska, Matica Srpska, *Pravopis Hrvatskosrpskog Jezika* (Zagreb, Novi Sad, 1962).

Pulkina's words[11] "Russian spelling is mainly based on the morphological principle, i.e. it tends to preserve unchanged every meaningful part of the word (the root, prefix suffix and the ending) even if in actual pronunciation the sound value of the letters representing this or that part of the word is changed due to a shift of stress or a different combination of sounds. Thus, in the root of the word ДОМ 'house' o is written in the nominative plural (ДОМá) just as in the singular though the stress in the plural has shifted to the final syllable, changing the pronunciation of the unstressed o to a." This is somewhat of an oversimplification, but the basic principle holds for many other orthographies as well, at least to a considerable degree. In German,[12] for example, we could argue that the letter *ä* or the letter combination *äu* are superfulous, and that only *e* and *eu* should be retained for spelling /e/ and /oi/. But should the singular-plural relationship between *Apfel* and *Äpfel* or *Baum* and *Bäume* be obscured in writing? Probably not, or at least we should defer any decision in this regard until we know more about the variables which are important to the reading process.

This is not to say that alphabetic writing systems have no relationship to the phonemic entities of a language. They certainly do, alphabets are phonemically based, but if the alphabetic (or phonemic) principles were the only ones employed, the resulting orthography would obscure many other important structures, like the relationships of allomorphs to a given morpheme. Before we look at the much maligned orthography of English, it may be useful to recall some of the functions of an orthography. Joos[13] and Francis[14] have enumerated some of them, and we want to state them here again: (1) An orthography of a given language is virtually standard for all dialects of a language. It translates between diverse speech habits within that language and its function is uniformity, a sort of written lingua franca, whatever the differences in the sound systems of the dialects of a given language may be. (2) In addition to the difficulties already mentioned in an orthography with purely one-to-one phoneme-grapheme relationships, it would seem impossible to acquire any great reading skill by having to decode each phoneme separately. Fries[15] has suggested the existence of spelling patterns consisting of sequences of letters representing word patterns, but not necessarily duplicating the sequence of phonemes in the word pattern. It seems to us that one of the crucial principles of orthography is to bring morphemically related words closer together than is done in speech. The morphemic relationships between words are usually much more apparent in writing than they are in speech, thus permitting the native speaker much more rapid scanning of the writing than an orthography based on a strict adherence to the phonemic system alone would. An orthography then should be basically morphophonemic, and account for both the phonemic and morphemic structures.[16]

[11] I. M. Pulkina, *A Short Russian Reference Grammar* 3 (Moscow, 1960).
[12] Joseph Lammertz, *Vollständige Rechtschreiblehre*, 18th ed. (Paderborn, 1962).
[13] Joos, *op. cit.*, 257.
[14] W. Nelson Francis, *The Structure of American English* ch. 8.441-468 (N.Y. 1958).
[15] C. C. Fries, *Linguistics and Reading*, 146-199 (N.Y. 1962).
[16] See also A. Valdman, "Not All is Wrong with French Spelling", *French Review* 37.213-223 (1963).

How does English orthography fit into this pattern? Is it really as terribly irregular as spelling reformers have led us to believe? In an attempt to answer this question, we have been engaged in a study of the spelling-to-sound relationships of some 20,000 English words,[17] formulating and testing some hypotheses as to the nature of the English spelling system. One of the hypotheses on which this research is based is that English spelling relates not only to phonology, but also to morphology and syntax, and that, when viewed with this understanding, a much higher degree of regularity emerges than does appear when we confine ourselves to a simple letter-to-sound relationship. To this end we have constructed a model which is based upon three different levels: grapheme, morphophoneme, and phoneme. Before a word is subjected to analysis, it is broken down into its morphemic constituents. Since it is our hypothesis that spelling is essentially morphophonemic, single morpheme words are our point of departure. It is further hypothesized that hierarchically ordered rules must be applied to map the single morpheme graphemic word onto the morphophonemic level, and then, through the application of further appropriate rules, onto the phonemic level.

The major objectives then are to analyze the spelling-to-sound relationships in order to discover not only the basic patterns involved, but also, the levels on which these patterns operate. In dealing with so-called irregular spelling-to-sound relationships, it is crucial to establish the levels on which the irregularities occur.

It must be pointed out that this research at present, deals only with the one-way relationship of spelling to sound. Also, proper nouns, abbreviations and contractions have not been used in the analysis. Entries were selected on the basis of frequency of occurrence in running English texts, using the frequency counts in the Thorndike Dictionary[18] as a guide. Pronunciations are drawn chiefly from Kenyon and Knott's *Pronouncing Dictionary of American English*,[19] with modifications based upon dialect atlas material for the upper Midwest.

Some samples of the types of correlations found follow, together with a model for spelling to sound correspondences.

In presenting the phonological patterns we have selected rather arbitrarily the divisions of *regular phonemic*, *irregular phonemic*, and *phonotactics*. In all cases phonological correspondences apply to single morpheme words. *Word* in this discussion is defined graphemically — *graphemes* being class definitions, related to graphs which appear on a printed page, in a manner analogous to the way that phonemes relate to allophones.

In the category of *regular* phonemic correspondences we have first *invariant* patterns, that is, graphemes that have one general pronunciation, regardless of their environments. Of the 2,000-odd occurrences of the grapheme ⟨b⟩, for example, all

[17] *U.S. Office of Education Contract OE-4-10-213.* Work under this contract is a joint effort of the writer and Mr. R. L. Venezky of Stanford University.
[18] *Thorndike Dictionary*, Revised Edition (Chicago, 1942).
[19] Kenyon and Knott, *A Pronouncing Dictionary of American English* (Springfield, Mass., 1951).

but a few are pronounced /b/. (There is a general rule that accounts for geminate consonant clusters like ⟨bb⟩). The graphemes ⟨f, k, m, n, v, y, z⟩ also fit into this class.

The second subdivision of regular phonemic correspondences is *variant* and in this category there are two further classes, each based upon the conditioning factor that determines the variation. Graphemic environment is generally the most important determiner of the various pronunciations for a single grapheme. The grapheme ⟨c⟩, for example, when it appears before the graphemes ⟨e, i, y⟩ plus consonant or juncture, is pronounced /s/ as in *cent*, *city*, and *cycle*, while in word final position, or before ⟨a, o, u⟩ and any consonant except ⟨h⟩, it is pronounced /k/. (There are a few exceptions to this pattern like *cello* and *facade*.)

The position of a grapheme or grapheme cluster in a word — still a case of graphemic environment — is also a major conditioning factor. Interconsonantal ⟨a⟩, for example, in monosyllables not ending in ⟨e⟩ is always pronounced /æ/ as in *back*, *bag*, *band*.

The second category of variant regular phonemic correspondences is the stress conditioning category. The patterns for intervocalic ⟨x⟩ are examples of stress conditioning. If the primary stress is on the syllable preceeding ⟨x⟩, then the corresponding phoneme consonant cluster is /ks/ (*exit*, *exercise*), while if the stress is anywhere else, the cluster is voiced to /gz/ (*exert*, *examine*). This follows directly from Verner's Law for the Germanic voiceless spirants.[20] The cases of ⟨x⟩ before a consonant are also regular, but are not stress conditioned.

The other major subdivision of phonological correspondences is the *irregular class*. This class, though accounting for only a small portion of the total phonologica category, receives the greatest attention in educational and popular writings on the general subject of orthography. There are two and possibly three seemingly natural categories for this class. The first contains frequent spellings that have various pronunciations which can only be predicted by knowing the whole word. Most occurrences of the digraph ⟨ch⟩ fit into this class.

The second subdivision of the irregular class is composed of such nonce forms as *debt*, *doubt*, *thyme* and *island*. As a general description of this class, 'rare-irregularities' should suffice. Number of tokens is what distinguishes this subdivision from the first one mentioned.

It may also be feasible to set up a third subdivision of irregularities to contain those spelling-to-sound irregularities that occur in homonym pairs, e.g. *sighs* and *size*, *would* and *wood*, *tolled* and *told*, etc.

In the third major category of phological correspondences are contained those spelling-to-sound correspondences which can be predicted upon the basis of phonotactics. The /š/ and /č/ pronunciations in *sugar*, *sure*, *mature*, and *bastion*, fit into this category. The rule (with certain conditioning factors which are not mentioned here) that applies to *sugar* and *social* is $\{s+y+V\} \rightarrow /š/+V\}$. A similar rule accounts for the /č/ in *mature* and *bastion*.

---

[20] "For the study of spelling ... an historical appraisal would be more enlightening than a phonemic one", C. A. Lefevre, *Linguistics and The Teaching of Reading* (N.Y. 1964), p. 166.

The most commonly mentioned morphemic elements in the orthography are the final ⟨—(e)s⟩ used as the regular noun plural marker, or as the third singular present indicative marker for the verb, and the regular past tense marker ⟨—(e)d⟩. Both of these graphemic forms represent single morphemes. There are simple phonotactic rules in English for predicting the pronunciations of these forms, once their morphemic identity is ascertained. Without this information, there is little regularity in their behavior.

The final consonant clusters in the words *paradigm*, *damn*, and *bomb*, are morphophonemic spellings. In a pure spelling-to-sound analysis, one is forced to the conclusion that the ⟨g⟩ in *paradigm*, the ⟨n⟩ in *damn* and the final ⟨b⟩ in bomb are functionless graphemes. When viewed, though, from a morphophonemic standpoint, the pairs paradigm — paradigmatic

damn — damnation
bomb — bombardier

reveal a regular morphophonemic alternation that is preserved in the orthography. This consonant pattern is quite common in English. Besides the three examples given, there are, for example

malign — malignant
design — designate
sign — signify
autumn — autumnal
condemn — condemnation
hymn — hymnal

Without the retention of the full consonant cluster in final position, the identity of the common morphemic element in such pairs would be lost on the graphemic level.

Another fairly regular pattern is a voiced - voiceless morphophonemic alternation as is reflected in

house — houses
north — northern
south — southern
worth — worthy

It should be evident from the foregoing material that any model that attempts to describe spelling-to-sound correspondences must account for both phonemic and morphemic patterns. Such a model must also handle irregularities, that is, it must show on what level the irregularity occurs. For example, given the irregular forms *arcing* and *facade*, one necessary condition for the model is that it distinguish the different types of irregularity which are reflected in the pronunciations of the grapheme ⟨c⟩ in these words. The irregularity in *arcing* enters with the irregular formation of the graphemic allomorph ⟨arc-⟩ before a suffix beginning with ⟨i⟩. This is an exception to a general orthographic rule that requires a ⟨k⟩ to be inserted in this environment, as in *trafficking*. *Facade* is irregular in the basic graphemic word — ⟨c⟩ before ⟨a⟩ is pronounced /s/ instead of the usual /k/. This is an exception to a basic environmentally conditioned grapheme → phoneme correspondence. In essence, the model that we are suggesting is an economical way to account for the workings of the current orthography which also predicts certain things about reading habits and regularity — or the lack of regularity.

Exactly how much this model will predict about reading habits, we cannot say at present. Some pinwork rogress hopefully will shed some light upon this problem. We are guided to a limited degree, however, in searching for regular patterns, by the notion of reading habit. Thus, in accounting for the various pronunciations of initial ⟨ch⟩, one could simply state that in words derived from Old English or borrowed from Old French before such and such a time, the pronunciation is /č/, and so on. But such a rule obviously does not reflect the habits of the average reader.

The selection of appropriate units perhaps best reflects the attempt — and some of the uncertainties — of using reader habits as a guide to rule formation. For example, the choice of a rule that says that the initial grapheme cluster ⟨rh⟩ is mapped into the morphophoneme {r} (the mapping rules will be explained shortly) rather than the rule that ⟨h⟩ after initial ⟨r⟩ is mapped into a zero morphophoneme is based upon a notion of how a reader operates. We do not really know that this is true — but we predict that it is, that is, we predict that initial ⟨rh⟩ is perceived as a unit rather than as two distinct units, ⟨r⟩ and ⟨h⟩.

In this example, either rule could be chosen on the basis of economy or simplicity. That is, for a pure competence model, either rule would suffice. But obviously, we are not interested in competence alone. If we were, we would attempt to formulate any rule possible based upon graphemic shape or upon morphology to show as much regularity as possible in the spelling-to-sound relationship. Rules of the type 'grapheme ⟨x⟩ in words of length y, or in words having no graphemes that open to the left is mapped into morphophoneme Z' — could be formulated and certainly would add regularity in many cases, but we are sure that most people would agree that such a rule could serve no useful purpose.

The actual model that we have constructed is based upon three different levels: grapheme, morphophoneme, and phoneme. For the present we are using the term phoneme to represent elements on the phonological level; broad phonetic may be a more accurate formulation, but a clumsy one as well. The term morphophoneme is used in an extremely broad sense here. What is meant by the morphophonemic level is an intermediate level between grapheme and phoneme that contains what are traditionally called morphophonemes plus additional things that deviate slightly from the traditional concept of the morphophoneme. What these other things are and how much they deviate from the classical view is not too important at the moment, and should offer no obstacle for understanding what we are attempting to do. Single morpheme graphemic words are mapped, by the application of appropriate rules, onto the morphophonemic level, and through the application of appropriate morphophonemic rules onto the phonemic level. This can be illustrated by two words like *haste* and *hasten*. As for ⟨hasten⟩, it first has to be broken down into its morphemic constituents, ⟨haste⟩+⟨en⟩. We then establish the morphophoneme $\{T_1\}$ in $\{hesT_1\}$ + $\{ən\}$ which follows the rule $\{-T_1\} \to /t/$ $\{-T_1\}$ else $\to$ zero. We thus obtain the form $\{hesən\}$ and by adding stress, /hésən/. In the case of $\{⟨haste⟩\}$ the rule is applied again, $\{-T_1\}$ now $\to /t/$ and the result is /hest/.

It must be emphasized that the rules we are writing at present for English are preliminary ones — a great deal more work is necessary to refine them. However, we are certain that English orthography is subject to morphophonemic rules, and that no one-to-one phoneme-grapheme correlation can account for its system.

Stanford University

JANUA LINGUARUM

STUDIA MEMORIAE NICOLAI VAN WIJK DEDICATA

Edited by C. H. van Schooneveld

SERIES MAIOR

2. DEAN S. WORTH: Kamchadal Texts collected by W. Jochelson. 1961. 284 pp. Cloth.
   Gld. 58.—

3. PETER HARTMANN: Theorie der Grammatik. 1963. 552 pp. Cloth.   Gld. 82.—

6. TATIANA SLAMA-CAZACU: Langage et Contexte: Le problème du langage dans la conception de l'expression et de l'interprétation par des organisations contextuelles. 1961. 251 pp., 5 figs. Cloth.   Gld. 48.—

8. THOMAS A. SEBEOK and VALDIS J. ZEPS: Concordance and Thesaurus of Cheremis Poetic Language. 1961. 259 pp. Cloth.   Gld. 58.—

9. GUSTAV HERDAN: The Calculus of Linguistic Observations. 1962. 271 pp., 6 figs. Cloth.
   Gld. 42.—

10. Proceedings of the Fourth International Congress of Phonetic Sciences, held at the University of Helsinki, 4-9 September 1961. Edited by ANTTI SOVIJÄRVI and PENTTI AALTO. 1962. 855 pp., numerous figs. and plates. Cloth.   Gld. 125.—

11. WERNER WINTER (ed.): Evidence for Laryngeals. 1965. 271 pp. Cloth.   Gld. 45.—

12. Proceedings of the Ninth International Congress of Linguists, Cambridge, Mass., August 27-31, 1962. Edited by HORACE G. LUNT. 1964. 1196 pp., plate. Cloth.   Gld. 125.—

14. RUTH HIRSCH WEIR: Language in the Crib. 1962. 216 pp. Cloth.   Gld. 32.—

15. Approaches to Semiotics: Cultural Anthropology, Education, Linguistics, Psychiatry, Psychology. Transactions of the Indiana University Conference on Paralinguistics and Kinesics. Edited by THOMAS A. SEBEOK, ALFRED S. HAYES, MARY CATHERINE BATESON. 1964. 294 pp. Cloth.   Gld. 40.—

16. A. ROSETTI: Linguistica. 1965. 268 pp., 19 figs. Cloth.   Gld. 58.—

17. Proceedings of the Eighth International Congress of Onomastic Sciences, Amsterdam, 1963. Edited by D. P. BLOK. LVI + 611 pp., 23 figs., 2 plates. Cloth.   Gld. 110.—

18. PIERRE DELATTRE: Studies in French and Comparative Phonetics: Selected Papers in French and English. 1966. 286 pp., 2 tables, 35 figs. Gld. 48.—

20. Sociolinguistics: Papers of the UCLA Conference on Sociolinguistics, May 1964. Edited by WILLIAM BRIGHT. 1966. 324 pp., some figs. Gld. 52.—

21. JOSHUA A. FISHMAN: Language Loyalty in the United States: The Maintenance and Perpetuation of Non-English Mother Tongues by American Ethnic and Religious Groups. 1966. 478 pp., 5 figs., many tables. Gld. 64.—

MOUTON · PUBLISHERS · THE HAGUE